P9-AQT-700

Tolstoy

Tolstoy

T. G. S. Cain

891.
733
TOLSTOY

BOOKS
10 East 53d St., New York 10022
(a division of Harper & Row Publishers, Inc.)

78-15283

Published in the U.S.A. 1977 by
Harper & Row Publishers, Inc.
Barnes & Noble Import Division

ISBN 0–06–490890–9
LC   76–53287

First published in Great Britain 1977 by
Elek Books Limited, London

Copyright © 1977 T. G. S. Cain

All rights reserved. No part of this
publication may be reproduced, stored in
a retrieval system or transmitted, in any
form or by any means, electronic, mechanical,
photocopying, recording or otherwise, without
the prior permission of the publishers.

Printed in Great Britain by
Latimer Trend & Company Ltd Plymouth

Contents

Preface

Tolstoy often seems to disarm criticism, rendering it unnecessary by the apparently effortless lucidity of his art, and one would feel somewhat suspicious of the critic of Tolstoy who never felt any doubts about the possible superfluity of his activity. There are occasions when everything appears so clear that neither commentary nor evaluation seems called for. But that lucidity which is so much a part of his greatness is not accidental: it is a product of the highest kind of art, and his work is, like Shakespeare's, as complex as it is great. For this reason, as with Shakespeare, there are and will be no 'definitive' books on Tolstoy, only a continuing discussion. This book is conceived of as part of that discussion. Its emphasis is literary critical, and its scope that of a general introduction to Tolstoy's fiction. In it I have tried to trace his evolution as a novelist by taking what seem to me the most important works of fiction in an approximately chronological order, and examining them with a sense of the separateness, the individuality of each one, while yet trying to place them in the total context of Tolstoy's career. That career is seen throughout as one motivated by an ongoing, introspective quest for a stable concept of truth and moral order. The word 'introspective' indicates my overall emphasis: such critics as Merezhkovsky and Eykhenbaum were, I believe, right in insisting on the essentially autobiographical nature of Tolstoy's art. In few writers is the greatness of the art so closely related to what may reasonably be called the greatness of the life, the intense spiritual struggles, the doubts, desires and vicissitudes of the man himself.

This emphasis has largely governed my choice of the work with which I deal, since choice is inevitable in a book of this kind. Of his voluminous work outside the novel I have given detailed attention only to *A Confession*, that crucial document of spiritual autobiography, because it is immediately relevant to Tolstoy the novelist in a way that the more objectively philosophical work, such things as *What is Art?* or *The Kingdom of God is Within You*, is not. To have attempted to cover the philosophical, social and religious writings as well as the novels would have entailed a book not only of excessive length, but of some diffuseness. The drama is yet another field of considerable achievement which I have excluded in order to focus the more clearly on what is indisputably Tolstoy's most important sphere of activity, the novel. My belief that the element of explorative spiritual biography is central in the development of the novelist has meant that amongst the minor fiction, too, I have concentrated on those works in which he is most clearly present, working out his own problems, rather than on those, like *Polikushka* or the *Sevastopol Sketches*, in which he is a more detached, if impressive, observer.

Within this sphere, the important works choose themselves, and I have tried throughout to approach them with as few preconceived theories as possible as to their nature or their place in Tolstoy's *oeuvre*; he is too large and too protean to be fitted neatly to any *a priori* critical theory, and the important patterns that are certainly discernible in his work will, I hope, emerge clearly enough in the course of the book.

Except where indicated, translations from Tolstoy are my own, and are from the standard Russian edition of the complete works, *Polnoye Sobraniye Sochineniy*, ed. V. G. Chertkov *et al.* (90 vols, Moscow, 1925–58), referred to in the text as *Works*. I have given volume and chapter references after quotations of any length to facilitate the use of English translations. In making the translations, I have erred on the side of literalness, partly because Tolstoy's intentions are often made more clear thereby, if not more graceful, and partly because the quotations may give the reader who has no Russian at least some sense of the very distinctive flavour of Tolstoy's rhetoric, which, with its repetitions, its runs of nouns, verbs and adjectives, and its somewhat involved syntax, is inevitably smoothed over in even the best translations.

Though I have not tried to write a critical biography, nor to examine Tolstoy's thought except as it bears directly on the issues of his fiction, I am aware of a considerable debt, which may not always be obvious, to those who have worked in these areas, particularly to the biographies by Aylmer Maude and Ernest J. Simmons, and the studies of various aspects of Tolstoy's ideas by Sir Isaiah Berlin and G. W. Spence. Of critics who have written on Tolstoy in English, I am most indebted to (though not always in agreement with) John Bayley and R. F. Christian. I am grateful in a more immediate way to Dr R. K. R. Thornton for reading through the typescript and offering many helpful suggestions. But most of all, though it has become something of a minor literary convention to end thus, it is undoubtedly true that I am most indebted to my wife, whose native knowledge of Slavonic languages has been invaluable, and whose patience and encouragement have helped me to complete the book. It is to her, therefore, that it is dedicated.

T.G.S.C.

4-29-82

LED-ZEPPELIN
RULES
FOREVER

Table of important dates

brother Sergey. Attacks Russo-Japanese war in *Bethink Yourselves!*

1905　Attempted revolution in Russia; Tolstoy attacks all sides involved.

1908　*I Cannot Be Silent*, protest against capital punishment.

1909　Intensification of animosity between Sonya and Chertkov; Sonya threatens suicide. Tolstoy persuaded by Chertkov to make will leaving copyright in his works to daughter Alexandra and not Sonya.

1910　Final breakdown of relationship with Sonya, aggravated by Chertkov; Tolstoy leaves home on October 28th, dies at Astapovo railway station November 7th (O.S.).

Tolstoy and his world

In one of his letters Tolstoy's contemporary Flaubert comments on the then fashionable trend of regarding the artist as merely the product of the world into which he was born. 'There is something else in art' he writes

> 'beside the milieu in which it is practised and the physiological antecedents of the worker. On this system you can explain the series, the group, but never the individuality, the special fact which makes him this person and not another . . . People used to believe that literature was an altogether personal thing and that books fell out of the sky like meteors. Today they deny that the will and the absolute have any reality at all. The truth, I believe, lies between the two extremes.'[1]

There are few writers to whom Flaubert's *caveat* is more relevant than to Tolstoy, few who stand so clearly independent of the intellectual currents of the age to which they belong, and the critic who tries to define the influences which worked to shape Tolstoy the novelist is treading dangerous ground. For Tolstoy was above all, and at all times, an individualist, a man who believed that the truth was to be found within himself and not in the doctrine of others, and a man who had the necessary courage and integrity to follow through all the difficult implications of that belief. Though, like any great writer, he made creative use of what he read, one rarely finds it possible to speak confidently of any writer influencing him in the sense of decisively modifying his outlook or his literary technique. Rather, he seems to find in other men's work the expression of ideas that already, in some sense, belong to him. The truth did not, in the first instance, normally come to him through reading: it came from his own many-sided experience, and from his habit of remorseless self-analysis. Other writers might articulate or confirm what he already knew, encourage him in the direction in which his own conclusions were already leading him, but he remains in all senses one of the most independent of all great writers.

Despite this it remains true that, as Flaubert says, books do not fall out of the sky like meteors, any more than novelists do; even the most independent of writers must be in some sense the product of the world in which he lives, shaped consciously or unconsciously by his time and milieu. In Tolstoy's case it is even possible to see that very independence which is so clearly a matter of individual character being encouraged both by the external circumstances of his background and early life, and by his most enduringly formative reading.

Few writers can have been endowed with such advantages of birth and family as was Tolstoy. He was born in 1828 into one of the great Russian families, a family which was to provide him both with a range of profoundly interesting figures to people his novels, and, equally important, with an instinctive and deep-rooted patrician outlook which, even in those later years when he preached humility and the equality of all men, he was never to lose. At his home Yasnaya Polyana, Tolstoy's father and his maternal grandfather had both consciously cultivated the patri-archal way of life of the old Russian nobility, and he inherited much of their rich conservatism, scornful, as they had been, of the new powers that were abroad. It is no accident that he despised lawyers and doctors more than any other class, for they typified those new professional groups which most threat-ened the old aristocracy through their dubious power over them. The entrenched bureaucracy of Petersburg, the rising merchant classes, and the liberal intelligentsia which opposed them, were alike alien to him. It is Tolstoy who is speaking when Levin in *Anna Karenina* bitterly attacks Oblonsky's descrip-tion of Vronsky as an aristocrat, saying 'I consider myself and people like me aristocrats: people who can point back to three or four honourable generations of their families, all having a high standard of education (talent and brains—that's a differ-ent matter), and who have never cringed before anyone, never depended on anyone, but lived as my father and grandfather lived,' (II.17) just as it is Tolstoy who, in *War and Peace*, shares Prince Andrey's justifiable pride in the honour and in-dependence of that family which so much resembles his own. Andrey's father, the old Prince Bolkonsky, is very largely, though not exclusively, based on Tolstoy's grandfather Prince Nikolay Volkonsky, who built Yasnaya Polyana and lived there in proud, eccentric withdrawal from the political world in which he had been a powerful figure. Tolstoy's father Nikolay, who was in part the model for Nikolay Rostov in *War and Peace*, continued the tradition in a less eccentric and aggressive form, farming his estates along old-fashioned but thorough lines. Both men had a respect and sympathy for the serfs they owned, a respect which Tolstoy was to inherit (along with 350 of the serfs) and which in him was to take at times the form of a kind of idolatry which saw the peasants as the only recipients of true wisdom.

Family tradition, then, was of immense importance to Tolstoy, all the more so, perhaps, because of the death of both his parents while he was still a child, as a result of which Yasnaya Polyana became, like Levin's home, a living memorial whose continuity helped preserve all that he believed they had stood for. His zeal for family life—like Levin he loved the idea of a family long before he loved his wife—grows out of this background, another kind of continuity which is celebrated so richly in the two great novels, *War and Peace* and *Anna Karenina*. The subsequent breakdown of harmony within his own family as a result of his moral and religious doctrines, which his wife and many of his children could not share, becomes all the more tragic when viewed in the context of those early aspirations.

Tolstoy's essentially patrician outlook had, as will be seen, manifold consequences for his work as a novelist. An immediate one was that he never saw himself as a member of that circle of liberal literary intellectuals who dominated the Russian literary scene in the mid nineteenth century. Though he wrote so copiously all his life, though he was a consummate master of his craft, and though he earned a great deal of money from his writings, he never quite saw himself as a writer by profession as Turgenev or Dostoyevsky did. He was an army officer who wrote, a landowner who wrote, a prophet of social, educational, moral or religious reform who wrote, but he was not a professional man of letters, and felt a certain contempt for those who were. When he first began to publish he was an awkwardly alien figure in that circle of writers which centred on Nekrasov's periodical *The Contemporary* (*Sovremennik*). Turgenev in particular, who had at first seen himself as something of a patron of the young Tolstoy, could never accept his refusal to dedicate himself to art in the way that he, like Flaubert, had done. Tolstoy for his part had an underlying contempt for Turgenev's aesthetic creed, and for what he regarded as his rather facile liberalism, which frequently overcame his admiration for Turgenev's work, and occasionally issued in a bristling animosity, leading to insults and projected duels. Later in his life Tolstoy's alienation from the fashionable intellectual life of his time was to be matched by his alienation from his own class, whose life came to seem to him more and more criminally parasitic on the toil of the peasants, so that the final spectacle we have of him is of a man very much alone, surrounded by those numerous disciples with whom he had so little in common. It is no accident that so much of his later work deals with some sort of loneliness, whether it is society's ostracism of Anna Karenina, Nekhlyudov's withdrawal from fashionable society in *Resurrection*, Ivan Ilyich's loneliness in the face of death, or Hadji Murat's fierce individualism, which leaves him trapped between opposing factions: all are reflections of Tolstoy's own isolation.

That isolation owes something also to another facet of his character which should be mentioned here and which, if it is certainly innate, we may yet see as being encouraged by his patrician background: this is his tremendous egoism. In a sense Tolstoy's world was most of all within himself: acute though his observation of those around him was, he spent his whole life looking less at others than into the depths of his own protean nature, in which so much could be discovered of such a conflicting character—arrogance alternating with humility, a massive appetite for life with a powerful leaning toward the ascetic, strong sexual desire with a longing for a state of chastity and innocence. His egoism was rarely of an ungenerous kind, and he never seems to have been really conscious of it in himself— perhaps the only gap in his otherwise extremely acute self-awareness. But his life, probably better documented than that of any other writer, his diaries, journals and letters, and especially his creative work, all speak eloquently of a world whose centre was always himself. That he should have kept a diary for so many years is significant: his novels grow out of the early habits of self-analysis which were fostered by it, and can, indeed, be seen as themselves a kind of diary. That diary is always profoundly interesting, because there was always so much to record; the self-absorption rarely seems narrowly irritating, because it is wide-ranging as well as deep. Unlike Dostoyevsky, who penetrates further into the dark, abnormal areas of human

4

experience, Tolstoy always gives the impression of thinking and feeling as other men do, but more so. This is why his preoccupation with his own feelings issues in most cases in an art of supreme sanity, normal without being mundane. Such an egoism as this is obviously a deep-rooted psychological trait, but it must surely have been encouraged by the fact that his birth ensured that he was always an object of the concern and interest of others, as well as of himself.

His aristocratic background seems to have had its effect, too, in more purely intellectual matters, for in these also he tends to show an independence of fashionable influences, and a range of tastes that sometimes seems more in keeping with that of a cultivated eighteenth-century gentleman than a post-Romantic novelist and thinker. Enough has already been said of his independence of mind to show that any attempt to ascertain the extent to which he was influenced by his reading must be more, if it is to be at all useful, than a list of the books that he read and was impressed by at various stages of his life, the kind of list that he himself obligingly drew up at the request of a Petersburg bookseller in 1891.[2] Sterne, Stendhal, Dickens, Schopenhauer and many lesser figures made a considerable impression on him at various times without in this sense fundamentally affecting his outlook. Two aspects of his cultural background do, however, seem to stand out as playing a truly formative, shaping role in his thought. One of these is his early and enthusiastic reading of Enlightenment philosophy in general, and Rousseau in particular. The other, much more difficult to assess, is the heritage of the Russian cultural tradition, not merely the relatively modern literary tradition in which Pushkin and Gogol were the greatest figures, but that older body of attitudes and beliefs which were part of his life from childhood, enshrined in the Orthodox religion, and in the folk tales and narrative poems which he tells us made an enormous impression in his early years, and which found contemporary expression in custom, ritual and superstition among both peasants and aristocracy. This essentially Russian background is one that makes Tolstoy's world significantly different from that of any writer born outside Russia, but, as will be seen, it combined easily with his reading of Rousseau in shaping the fundamental attitudes and beliefs that were to run through his work.

Most writers on Tolstoy have noted his indebtedness to the Enlightenment tradition, though not all have given adequate weight to the part it played in his work. Certainly, it seems a very surprising allegiance if we consider that when Tolstoy was born, in 1828, Byron had already been dead for four years; Goethe was seventy-nine, Wordsworth fifty-eight. The high period of European Romanticism, both product of and reaction against the Enlightenment, was already over. By 1852, when his first published work appeared in the pages of *The Contemporary*, it was long dead, succeeded by an age which, if it was uncertain about the values maintained by the great Romantics, was even more uncertain about those proposed by the Age of Reason. It brings a salutary and freshening sense of surprise, therefore, to meet the proposition that the greatest writer of this age is as much a child of the eighteenth as of the nineteenth century, a man who until the end of his life held as firmly as any *philosophe* to his belief in the power of natural, uncorrupted reason to search for those universal truths in which lie man's ultimate happiness.

It remains true, though, that both in temperament and philosophy Tolstoy does in many ways belong to the eighteenth century, and that, far from being damaging, it is partly from the peculiarly independent angle of vision which his unfashionably anachronistic stance allows him that his greatness arises. For it is his belief in the existence of a stable, objective realm of human values that are eternal, and not constantly shifting, that enables him to ask with the confidence that they are answerable the most fundamental questions about human experience. It is his belief in the power of natural reason that enables him to pose those questions with uncompromising realism, with a clarity of vision that is often so striking that he seems to be seeing experience from an angle that has never been adopted before, but which yet seems to render the essence of that experience more accurately than would a conventional view.

This clarity and freshness of vision, which has struck all readers of Tolstoy, is a product of his independence, his faith in the individual's ability to discover the truth of things afresh. He often seems to be looking at the world as if seeing it for the first time, his remorselessly rational eye cutting through the web of assumptions and prejudices through which we normally view even the most commonplace events. In Mirsky's words, he 'strips the world of the labels attached to it by habit and social convention and gives it a "dis-civilised" appearance, as it might have appeared to Adam on the day of creation, or to one blind from birth who received his sight.'[3] The Russian formalist critic Viktor Shklovsky coined the much-used phrase 'making it strange' (*ostraneniye*) to describe this strategy; it is, as Mirsky says, akin to anarchism. But it is an anarchism Rousseau or Voltaire would have recognised, a rational anarchism which replaces habitual assumption with freshly observed fact, and which makes so much of Tolstoy's work seem like an exemplification of Samuel Johnson's characteristically eighteenth-century definition of wit in the *Life of Cowley* as that 'which is at once natural and new, that which though not obvious is, upon its first production, acknowledged to be just, . . . that, which he that never found it, wonders how he missed.'

Johnson's definition rests on two major assumptions about the world which he shares with most eighteenth-century thinkers, and with Tolstoy: that there is a realm of eternal values, and that all men, unless corrupted by false values, will recognise them and respond to their discovery by the writer. It is because Tolstoy too shares these assumptions that he fulfils so many of the eighteenth-century critic's terms of praise, so that it has become commonplace for writers on Tolstoy to echo the familiar Johnsonian terms, saying in effect that he deals with universal themes, rather than those limited by time or place, that his sentiments find an echo in every bosom, that his mind at once comprehends the vast, and attends to the minute, and that his characters are the genuine progeny of common humanity. Most of all, Tolstoy would have understood and shared Johnson's belief, as expressed in the *Preface to Shakespeare*, that 'the pleasures of sudden wonder are soon exhausted, and the mind can only repose on the stability of truth.'

All of Tolstoy's work is, in an important sense, a dramatisation of his search for that stability. It is his own explorative moral quest that lies at its centre. Truth is the ultimate aim, the hero, as Tolstoy himself says early in his career, of his story: and the great *philosophes* of the Enlightenment were prominent among those writers who pointed the way towards that truth.

Rousseau is by far the most influential, but by no means the

7

only figure of the Enlightenment who was read with enthusiasm by the young Tolstoy. We know from a statement made much later, for example, that Montesquieu played a significant part in his unhappy years at Kazan University. While there, he worked on a comparison of Catherine the Great's legal system with Montesquieu's *Esprit des Lois*: this work, he says, 'opened up for me a new area of independent intellectual activity, but the University with its demands not only did not help in this activity, but actually hindered it'.[4] That his thinking should follow independent lines was, and remained, essential for him, and it was never likely that he would fit happily into the hide-bound university system. Like so many eighteenth-century thinkers, he rejected the curriculum of organised higher education as a compendium of facts which no reasonable man could ever wish to know, and set out instead to teach himself. His reported comment to a fellow student that 'History is like a deaf man answering questions which nobody has put to him'[5] summarises his attitude towards almost the whole university course, and prefigures the attitudes of *War and Peace*.

Another great figure of the French Enlightenment, Voltaire, figured at least as prominently as Montesquieu in Tolstoy's reading. He reports in *A Confession* that he read him when he was very young, and that his irony was partly responsible for destroying his childhood Christianity. A more positive contribution which that rational, ironic approach had to offer him, though, was the strategy of which Voltaire makes use so often in his *contes*, the strategy of seeing conventional experience through the eyes of an *ingénu*. In the story actually called *L'Ingénu*, the innocent concerned is a Huron Indian, whose simple but wholly reasonable vision enables him to see the absurdity of much conventional 'civilised' behaviour. This technique has obvious affinities with Tolstoy's strategy of 'making it strange', and Voltaire's Huron may be seen in some respects as a prototype for such characters as Eroshka and Lukashka in *The Cossacks*, or Hadji Murat in the short novel of that name, as well as for his more sophisticated *ingénus*, Pierre and Levin.

Voltaire's use of the Huron Indian is a reminder that, despite his sardonic distaste for Rousseau's natural man, he shared with many of his contemporaries a view of man that was quite close to Rousseau's. It is a view that is put most succinctly by another great *philosophe*, Diderot, when he writes:

'Vous voulez savoir l'histoire abrégée de presque tout notre misère? La voici. Il existait un homme naturel: on a introduit au dedans de cet homme un homme artificiel, et il s'est élevé dans la caverne une guerre continuelle qui dure toute la vie.'⁶

Diderot's words might be taken as an epigraph for Tolstoy's life and work, so closely do they seem to reflect his own views. Significantly, though, they might also be a summary of Rousseau's philosophy; and it is undoubtedly in Rousseau that we find the writer who stands closest of all to Tolstoy.

We can see from various fragments of autobiography the kind of impression that a reading of Rousseau made on him at a relatively early age. What he felt for Rousseau, he told Paul Boyer, 'was more than enthusiasm, it was worship. At fifteen I wore round my neck, instead of a cross, a medallion with his picture. Many of his pages are so close to me that I feel as if I had written them myself.'⁷ This statement was made in 1901, but its accuracy may be gauged from a passage he wrote much earlier, in the first chapter of his projected sequel to the semi-autobiographical *Youth*:

'I will never forget the strong, joyful impression, the contempt for human lies, and the love of truth which Rousseau's *Confessions* made on me. "So all people are the same as me" I thought with delight, "I am not the only monster born into the world with an abyss of sordid qualities. Why then does everyone lie and pretend when they have all been exposed already by this book?" I asked myself . . . Rousseau's discourse on the superiority of the wild state to the civilised one was also very much to my taste. As if I were reading my thoughts and adding to them only something else of my own.'⁸

There are indeed many passages of Rousseau that are strikingly reminiscent of Tolstoy, many isolated dicta which seem to anticipate moments in the novels. This is particularly true of *Émile*, in which book the reflections of the Savoyard priest were particularly close to him throughout his life. Thus we find him writing in his diary on July 8th, 1853, 'Got up late, began writing, but did not get on: I am much dissatisfied with my aimless, disorderly life. Read *Profession de foi d'un Vicaire Savoyard*, and as always when reading it, it produced an immensity of useful and noble thoughts in me. Yes, my main misfortune is a great intelligence.'[9] On October 7th in the same year we have: 'After dinner I read the *Profession de foi*, and remembered the only way of being happy.'[10] The priest's claim that 'I am no great philosopher, nor do I desire to be one, I have, however, a certain amount of common sense and a constant devotion to truth', his passionate belief that 'conscience persists in following the order of nature in spite of all the laws of man', and his advice to 'listen to the inner voice of feeling' in order to understand the workings of the universe, must all have struck an immediate and powerful echo in Tolstoy's breast, so strongly do they prefigure his own characteristic attitudes throughout his life.[11]

Émile, with its emphasis on man's natural goodness and on the importance of a correct education if that goodness is to be brought to its proper fruition and not corrupted by society, probably had more to offer the young Tolstoy than the *Social Contract* or the rambling and not always ingratiating *Confessions*. Nevertheless, aside from the support they give to the central doctrines of *Émile*, the early part of the *Confessions* in particular did have much to teach him. Perhaps of most immediate value was the reassurance that he was not alone in harbouring an 'abyss of sordid qualities'. Just as important, Rousseau's account of his early life offered him the spectacle of a mind attempting to apply rational, disinterested analysis of the frankest kind to the early years of its life. Though one often doubts Rousseau's honesty (as did Tolstoy later), the attempt is one that is likely to have inspired his imagination, and its relevance for his own exploration of the youthful mind in *Childhood, Boyhood and Youth* is obvious.

We do not need Tolstoy's direct testimony, then, to tell us that Rousseau's influence on the development of his own ideas was, to use his own term, 'enormous'. The evidence is there for any objective assessment to discover. The belief that man is basically good rather than evil is no doubt a matter of individual character, an instinctive belief existing more deeply than the influence of philosophers can reach. But finding this belief shared by Rousseau, Tolstoy makes it one of the great foundations of all his subsequent work. 'Man is born perfect' he wrote in 1862 'that is the great word spoken by Rousseau, and it will, like a rock, remain strong and true.'[12] For him it does remain strong and true, and on the rock of that conviction he builds the novels, and the life, which are both a quest for the rediscovery of that natural goodness, in harmony with itself and the natural world, knowing instinctively the good from the bad, the only state in which true happiness is to be found.

Sharing Rousseau's belief in man's natural goodness, Tolstoy also shares his belief that the realm of values is something constant and eternal. He read Hegel thoroughly, and dismissed with some anger the argument that truth was in any way relative or historically evolving. He had no time for Hegelian metaphysics, or for any kind of mysticism. Truth was something constant, something that was to be found in the individual's own experience, if he had not been too corrupted by the education imposed on him by a self-appointed élite of intellectuals. This mistrust of progressive intellectuals, which he shared with Dostoyevsky as well as with Rousseau, was another of the factors which made his relations with contemporary writers, and especially with Turgenev, so notoriously difficult. Believing as he did that the essential truth of things might be more clearly seen by the innocent child than by the sophisticated man, he found it difficult to accept that the latter should be allowed to impose his supposedly advanced beliefs on the former. With a characteristic willingness to follow the logic of his beliefs to their limits, he based the school that he founded on his estate at Yasnaya Polyana on the principle that the children should be allowed to learn whatever they wanted to. When he discovered, not surprisingly, that the children were unimpressed by Pushkin and Gogol, he concluded, consistently but perversely, that there was something corrupt about the latter, and about all 'sophisticated' art. Art, like life, should be concerned with the simple, basic truth of things in a way that can reach not the sophisticated few, but the uneducated multitude. These conclusions, arrived at in the early 1860s and argued out in the magazine *Yasnaya Polyana*, anticipate the later attacks on sophisticated art which culminate in *What is Art?* in 1897. Again, though, they had been anticipated to some extent by Rousseau's *Discourse on the Sciences and Arts* and by his attacks on the fashionable theatre of his own times.

We can see, then, why Tolstoy should have worn Rousseau's picture like an icon around his neck at the age of fifteen. The commitment to the discovery of the truth, the emphasis on natural goodness, on the need to look inside oneself for the answers to the most important questions, on the corruption of so-called sophisticated man, and on the corresponding innocence of the child or the peasant, which are all features of both the early and the late Tolstoy, were all to be discovered in Rousseau.

Recognition of this indebtedness helps dispose of the belief that Tolstoy's views changed drastically as he grew older. Certainly they are modified in various ways, particularly with the spiritual crisis of the 1870s which is described in *A Confession*. But the old Tolstoy who made his own shoes and wore peasant clothes was already there in the seventeen-year-old boy who made his own clothes from coarse linen. Both were indebted to the discovery in Rousseau of a philosophy of life which chimed so exactly with his own existing, instinctive beliefs. That the process was of this kind needs emphasising; Tolstoy probably learnt little that was new to him from Rousseau. Rousseau's philosophy provided him with a channel along which his own ideas could run more confidently, developing into an art far richer than Rousseau's and far wider in its apprehension of the manifold complexities of human experience, but unchanged in its essential principles until his death. As he lay dying at Astapovo railway station his last audible words were 'Truth . . . I love much', and they look back significantly to the closing words of *Sevastapol in May*, written half a century before: 'The hero of my story, whom I love with all the power of my soul, whom I have tried to portray in all his beauty, who always was, is, and will be beautiful—is truth.'[13] During the fifty-five years that intervened, he had consistently sought that truth in novels, plays and essays, as well as in his actions, sacrificing his art, his peace of mind, and even his family in following wherever it seemed to lead him. And all he gained, as Sir Isaiah Berlin has said, was 'doubt, insecurity, self-contempt and insoluble contradictions'.[13]

It is often assumed that Tolstoy's sympathy with the Enlightenment is to be explained by the backwardness and isolation of nineteenth-century Russian culture, lagging a generation or two behind Western Europe. It is true that a conventional aristocratic education in Russia in the 1830s and 1840s might well have involved a reading of Rousseau and Voltaire, as it would probably have done in England. But it is a mistake to assume that sophisticated circles there would have regarded them as anything but old-fashioned. Older contemporaries of Tolstoy like Turgenev were well abreast of developments in

Western Europe. Indeed, when Tolstoy entered the literary scene in 1851, the Russian intellectual world had for some time been divided between those liberal progressives, like Turgenev or the critic Belinsky, who admired Western culture and institutions, and the reactionary Slavophils, of whom Dostoyevsky was to become the most famous, with their quasi-mystical regard for all that was Russian, and their distaste for materialist Western civilisation. Both groups testify by their existence to Russian involvement, albeit at a distance, in European movements of thought. Tolstoy belonged to neither group, and had little patience with either, though both wooed him for a time. But there can be no doubt that he was well aware of the cultural movements which he chose to disregard. *The Contemporary*, to which he sent his first work, lived up to the claims of its title by providing its readers with translations of the work of contemporary European authors, and with more general surveys of the foreign cultural scene. It was probably in *The Contemporary* that Tolstoy first read Dickens, whom he admired immensely, and George Eliot. Like any Russian aristocrat he spoke French fluently, and read the fashionable French novelists of his day— Hugo, George Sand, or Eugène Sue. Against this background his continued adherence to Rousseauan ideas can only be seen as a characteristically independent and unfashionable allegiance.

Just how anachronistic it was can be seen by the treatment of Rousseau in the greatest work of Russian literature before *War and Peace*, Pushkin's *Eugene Onegin*. Pushkin's 'novel in verse' was written twenty years before the young Tolstoy began to wear Rousseau's picture round his neck. Even in the 1820s, however, Pushkin's heroine Tatyana is old-fashioned and provincial in her taste for Rousseau and Richardson. Pushkin contrasts her reading with the fashionable Romanticism of Eugene and his circle. When Tatyana visits Eugene's deserted house, she finds in his study a statue of Byron, and the books on which he has modelled himself—Byron and the modern novelists in whom

> the epoch is reflected
> and modern man
> rather correctly represented
> with his immoral soul,
> selfish and dry,

> to dreaming measurelessly given,
> with his embittered mind
> boiling in empty action. (*VII*.22)[14]

In fact Pushkin's great poem is a critique of fashionable Byronism that testifies to the impact of Western European culture on literate Russia a generation before Tolstoy began to write.

A reading of *Eugene Onegin* is also important in introducing us to a more significant fact about Tolstoy's admiration for Rousseau than its independent unfashionableness. This is the extent to which Rousseau's ideas are so easily identifiable with a set of values which both Pushkin and Tolstoy, and after them Pasternak, see as essentially Russian. His heroine Tatyana, as Edmund Wilson has said, represents for Pushkin the good 'Rousseauist Nature', as opposed to the deadly Byronism of Onegin or the foolish idealism of his friend Lensky; but she also represents something beyond this: 'both Evgeny and Lensky are half foreigners, they think in terms of the cultures of the West, whereas Tatyana, who has spent her whole life on the wild old feudal estate, is for Pushkin the real Russia.'[15] Tatyana's goodness lies in her simplicity: her behaviour towards Onegin is honest, loving and natural. Further, she has, despite her naïveté as it seems to Onegin, a deeper insight into the truth, the hidden reality of things, than does either he or Lensky, for all their education. In all these ways she is strikingly similar to Tolstoy's Natasha, who is in the same way instinctively closer to the real truth of things than is either of her highly educated lovers, Pierre and Andrey. In both cases the writers associate these Rousseauan virtues with the essentially Russian character of their heroines.

In Tolstoy there are many more examples of such an association. In *War and Peace*, both Platon Karatayev and Kutuzov, for all their difference in rank, have a simple wisdom that is based on this same essential Russianness, as to a lesser extent does Nikolay Rostov. In *Anna Karenina*, the peasants from whom Levin learns, as well as his wife Kitty, and Stiva Oblonsky's wife Dolly, have the same kind of insight, the same kind of Russian character on which Western European ideas either have never impinged, or have only touched superficially.

Here and in the shorter novels and stories, the Russian soul is celebrated as something simple and close to nature, wise in a way denied to the mind that is corrupted or bewildered by Western European culture. The virtues that are praised by Rousseau are identified with Russia, and particularly Russian womanhood, the corrupting artificial world with that which is not Russian.

Much later, in *Dr Zhivago*, Pasternak makes the identification of his heroine with both Russia and with the natural world still more explicit. When Zhivago asks himself what Lara means to him, the answer comes easily—she stands for Russia, 'his incomparable mother', and at the same time for life itself: 'You could not communicate with life, but she was its representative, its expression, the gift of speech and hearing granted to inarticulate being.'[16] In this she stands in the tradition of Pushkin's and Tolstoy's heroines, and also in a still older Russian tradition, for the cult of the Earth Mother which comes out so clearly in *Dr Zhivago* had since earliest times been what G. P. Fedotov calls 'the core of Russian religion' in which 'converge the most secret and deep religious feelings of the folk'. As Fedotov goes on to point out, it is the fertility of the earth, not its outward appearance that is important:

> 'The very epithet of the earth in the folk songs, "Mother Earth, the Humid," . . . alludes to the womb rather than to the face of the Earth. It means that not beauty but fertility is the supreme virtue of the earth . . . Earth is the Russian "Eternal Womanhood," not the celestial image of it: mother, not virgin; fertile, not pure . . .'[17]

Christianity never altogether supplanted this early worship of the Earth Mother. Instead she was assimilated to Russian Christianity as the image of motherhood, still identified in the folk songs, and in the non-religious lyric poetry, with the world of nature—that is, with the Russian land.

It seems very likely that it was in part the lost religion of his childhood, for which Tolstoy always had such a powerful nostalgia, that instilled in him an enduring sense of womanhood as associated with a special kind of natural, intuitive wisdom, and with the beauty and fertility of the earth. As in the religious tradition Fedotov describes, so for Tolstoy, the idea of womanhood was always inseparable from that of motherhood, and this larger context helps us to understand better his treatment of Anna Karenina, who abandons her role of mother, or Sonya, who becomes a 'sterile flower', and whose love is too generalised to be productive, so that she can be neither wife nor mother.

This attitude towards women is one of the clearest examples of the way in which values that are peculiarly Russian in origin influence Tolstoy's outlook, shape his world. Another example, arising from the same sense of the earth as mother of all things, is his acute awareness of a harmonious relationship between man and the beneficent physical world around him. It is a relationship Olenin perceives in *The Cossacks*, which Andrey discovers when he passes the newly-leafed oak on his return from the Rostov's estate, or which Natasha and Nikolay experience in the hunt in *War and Peace*. There are many more examples in the major novels and the shorter works of the way in which, in Thomas Mann's words, 'the strength of his mother the earth streams through him',[18] but probably the best known of all is the mowing episode in *Anna Karenina*, where Levin's hard, rhythmical labour as he moves through the field with the peasants takes him deep into that harmonious state which his companions already know. That experience is both Rousseauan and Russian. Tolstoy himself, staying at Clarens, where Rousseau had set *La Nouvelle Héloïse*, describes how the beauty of the evening scene acted upon him with the power of the unexpected:

'At that moment I wish to love, and I even feel love for myself, and I regret the past, hope for the future, and there is joy in me at being alive. I want to live forever, and thoughts about death are filled with a childishly poetic horror. Sometimes, while sitting alone in the shade of the little garden and gazing, always gazing on the shores of the lake, I experience a kind of physical impression, as though the beauty "pours through my eyes into my soul." '[19]

One would hardly need to know the significance of the location to associate this experience with Rousseau. But there is a difference; Tolstoy goes on to express his indifference to the dramatic views beloved of the English tourists, and to link his love for nature with a landscape that is recognisably Russian, not Swiss. He does not want to look at scenery, but to be part of it: 'I love nature when it surrounds me on all sides and extends unendingly, and when I am a part of it. I love it when I am surrounded by warm air, and when that air rolls away into the measureless distance.' The Russian experience of nature differs from the Western European one in this strong emphasis on being a part of a vast, measureless whole. As Fedotov says, 'the beauty of nature for the Russian is the embracing, the enveloping, rather than the contemplated. Man is lost in nature, unwilling to master her.'[20] Again this attitude is found in Pushkin and Pasternak as well as in Tolstoy: it is part of his specifically Russian heritage, to be reinforced rather than originated by what he could find in Rousseau.

The asceticism which was always a strong element in his moral nature, existing uneasily alongside an equally strong appetite for sensual fulfilment, is another characteristically Russian quality that Rousseau's ideas may only have helped to clarify. Asceticism was a major virtue in the Russian Christian tradition, embodied in the hard monastic life, and preached by its founder and greatest saint, Theodosius, a man who is in many ways strikingly similar to the later Tolstoy. Theodosius preached and practised asceticism, humility and self-impoverishment; he wore simple clothes and associated with the poor. Through his influence these typically Tolstoyan characteristics entered the Russian religious tradition at an early stage and remained so strongly embedded that they can hardly have failed to influence Tolstoy's own moral attitudes. When Levin tells Oblonsky, while the latter is ordering dinner with all the relish that only Tolstoy's characters can muster, that he likes 'buckwheat porridge and cabbage soup best' he is not just a projection of his creator's idiosyncratic tastes; he is also reflecting a Russian ascetic tradition of which Tolstoy and Dostoyevsky, and after them Pasternak and Solzhenitsyn, are the inheritors and developers.

In many ways then, Tolstoy's early and enduring respect for Rousseau seems likely to have been founded not only on an innate temperamental affinity between the two men, but also on the similarity of many of Rousseau's ideas to those typically Russian values which Tolstoy would have drunk in from early childhood. In retrospect it seems likely that it is the latter, vague and ill-defined though they must remain, which exercised the greatest influence over his essentially religious sensibility, offering him the basic moral attitudes from which he never diverged. What Rousseau offered was a philosophical system which rationalized and channelled these beliefs, the two combining to make his faith in the existence of an eternal moral order, in the virtues of the simple natural life, and in man's essential goodness, the foundations on which his novels and his life were to be based.

Childhood, Boyhood and *Youth*

After withdrawing from Kazan University in April, 1847, the young Tolstoy spent four indecisive years in Moscow, Petersburg, and on his newly inherited estate at Yasnaya Polyana, before in April, 1851, he left for the Caucasus in the company of his brother Nikolay, whose regiment was stationed there, part of the Russian attempt to subdue the still independent mountain tribes. During these years, Tolstoy shows no sign of interest in the very active intellectual and political life of the two capitals. At the same time as Dostoyevsky was being taken to his own pretended execution before being exiled to Siberia for his political activities, Tolstoy was living the life of a fairly typical young man of his background, the polite social round being heavily augmented by brothels, gambling, and a fashionably dissolute life-style in general. Despite the decidedly non-intellectual character of his associates, however, his intellectual development went on in its own typically self-centred way. Just as he threw himself with gusto into the life of the city, so he would frequently recoil from it in disgust, recording in his diary his violent self-criticisms and his rules for a new life, and retiring periodically to Yasnaya Polyana with the aim of leading a simple, pure life as the mentor of his peasants.

Both then and later his life during these four years seemed to him an aimless and vicious one; but it was the conflicting and complex character of the new experiences with which he was then being confronted that gave rise to his first serious efforts to write, and it was just before dissatisfaction and mounting gambling debts drove him to the Caucasus that he began the unfinished fragment, *A History of Yesterday*, an experiment in the detailed recording of a single day's experience, full of digressions and a rather self-conscious whimsicality, which owes a good deal to Sterne, by whom he had long been impressed. Once in the Caucasus, where he eventually decided to enter the army himself as an officer-cadet, he turned to the first part of what he intended to be a much more substantial novel in four sections, based loosely on his own life up till that time, which we now know in the three sections which were completed—*Childhood*, *Boyhood* and *Youth*.

Though these three sections were published separately in *The Contemporary* over a period of five years, from 1852 to 1857, Tolstoy seems always to have seen them as a single, coherent work, a *bildungsroman* that was neither strictly autobiographical, nor yet more than superficially fictionalised. He calls it 'my novel up to Tiflis' (i.e. the end of 1851, when he took the examinations to enter the army at Tiflis), and toys with the idea of calling it *Four Epochs of Life*.[1] Though its final section was never finished, it still retains in its tripartite form a simple and obvious homogeneity that justifies us in taking it as a single novel, rather than as three loosely related sketches.

Taken thus, *Childhood, Boyhood and Youth* is one of Tolstoy's most substantial achievements before the writing of *War and Peace*. It provided him with a very open setting in which he was able to explore, through the apparently simple series of recollections of which it consists, the significance which his formative experience held for him. In this respect, it is worth making the comparison which suggests itself with Joyce's *Portrait of the Artist as a Young Man*: for, different though the two men seem in so many ways, to make the comparison is to recognise more clearly what is often passed over in discussion of *Childhood, Boyhood and Youth*—that is, the extent to which it, too, is very much a portrait of the artist as a young man, or at least of an individual who is in many ways different from those around him, isolated by virtue of his greater sensitivity, the greater complexity of his character. Professor Christian has emphasised the relative normality of Tolstoy's narrator, the young Nikolay Irtenyev, and the inevitable universality of much childhood experience.[2] But if that experience is in one sense normal and universal, it nevertheless bears down on Nikolay, as it does on the young Stephen Dedalus, with an urgency that it doesn't have for their contemporaries. This is brought out if we look at Nikolay's brother, the quintessentially normal Volodya, who is introduced as a foil to his younger brother; none of Tolstoy's brothers, it is worth noting, could reasonably have been described as normal.

That we don't on the whole recognise this greater intensity of experience, and with it the figure of the young artist, in Tolstoy's novel is partly because, as has been said, he never saw himself in that role in the way that Joyce or Flaubert did. But it is also because that figure is so firmly embedded in a matrix of apparent normality. Tolstoy's strategy, here as so often, is to invite the reader to recognise and share in his experience, to convince him that he, too, has felt just these emotions, or that he, too, would have reacted in just this way. With Joyce it is precisely the opposite: we are always aware, always encouraged to be aware, of the difference that exists not only between the artist and those around him, but also between the artist and those who read his book. We are never, for example, tempted to feel kinship with Stephen's period of intense religious commitment, minutely though his feelings are described. However much we may sympathise and respect, we feel his experience as something remote from our own. And yet, when Tolstoy describes a not dissimilar period of religiosity in the opening chapters of *Youth*, culminating in his visit to the monastery to make a second confession, the reader does feel such a sense of kinship, and this despite the fact that he would probably not have felt or acted in this way any more than he would in the way Joyce describes. Tolstoy's experience, here and elsewhere, is as far from the normal in its intensity as is Joyce's: the difference lies in the self-consciousness of Joyce's role as artist, compared with the sense we have in reading Tolstoy that he is simply as other men are, but more so. It is only on sober reflection that we recognise that the protagonist of *Childhood, Boyhood and Youth* is really as far from the 'common reader' as is Stephen Dedalus, but that Tolstoy would never have thought for long of presenting him as 'Nikolay Hero'. The result is that instead of witnessing the development of the artist from a respectful distance, we are immersed in it in a way that invites familiarity, sympathy and judgement, but which rarely if ever seems to be asking for a special degree of respect.

To recognise this sense of familiarity and immersion in his first novel is to recognise one of the major defining characteristics of Tolstoy's fiction. It is the recognition not only that we know the details of the inner life of Nikolay, Pierre, Andrey or Levin, but that we are familiar with them, have a sense of kinship with them, to a greater extent than we do with the characters of Flaubert or Stendhal, Dickens or George Eliot. Tolstoy's are the least heroic of heroes, and therefore in many ways the most heroic; for if we finally come to respect them, as we so often do, we do so with a full and familiar knowledge of their weaknesses, having seen them tread a path of self-discovery in which we have been continually invited to see a reflection of our own actual or potential experience. It is an aspect of that mixture of egoism and humility, which becomes more evident in Tolstoy as he grows older, that leads him thus to offer up much of his own character, in the guise of Nikolay, for consideration by a reader who is encouraged to feel that he is his peer, just as later he is encouraged to feel a familiar equality with, or even at times an indulgent superiority to, Pierre or Levin. In all three cases the feeling is likely to be deceptive: their capacity for experience, the degree of intensity with which they feel love, anguish or happiness, is likely to be greater than our own. But it is an innocent and profitable deception: by encouraging the sense of familiarity and kinship Tolstoy makes us participate in the experience of his characters in a way that we rarely do with those of other novelists, a way that enlarges our own experience, since we see our own potential actions and feelings in the world he creates.

This process of immersion in his world is one of the most important factors in bringing about the sense of immediacy in the novels, the sense testified to by so many readers that his work is, in Matthew Arnold's phrase, not art but 'a piece of life'.[3] Arnold, Henry James and others were wrong—quite indefensibly wrong—in failing to see that Tolstoy's is in fact a highly considered and accomplished art; but Arnold's formula directs us usefully towards one of the main distinctions that can be made between Tolstoy's work and that of his great contemporary, Dostoyevsky. It seems unlikely that Arnold would have described a Dostoyevsky novel as 'a piece of life', not because of the evidence of any clearer formal discipline, but because of the absence of this kind of familiarity, this sense of normality. The point may be made by saying that we have sympathy *for* Dostoyevsky's characters, we have sympathy *with* Tolstoy's. If we consider the way Tolstoy would have handled the events of *Crime and Punishment*, for example, we can see that the difference would almost certainly have lain in the reader's greater sympathy and sense of kinship with Raskolnikov. Dostoyevsky, of course, goes far into the mind of the murderer, but he, and we, observe rather than participate. Tolstoy's murderers, Pozdny-shev in *The Kreutzer Sonata* or Irtenyev in *The Devil*, drag us into a kind of complicity with them, despite the fact that in the case of the former, at least, few readers are likely to sympathise with his views.

This sense of kinship with his characters that is so important to Tolstoy's work is the more easily achieved in *Childhood, Boyhood and Youth* because we see the world exclusively through the eyes of a single character. We share Nikolay's experience and so, inevitably, we tend to identify ourselves with it more easily than if the story was being told in the third person, even a third person as transparently close to the hero as that of Joyce in *Portrait of the Artist*. Dickens uses the same technique in that other great nineteenth-century work of fictionalised autobiography, *David Copperfield*, a book which Tolstoy read just before he began *Childhood*, which he admired enormously, and which, as has often been pointed out, he seems to echo at times. Just as important for examples of the first person narrative being used to engage the reader's sympathy, and even complicity, were those two short novels which Tolstoy was later to say had exercised a disproportionate influence over him when he was writing *Childhood, Boyhood and Youth*—Sterne's *Sentimental Journey* and the Swiss writer Topffer's *Bibliothèque de Mon Oncle*.

The fact of the young Tolstoy's indebtedness to Laurence Sterne has become a commonplace, and yet it has probably done so only because Tolstoy himself drew attention to it. It seems unlikely that any reader of his published work from *Childhood* onwards would otherwise be reminded in any significant way of the *Sentimental Journey* (the work of Sterne with which he was most familiar), so different in temperament do the two men seem. Once alerted to the debt, though, both by Tolstoy's own statements, and by the very Sternian *History of Yesterday*, it is easy to see how the organisation of *Childhood, Boyhood and Youth* into a series of short, cameo sketches within a very loose first person narrative frame parallels the structure of the *Sentimental Journey*. We can see, too, that however different the tone may be, Sterne's 'quiet journey of the heart in pursuit of NATURE, and those affections which arise out of her, which make us love each other—and the world, better than we do' does have much in common with Tolstoy's record of his own spiritual journey of the heart from childhood to youth. It moves through the same succession of brief sketches, searching for the natural feelings that underlie the hypocrisies of the civilised world, and laying open for close inspection those epiphanic moments of happiness, grief or generosity when *la sensibilité* flourishes most. We can see why Tolstoy would have admired Sterne; and yet from the very outset of *Childhood*, despite the fact that it begins with a mixture of tears and happiness which followers of the cult of the sentimental would doubtless have admired, we are aware of a voice that differs fundamentally from the wry, almost bantering tone of the *Sentimental Journey*. Tolstoy, it is true, is often an ironist, but his irony is almost as different from Sterne's as it is possible for irony to be. Not only does he use the device less frequently than Sterne, in whose work one is aware of almost every statement being undercut by the gently ironic voice, but his irony is pungent and committed where Sterne's is bland and elusive, angry where Sterne's is tolerant. The description of Nikolay's ridiculously boorish behaviour when first visiting his friend Nekhlyudov's family, in Chapter 23 of *Youth*, for example, has none of Sterne's wry urbanity about it, though it is not the less deftly or amusingly handled, as Nikolay stoutly insists that he always prefers to begin reading books from the middle, because they are more interesting that way. The irony comes from the discrepancy between what the young Nikolay thinks is a 'clever and original manner' and what his behaviour looks like to those around him, to the mature Tolstoy, and to the reader. It is not, as Sterne's irony is, the medium through which he views all human experience.

It may be that much of what seems to us to be alien to Tolstoy's temperament in Sterne was blunted for him because he read him in French translation, or in his relatively limited English. It seems likely, for example, that he slightly misunderstood his favourite quotation from Sterne, which he uses in *The Cossacks* and quotes twice in his own diary:[4] 'If nature has so wove her web of kindness, that some threads of love and desire are entangled with the piece, must the whole web be rent in drawing them out?' Sterne was thinking of the decidedly physical temptations with which the *fille de chambre* presented him, but Tolstoy seems to have taken the 'love and desire' on a more spiritual plane, or at any rate a less ironic one, as the context in *The Cossacks* shows. It may thus have been a somewhat cruder and more overtly serious Sterne that influenced him, and it is interesting to reflect that this is not an altogether unfair description of the other novel which he was later to say had over-influenced *Childhood, Boyhood and Youth*, Topffer's *Bibliothèque de Mon Oncle*.

As with Sterne, one can see the link with Topffer once Tolstoy has pointed to it. Though it now wears an air of pleasant mediocrity, Topffer's novel tells, if not of childhood, at least of boyhood and youth, without profundity, but with an ironic humour that tries to imitate Sterne, but has none of his poise or panache. What is important is that he is far more overt a moralist than Sterne, and such things as the last sentence of *Childhood*—'The thought comes to me: is it possible that Providence united me with these two beings, only to make me for ever mourn them?'—are much closer to Topffer than to Sterne.

The influence of Rousseau as well as Sterne is apparent in *La Bibliothèque de Mon Oncle*, and the combination is obviously one that would have appealed greatly to the young Tolstoy. Indeed, the tone of Topffer already seems to be there in the *History of Yesterday*. His novel could have offered Tolstoy in 1850 far more than it could offer any reader now. For him, it must have provided a valuable example of a sympathetic and gentle sensibility exploring the emotions of boyhood and youth, and recounting them in a first person narrative that on the whole manages to avoid condescension.

There is no question but that Tolstoy's own narrative consistently avoids any such condescension, however much direct or ironic disapproval of his earlier behaviour the narrator may display. The first person narrative does, nevertheless, present some fundamental problems: one simple one has been pointed to by Professor Christian, who rightly comments on the fact that since we only see other characters through Nikolay's eyes, we often have the sense of coming into only brief and superficial contact with them.[5] This is less true of the closer members of his family, but it is tantalisingly so of, for example, Nekhlyudov's aunt, Sophia Ivanovna, whose physical appearance—'she had that peculiar over-full type of figure which is only found in short, very stout old maids who wear corsets. It was as if all her healthfulness had risen upwards with such force that it threatened to choke her at any minute'—overawes the young Nikolay, but whose 'habit, after uttering a few words, of sighing deeply, opening her mouth a little and slightly turning up her large blue eyes' puts him at ease: 'such sweet kindliness was somehow expressed that following that sigh I lost all fear of her, and even liked her very much. Her eyes were charming, her voice sonorous and pleasant, and even the very rounded lines of her figure, at that period of my youth, seemed to me not devoid of beauty.' (*Youth*, Chapter 23)

Sophia Ivanovna, though she is splendidly bodied forth here, clearly also has an inner life of her own of which we know nothing, but of which, if this were *War and Peace* or *Anna Karenina*, we would learn and understand something more, perhaps a good deal more. Now, although she precipitates a short digression on the three different kinds of love Tolstoy believes to exist (he is exceptionally fond of such orderly, tripartite classifications) we see Sophia Ivanovna and her inexhaustible store of love for those around her only briefly. Because of the framework of the novel she cannot, as we see by the very nature of this description, exist independently of Nikolay and the impression she makes on him. This is true too of other peripheral characters in the novel—the rest of Nekhlyudov's family, the university students Zukhin and Semyonov, Prince Ivan Ivanych, and many others to whom Tolstoy gives a brief vitality that cries out for the kind of objective enlargement that a more conventional third person narrative could provide. It is one of his greatest strengths as a novelist that he is able to give his characters this kind of independent existence, so that his reader seems actually to know what it feels like to be Oblonsky or Levin, Natasha or Princess Maria. In choosing the first person narrative form of *Childhood, Boyhood and Youth* he has largely cut off the possibility of doing this in all but the case of the narrator himself.

The other major problem to which the first person narrative gives rise has to do with the character of this narrator. *Childhood, Boyhood and Youth* inhabits a rather uneasy area between autobiography and fiction, so that the story we are told is not that of Tolstoy's own youth. It is, as he himself said many years later, partly his own experiences and partly those of his boyhood friends, the Islenyev brothers, that are described. Nikolay himself is not directly identifiable with Tolstoy—he did not, for example, remember his mother's death, nor was his father a gambler. He had three elder brothers, none of whom is identifiable with Nikolay's brother Volodya. These and many other elements are either fictional, or derive from the circumstances of the Islenyev brothers, and they justify his annoyance when he found that Nekrasov had published *Childhood* under the title *The History of My Childhood*. Nevertheless, Nekrasov's action is understandable, as is that of those biographers who use *Childhood, Boyhood and Youth* as source material. For, though the stuff of the narrative is partly fiction, the 'I' that tells the story is often recognisably Tolstoy himself. What we have, in fact, is a mixture of narrators that corresponds roughly to the mixture of autobiography and fiction, or (since Tolstoy disliked 'inventing' and rarely wrote wholly imaginary fiction) autobiography and biography, of which the novel consists.

At about the same time as he wrote *Childhood*, he also wrote the fine short story *The Raid*, one of the most impressive aspects of which is the extremely sensitive use of a narrator who, the reader gradually realises, doesn't understand the full implications of the story he is telling. The result is a controlled objectivity, an irony which exposes the futility of the military operation being described much more tellingly than a narrative by a character more closely identified with the author could have done. In *Childhood, Boyhood and Youth* he could not, and would not have wanted to, make use of this controlled distance between the perceptions of the narrator and those of the author. He was concerned with sincerity, with an honest attempt to reflect the crucial, formative aspects of childhood as accurately as possible, and he therefore required a narrator in whom the reader has a complete trust. Narrator and author are very close, so close that it is probably inevitable that they will merge into each other from time to time. We thus have two 'I's co-existing uneasily together in the novel, one the fictional character Nikolay Irtenyev, who has his existence as a central part of a work of art, the other Leo Tolstoy, whom we know as a historical, not a fictional character. It may have been to this that he referred when he later said, rather cryptically, that it was 'in a literary sense, insincere'.

So close are the two 'I's who tell the story that this might in any case seem a very minor flaw, the transitions between them scarcely noticeable, were it not for the fact that *Childhood, Boyhood and Youth* has no overall principle of structure that is strong enough to compensate for this lack of objective detachment on the part of the author. Consisting as it does of a series of sketches and digressions, Sternian in origin if not in tone, it never, at least after *Childhood*, gives any real sense of being shaped by the novelist. This is, it is true, largely a conscious decision on Tolstoy's part. Extending the method of *A History of Yesterday*, his concern was an experimental one, a concern with truth in the sense of an immediate accuracy to life, rather than with any of the distortions of that truth that the shaping of a work of art seemed to him to involve. But the fidelity and accuracy, though impressive, are dearly bought. The series of cameos, held together after the first book by no more than chronological sequence, give scope for his realism, his psychological insight, his ability to convince his reader that he is immersed in a real world which he recognises and understands, even though he may never have seen it before. But all these strengths and many others are working outside the formal discipline of any but the loosest of frameworks. And it is this, more than anything else, that makes *Childhood, Boyhood and Youth* at once clearly the work of a potentially great novelist, and yet not itself a major novel— makes it, in fact, precisely what one might expect such an early work to be. 'When this wine has ripened,' Turgenev wrote, 'there will be a drink fit for the gods.'

From the very outset the wine was of an undeniably impressive quality. *Childhood* attracted a good deal of attention, and received a warmer welcome than did its two sequels, partly no doubt because it was the first published work of an unknown and still anonymous writer—'who is this mysterious L.N.T.?' Dostoyevsky wrote from Siberia—but partly, too, because though it is the more clearly flawed in some respects, it is also the freshest and most closely organised of all three books. From the very first page one is impressed by the sensitive accuracy of Tolstoy's picture of childhood. That convincing physical detail that always provides the matrix of his work is there from the beginning: 'On the 12th August 18— exactly three days after my birthday, on which I was ten, and on which I was given such wonderful presents, Karl Ivanych woke me up at seven o'clock in the morning, having hit at a fly just above my head with a flap made of sugar-bag paper on a stick.' The child's feelings are rendered with the same kind of precision, a pre-

cision that requires considerable tact if it is to avoid condescension:

> ' "Granted" I thought "I am small, but why does he disturb me?
> Why doesn't he flap at flies around Volodya's bed? There are lots
> there. No, Volodya is older than me; and I am the smallest of all:
> and that's why he tortures me. He spends his whole life thinking
> about how to make things unpleasant for me," I muttered. "He
> can see very well that he woke me up and startled me, but he acts
> as if he hasn't noticed it ... disgusting man! And his dressing-
> gown and the cap and the tassel—they're disgusting!" ' (*Childhood*,
> Chapter 1)

So accomplished and unlaboured, so inevitably right, is the tone
of these opening pages that it is difficult to believe that they
begin the first novel of a young man of twenty-four. Perhaps the
greatest compliment one can pay them is to say that they easily
stand the comparison, which the author himself half invited,
with the justly famous opening of the *Sentimental Journey*. We
are plunged, as there, *in medias res*, into a world of compelling
reality, a world in whose dealings we remain engaged until the
last pages of *Youth*. This reality is the more compelling because
it is a world notably, and rather surprisingly, considering
Tolstoy's later reputation, undistorted by any didactic formula:
the novel does not set out to teach us anything in any simple,
overall sense. We don't feel, for instance, that it is primarily
about childish innocence growing corrupt, as we might expect
from his enthusiasm for Rousseau. Though that element is
there, Rousseau's influence works more in the reflective honesty
of the account, and in the very conception of the work, in so far
as it differs from the family memoir popular in Russian literature at this time. The didactic impulse is only noticeably present
in isolated observations of a generalised kind, or in such wholly
acceptable and moving instances as the life and death of the old
housekeeper, Natalya Savishna. The overall impression we have
is the one Tolstoy intended, that of a scrupulous sincerity in de-
tailing events and the feelings that went with them, without any
heavy underlining of their significance. This is why the novel,
as in all his later work, is often at its best in the least obvious
places, where we are wholly convinced by the simple trans-
parency of the narrative, rather than in the more generalised
observations where, as one might expect even in Tolstoy at this

stage of his career, there is sometimes a certain lack of weight. Some of these generalisations, though, have their own magnificent nonchalance, as when we are told of Papa that 'like all retired military men he did not know how to dress fashionably'. It is a strategy Tolstoy was often to use later, with equally dubious statements—in the famous opening of *Anna Karenina*, for example, which might be reversed and still invite nods of profound agreement. They cajole the reader into an acceptance he might well withhold were it not for the air of urbane assurance, the assumption of ready agreement, with which they are made. Indeed, the importance of this kind of generalisation rarely lies in what is being said, so much as in this comforting impression it gives of the worldly wisdom of both author and reader.

If it is not shaped by any didactic intent, however, *Childhood* is given another kind of form, one which probably derives from the *History of Yesterday*. For it is basically an account of two important days in the young Nikolay's life, the first that preceding his departure from the family estate which, up to that point, had been all that he had known, and the second that of his grandmother's name-day in Moscow. The accounts of these two days are separated by a short reflective chapter, also called 'Childhood', which is filled with nostalgic memories of motherly love, while the book ends with the event which, as Nikolay says, ended his childhood—his mother's death. It thus has a relative tightness of form which is lacking in *Boyhood* and *Youth* where, although the scrupulously detailed scrutiny of the events of a short period is still the basic strategy, these periods are themselves selected from a much wider span of time than is the case in *Childhood*, so that they represent a succession of focal points in Nikolay's life. In this sense their structure is simply that of an album, sometimes introducing scenes and characters which never recur again, sometimes showing us faces we have seen many times before, but never needing to make any more solid connection between the pictures than their appearance beween the covers of the same album, the story of the young Nikolay Irtenyev's life.

It was perhaps inevitable that *Childhood* should be more shaped as a work of fiction than the other two parts, since it was further removed from the circumstances of Tolstoy's own life: his parents had both died when he was young—his mother when he was two, his father when he was nine. *Childhood* begins three days after Nikolay's tenth birthday, as we have seen, and much of it revolves around his relationship with his mother, the anticipation of whose death hangs rather heavily over the whole book.

Though she brings Tolstoy's invention into play, Maman is also the source of most that is flawed and awkward in *Childhood*. She is an idealised, sentimentalised figure, never as substantial to the reader as is her husband, with his twitching shoulder and slightly eccentric manner of dressing. Part of this lack of substance is no doubt due to Tolstoy's own reverence for the mother he never knew, and whom he was to present altogether more convincingly in the shape of Princess Maria in *War and Peace*. Part of it may be due, too, to his reading of *David Copperfield*, with its presentation of an equally sentimentalised mother. It has often been pointed out that when we first see Maman, she is sitting absentmindedly allowing the water from the samovar to overflow the teapot and flood the breakfast table, in precisely the same way that Betsey Trotwood does in Dickens's novel. Another close parallel is to be found in the description of the two boys' grief at their mothers' deaths: both writers reflect on the element of egoism and self-congratulation that is present in even a child's response to death, recording with considerable insight and honesty the feeling of dignity and importance in which they took a certain pleasure. The penultimate chapter in *Childhood*, called 'Grief', was the only one which Tolstoy was able to re-read later with pleasure, and it is indeed one of the high points of the whole novel, showing more clearly than anything else the qualities of the best work that was to follow it. Short, selective quotation misses the effect of a chapter that needs to be read as a whole, but one of the more readily isolable passages is that in which he describes the child's feelings as he stands on a chair and looks down at his mother lying in the coffin:

'I stared and felt that some incomprehensible, irresistible power drew my eyes to that lifeless face. I did not take my eyes from it, but my imagination drew pictures that blossomed with life and happiness. I kept forgetting that the dead body which lay before me and at which I stared absently, as on an object which had nothing to do with my memories, was *she*. I imagined her in one situation, and another: vital, happy and smiling; then suddenly I was struck by some feature in the pale face on which my eyes rested: I remembered the dreadful reality, and shuddered but did not stop looking. Then again dreams replaced the reality, and again consciousness of the reality dispersed the dreams. In the end my imagination became weary, it ceased to deceive me. The consciousness of the reality disappeared too, and I became oblivious of everything. I do not know how long I remained in this state, do not know what it was; I only know that for a time I lost consciousness of my own existence and experienced a kind of exalted, ineffably pleasant and sad happiness.'

This is superb in the fidelity with which it creates, or re-creates, the succession of feeling. The situation is hardly a commonplace one, and yet there can be few who read it for whom the experience described is not rendered absolutely real, true in the sense in which we know our own immediate experience to be true. This is the way in which the great Tolstoy is to work, reproducing the stuff of experience in a way that makes us forget the intervention of art between it and ourselves; the Tolstoyan mimesis seems not imitation, but the thing itself. Here, as often later, the effect is gained largely through the paradoxical nature of the experience. We accept it as a likely account because its apparent paradoxes correspond in general to our own experience. Feelings, we know, are more often than not confused and unpredictable in just this way. Tolstoy himself was very conscious of this, reminding us in *Boyhood* that 'improbability in matters of feeling is the surest sign of their sincerity' (Chapter 23), and to see pictures of life while looking at the face of death, to wander from the one to the other, and finally to feel a 'pleasant and sad happiness', when we would expect something quite different, is, we feel, likely to be right just because it is unexpected.

In its context, one of the most striking things about this particular passage is the contrast it presents to the short one which follows it, and which is as starkly untrue to any kind of experience we can know or surmise as the other is true:

'It may be that as she flew towards a better world her beautiful soul looked back with sadness at the one in which she was leaving us; she had seen my grief, taken pity on it, and descended to earth on the wings of love with a heavenly smile of compassion in order to comfort and bless me.'

This is not what the child felt: it is what the author offers as an explanation of those feelings he has just described so discerningly. And its inadequacy, the roots of its cloying sentimentality, lie not so much in any doubts we may have about its theology, as in its evident artificiality. It is irresistibly reminiscent of Victorian funeral sculpture, its images second-hand, its language literary in the worst sense. Whereas the language of the preceding paragraph is always alert, always convincing us that we are in the presence of a sensitive, exploring mind, here it is inert, not discovering so much as echoing. We have all read phrases like 'as she flew towards a better world', 'a heavenly smile of compassion', and 'on the wings of love'. They can mean nothing to us, irrespective of our religious convictions, because they mean little in the most important sense to Tolstoy.

This paragraph stands out sharply from those that precede and follow it, but its essentially unreal, sentimentalising tone recurs often in *Childhood* when Maman is mentioned. Her unreality is made all the more obvious by the palpable reality of Karl Ivanych, Papa, Grandmother, or Natalya Savishna. We have no sense of her physical presence, a lack that is rare indeed in Tolstoy. Instead we have the impression of a vague, sad spiritual presence, the sadness being there, one feels, not so much because of the impending departure of her children, nor because she has a profligate gambler as a husband, but because throughout we are being prepared for her death. The hints of this come in the very first chapter, when Nikolay invents a dream of his mother's death to explain his tears to Karl Ivanych (they are really caused by the latter's kindness after Nikolay had been thinking such hard thoughts about him). The forebodings are reinforced by the cryptic prophecies of the 'holy fool' Grisha, who keeps 'saying as if to himself: "A pity! . . . she flew away . . . the dove will fly to heaven . . . Oh, a stone on the grave".' Several chapters later we are told that 'From the very moment [Grisha] entered our house he had not stopped sighing and weeping, which in the opinion of those who believed in his powers of prophecy portended some kind of calamity to our household.' All this means that when, on

Nikolay's departure for Moscow, his mother 'smiled sadly, and kissed me strongly, strongly, for the last time' the atmosphere is heavily loaded: we already suspect that it really is for the last time. The effect of all this foreboding is to make the reader feel there is something altogether unworldly about Nikolay's mother: Tolstoy seems to want us to share the opinion expressed by Natalya Savishna that 'she was not a human being, she was an angel from heaven'. There are times when Tolstoy himself seems to think in these terms, and however acceptable the words may be in the mouth of the old housekeeper, they can only be unsatisfactory as the serious opinion of a novelist who depends elsewhere on an honest and penetrating realism.

Since motherly love is intended to dominate and define the period of childhood—the reflective chapter called 'Childhood' is almost entirely devoted to it, and as has been seen Nikolay's childhood ends with his mother's death—this sentimentalising of the mother figure means that we are always uncomfortably aware of a certain softness at the centre of the book. It is, however, the only area in which Tolstoy does not seem to be in easy and total command of his characters, and of the medium in which they are presented. Nikolay's father, the obvious foil to his mother, is sketched in—it is little more than that—with a tact that has not always been recognised. His character, or rather, as is always the case, Nikolay's reactions to his character, develop through all three books. But the chapter in *Childhood*, 'What kind of man my father was', is written from the standpoint of the mature narrator, not the child, and is remarkable for its quality of wholly objective and yet generous appraisal. This is so in spite of the fact that we are told that 'the two main passions of his life were cards and women: he had won several million roubles in the course of his life, and had had affairs with countless women of all classes'. Tolstoy's description conveys exactly the feelings of love, respect, doubt, and a certain envy that we might expect Nikolay's father to inspire in him. The nearest he comes to judgement is in the last sentences, which catch precisely and delicately his simple, amoral qualities:

'In his old age he developed fixed opinions on things, and innumerable rules of conduct—but solely on practical grounds. Those actions and the way of life which afforded him happiness or satisfaction he considered good, and considered that everybody else should act in the same way. He spoke very eloquently, and this ability, it seemed to me, increased the flexibility of his principles: he was able to describe the same action as the most delightful prank or as the lowest kind of villainy.' (Chapter 10)

Moral judgement is hinted at rather than made direct, with a self-restraint that is unexpected in a young writer, especially one with the tendency towards didacticism that was always part of Tolstoy's character. On the few occasions when he does make moral judgements elsewhere in *Childhood* they are nearly always managed with a similar tact; we can accept them because they are elicited carefully from their immediate context. One example of this is found in the chapter on 'Grief', where Nikolay's analysis of his own mixture of real grief and insincere posturing gives him the right to comment on the mixed motives observable in others:

'My father stood at the head of the coffin, was as white as a sheet, and kept back his tears with obvious difficulty. His tall figure in a black frock-coat, his pale expressive face, and his movements, graceful and assured as ever, when crossing himself, touching the ground with his hand while bowing, taking a candle from the priest's hands, or approaching the coffin, were extraordinarily effective; but, I don't know why, I particularly disliked it in him that he could appear so effective at that moment. Mimi was leaning against the wall and, it seemed, was hardly able to hold herself up; her dress was crumpled and covered with bits of down, her cap on one side; her swollen eyes were red, her head was shaking; she did not cease sobbing in a heart-rending voice, and kept covering her face with her handkerchief and her hands. It seemed to me that she was doing this so that having hidden her face from the spectators she could rest for a moment from her forced sobs.' (Chapter 27)

Natalya Savishna's grief is in contrast to this: she has none of the mixed feelings of her masters, and 'Grief acted on her so strongly that she did not find it necessary to hide the fact that she could attend to secondary matters; she would not even have understood how such an idea could occur to anyone.' (Chapter 28) Again, it is because it grows so convincingly out of its context that the reader can be profoundly moved by Tolstoy's account of Natalya Savishna's grief and her own death. The concrete details of the circumstances of the latter—her argument with Foka over the amount of rice the cook is using, her brother's displeasure over the size of her legacy, her bequests to the three children—convince us of the reality of the situation and of the characters involved in it. It is thus that we can accept the generalised judgements of the closing paragraphs which, taken in isolation, might seem like the most empty and sentimental moralising:

> 'She left life without any sorrow; she did not fear death, but accepted it as a blessing. It is often said, but how rarely it actually happens! Natalya Savishna was able to be unafraid of death because she was dying with an unshaken faith and having fulfilled the law of the Gospels. Her whole life was pure unselfish love and self-sacrifice. What if her beliefs could have been more lofty, her life dedicated to higher aims; was that pure soul any the less deserving of love and admiration?
>
> She accomplished the best and greatest thing in life—she died without grief or fear.' (Chapter 28)

Tolstoy's powerful nostalgia for his lost, childhood Christianity comes through strongly here. But we can believe these sentiments because we have been convinced by the wonderful solidity of what has gone before. And this is perhaps the greatest testimony one could offer to the level which he has already reached in his first work. For a young man of twenty-three it was, as his contemporaries recognised, a truly impressive achievement.

When we move from *Childhood* to *Boyhood* and *Youth* we are brought more unequivocally into contact with the self-imposed limitations of the semi-autobiographical form Tolstoy has chosen. Not only does the confusion between the two narrators increase, but lacking the formal coherence of *Childhood*, its sequels spread out into a series of cameos illustrative of Nikolay's development through boyhood and adolescence, and only loosely connected by the theme of growth itself. The only gesture he makes towards formal organisation is the inclusion in each book of a generalising, reflective chapter on 'Boyhood' and 'Youth' which parallels the chapter 'Childhood' in the first book. But he eschews the many other possibilities open to him— the record of one or two representative days, for example, the treatment of parallel or otherwise recurring themes, the use of a plot, or at least of a connected narrative. In doing so, though, he has gained what he wanted to gain, an evident and impressive honesty. Here, truly, the novelist might be said to be holding a mirror up to life, reflecting it with scrupulous accuracy, and imposing no distorting organisation on his experience in order to fit it into the framework of art. In fact the process of selection necessarily does this itself to some extent: but it remains true that the dominant spirit of both books is that of an explorative, sensitive openness to the facts of experience as the author recalls them. If they are less organised than *Childhood*, they never strike the falsely sentimental note that sometimes mars the latter.

Art, however, is not absent from *Boyhood* and *Youth*: if it is consciously avoided in the shaping of the whole, it is always evident in the parts. Sometimes, indeed, it is a little too much so. In the first chapter of *Boyhood*, for example, one is conscious of something uncomfortably close to a literary exercise in the undeniably impressive descriptions:

'In the hall the samovar, into which Mitka the postilion, red as a lobster, is blowing, is on the boil: outside it is damp and misty, as though steam was rising from an odorous dungheap; the sun irradiates the eastern part of the sky with a cheerful bright light, and the thatched roofs of the spacious outhouses around the courtyard glisten with the dew which covers them. Underneath them our horses can be seen tied up around their mangers, and their regular chewing can be heard. A shaggy mongrel, which had settled itself down before dawn on a dry heap of dung, stretches itself lazily and, wagging its tail, goes at a gentle trot to the other side of the yard. A bustling woman opens the creaking gates and drives her ruminative cows into the street, on which you can already hear the stamping, lowing and bleating of the herd, and exchanges a word with her drowsy neighbour. Philip, with his shirt sleeves rolled up, winds a bucket from the deep well, and splashing the clear water, pours it out into an oak trough, round which some newly-awakened ducks are already paddling about in a puddle; and I look with satisfaction at Philip's expressive, full-bearded face, and the big sinews and muscles which stand out sharply on his strong bare arms when he exerts himself in any way.'

The whole, finely realised scene does indeed convey some of the freshness of a boy's apprehension of an awakening world. But Tolstoy seems also to be enjoying the deployment of his powers of selective description for their own sake. The accuracy, the concern for visual detail, seeing what is actually there rather than what we expect to be there (even if it is at the expense of syntactical smoothness) are reminiscent of Ruskin's descriptions in *Modern Painters*, and a morality similar to Ruskin's, the post-Romantic morality of clear sighted respect for the actual world, lies behind the appeal of such passages as this. But the name of Ruskin reminds us also of how much like a painting, separable from all around it, this piece is. At the same time as we share Tolstoy's enjoyment, we are aware that we are reading a piece of self-consciously fine writing. It is—again reminiscent of Ruskin—a purple passage, and one that is felt to have been conceived as such by the author.

At its best, though, his visual observation in all three books plays a more important role than this kind of virtuoso scene painting. Again and again he uses the details of the physical scene to define a psychological one, a *paysage intérieure*. A simple example of this can be found in the excursion to the monastery in *Youth*. As he waits in the confessor's cell, Nikolay feels the physical surroundings having their effect on him:

'The windows faced out onto a white wall which rose about five feet away from them. Between them and the wall was a small lilac bush. No sound from outside reached the room, so that in this quietness the pleasant, measured ticking of the pendulum seemed quite loud. As soon as I was alone in this quiet corner, all my earlier thoughts and recollections disappeared from my head as if they had never existed, and I subsided wholly into a kind of inexpressibly pleasant musing. That faded nankeen cassock with its threadbare lining, the worn black leather binding of the books with their brass clasps, those dull green plants, the carefully watered earth and washed leaves, and especially the monotonous broken sound of the pendulum, spoke to me distinctly of some new, hitherto unknown life, a life of solitude, prayer, quiet peaceful happiness . . .' (Chapter 7)

The details of the room have a similar effect on the reader—enough, at least, to enable him to understand and partially share Nikolay's feelings. This use of the concrete, physical world, especially of selective detail of it, to help locate and body forth a spiritual state is another factor of immense importance to Tolstoy's later work, and is intimately related to the strategy of 'making it strange'. We can see it at work at some of the most crucial points in *Childhood, Boyhood and Youth*, in, for instance, the description of the orchard in *Youth*:

'In that thicket it is always damp, with a smell of dense, constant shade, of cobwebs and fallen apples which are already blackening where they lie on the rotting soil, of raspberries, and sometimes of the forest bugs, which you swallow accidentally with a berry, quickly eating another one to take away the taste. Moving forward you startle the sparrows, who always live in this quiet wood; you hear their hurried twittering and the beating of their small, quick wings against the twigs; in one spot you hear the droning of a bumble-bee, and somewhere on the path the steps of the gardener, the half-witted Akim, and his eternal humming to himself under his breath. You think to yourself: "No! neither he nor anyone in the world can find me here . . .", while with both hands, to right and left you pluck the juicy berries from their little white cones and swallow them one after another with delight. Your legs are wet through even above your knees, your head is full of some frightful nonsense (you keep repeating in your mind a thousand times in succession "a-n-d by-y-y twenty-y-ies a-n-d by sevens"), your arms, and your legs through your wet trousers, are stung by nettles, your head is beginning to be burnt by the vertical rays of the sun that are penetrating into the thicket, the wish to eat is long gone, but still you sit in the thicket, looking about, listening, thinking, and mechanically plucking and swallowing the best berries.' (Chapter 32)

The difference between this and the passage quoted from the first chapter of *Boyhood* is that here the physical details are intimately related to the state of mind of the protagonist. As in the case of the confessor's cell, but more powerfully, they convey that physical and mental state, that complex nexus of joyful feelings, in a way the reader can at once recognise and respond to. Again we forget the intervention of art between us and the experience, which seems to be itself present as we read, fully individualised and yet, for that very reason, all the more available. The medium itself has become transparent, so that we no longer feel we are in the presence of self-consciously fine writing, but of a mature and functional art.

The development of this skill in bodying forth both interior and exterior landscapes, of what Sir Isaiah Berlin calls Tolstoy's genius for 'marvellously accurate reproduction of the irreproducible',[6] is perhaps the most impressive achievement of the whole novel. To put the final emphasis on description is, at any rate, proper, for it is through its marvellously sensitive, perceptive description of the protagonist's feelings and experiences that *Childhood, Boyhood and Youth* works. Because he is dealing with his younger self, a self whose enthusiasms and problems he has largely outgrown, Tolstoy rarely touches on the major, quasi-philosophical problems that preoccupy him in most of his later work. He describes how it was, not how it might or ought to have been, nor on the whole does he seek for the reasons why it was so and not otherwise. We see, it is true, the awakening of that explorative moral consciousness which dominates his later work, but it is described in a spirit of complete, even ironic detachment:

'I often imagined myself a great man, discovering new truths for the benefit of all mankind, and looked upon other mortals with a proud consciousness of my own worthiness; but, strangely, coming into contact with those mortals, I felt shy towards each of them, and the higher I put myself in my own estimation, the less capable was I not only of exhibiting the consciousness of my own worthiness to others, but even of accustoming myself not to be ashamed of my simplest word or movement.' (*Boyhood*, Chapter 19)

Nikolay's relationship with the serious-minded Nekhlyudov develops out of the moral and philosophical preoccupations which begin to appear in *Boyhood*; but that relationship, too, is well distanced from the narrator, and Tolstoy passes over the actual substance of their long conversations very briefly, concentrating instead on the emotional side of their relationship. Perhaps the passage which most anticipates the moral concerns of the later work is that in the second chapter of *Youth*, when, in 'that particular time of Spring which affects the soul of man most strongly of all', the physical world about him awakens the moral springs of Nikolay's soul:

'A feeling new to me, extremely strong and pleasant, suddenly penetrated my soul. The wet earth through which, here and there, bright green blades of grass with yellow stalks were pushing up, the rivulets glistening in the sun and carrying whirling bits of earth and chips of wood, the reddening twigs of lilac with their swelling buds, swaying just under the window, the busy twitter of birds bustling about in this bush, the blackish fence wet from melting snow, but mainly the fragrant moist air and joyous sun, spoke to me distinctly and clearly of something new and beautiful, which, although I cannot communicate it just as it was revealed to me, I will try to communicate just as I conceived it: everything told me of beauty, happiness and virtue, told me that one was as easy and possible for me as the other, that one cannot exist without the other, and even that beauty, happiness and virtue are one and the same. "How could I have not understood this? How stupid I have been till now! How good and happy I could have been, and can be in the future!" I said to myself. "I must quickly, quickly, this very minute, make myself a different person and begin to live differently." Regardless of this, however, I went on sitting for a long time on the window-sill, dreaming and doing nothing.'

This awakening is the prelude to Nikolay's period of religious enthusiasm, and it marks, as he says, the beginning of his youth. Its concern with the nature of happiness and its connection with virtue is reminiscent of much that is to follow, particularly in *The Cossacks*. Here, though, the ironic implications of that final sentence are enough to remind us of how firmly the experience is embedded in the narrator's and the author's past (it is one of those occasions when the two are very obviously one). Neither Tolstoy nor his central character is still enmeshed in that experience, still conducting the argument, as we feel is the case with Olenin, Pierre or Levin. What he is doing is simply describing, and doing so with the same understanding and accuracy as he describes the University or his preoccupation with being *comme il faut*. All are equally aspects of his past: 'I can', he wrote in his diary in November, 1852, 'write about it because it is far away from me.'[7] The problems which beset him very sorely during the 1850s were not the material for *Childhood, Boyhood and Youth*. Instead, they were explored in short stories and two short novels written during those years, *The Cossacks* and *Family Happiness*.

3
The problem of happiness:
The Cossacks and *Family Happiness*

At one of those relatively rare moments in *Childhood, Boyhood and Youth* where Tolstoy does touch on some aspect of his inner life which still affects him deeply, he writes of a year of his boyhood in which he had wrestled with 'abstract speculations', with the nature of human happiness and the destiny of man, and says:

> 'From all this heavy moral toil I gained nothing except a devious-ness of mind which weakened my strength of will, and a habit of constant moral analysis, which destroyed spontaneity of feeling and clarity of judgement.' (*Boyhood*, Chapter 19)

The bitterness of this gives some indication of the state of mind he seems to have been in during much of the 1850s and early 1860s. These were the years during which he served as a soldier in the Caucasus and at the terrible siege of Sevastopol, recording his experience of the latter in the three *Sevastopol Sketches* of 1855–6, which caused a considerable stir by the honesty with which they recorded the conditions under which the fighting was taking place. During this period, too, he developed and broke his relationship with the members of the *Contemporary* circle, and with Turgenev in particular, farmed his estate, de-voted himself to educational experiment, and travelled in England and Western Europe, starting the ironic story of serf-dom, *Polikushka*, while he was in Brussels. Finally, in 1862, he found at least temporary answers to some of the problems which pursued him through this period in his marriage to Sonya Behrs, soon after which he began work on the novel that was to become *War and Peace*.

The problems were many and various, and they increased in size as Tolstoy's relentlessly explorative conscience, remorseless in pursuing ideas to their logical conclusions, followed them through. This quality, which he calls somewhat disparagingly in *Boyhood* his 'habit of constant moral analysis', was given all the more material on which to work because of what he calls there his weakness of will, something which seems to the more distant observer a virtue and not a fault, involving as it does a refusal to rest satisfied with any particular answer, and, on another level, a massive appetite for experience, not only for what he calls the 'passions' of 'women, cards, and wine', but for the whole life of the senses, in all its irreducible variety.

These two 'faults' which he saw in *Boyhood* as the only product of his 'heavy moral toil', the causes of his loss of that simple spontaneity and clarity for which he so much yearned, were in fact at once the roots of his future greatness as a novelist, and the cause of his unhappiness during the decade before his marriage. If Tolstoy had been the spontaneous, unselfconscious man he always wished to be, he would never have been a great novelist; it was precisely because both intellect and appetite refused to allow him to rest easy for long with any solution to his predicament that things could not be as simple and clear as he would have liked. The urge to go on exploring, to recognise and put on paper the complexities of the situation, though it caused confusion and unhappiness at the time, was to issue later in the massive, all embracing complexity of *War and Peace* and *Anna Karenina*. But at this stage much of his work remains significantly unfinished or hastily completed, and it is only when he turns away from his own uncertainties, as in a story like *Polikushka*, that we find anything like the satisfactory formal completeness of the later years.

All of the problems which tormented him at this time, and indeed throughout his life, were subsumed under the one, great question: 'In what lies happiness?' Early on in *Youth* his *persona* Nikolay had, as we have seen, concluded that happiness was identifiable with virtue, that 'beauty, happiness and virtue are one and the same', and this was a conclusion that remained true for him when he wrote in the 'Introduction for the Author, not the Reader' to his *Novel of a Russian Landlord* 'The main idea of the work: happiness is virtue'.[1] The *Novel of a Russian Landlord* was intended to convey this idea through its narrative; it was to be, unlike *Childhood, Boyhood and Youth*, an overtly didactic book: but it was never finished, and its twenty completed chapters were published in 1856 as *A Landlord's Morning*. Its abandonment was significant, for to write a didactic novel you must have real confidence in the truth of what you teach, and Tolstoy was not completely satisfied with his formula that 'happiness is virtue'—it not only begged the question as to what virtue is, but it tended to exclude that 'spontaneity of feeling' which seemed to him an essential part of any really satisfactory answer to the problem.

It was this very question which was taken up in the other novel he was writing over this period, *The Cossacks*. This too was intended to form the opening section of a longer novel containing, like the *Novel of a Russian Landlord*, large elements of autobiography. Not only were its sequels never to be written, but he almost abandoned *The Cossacks* as well, completing it as late as 1863 only under the pressure of a gambling debt. It centres on the question of happiness with less overtly didactic intent than *A Landlord's Morning*. In it Tolstoy moves uncertainly and unwillingly away from his earlier definition, going on to Olenin's belief in 'self-sacrifice', which is itself criticised, and at least partially replaced by the latter's final conclusion that happiness lies in a high form of selfishness, a self love that issues naturally as a spontaneous love for others. In this, *The Cossacks* anticipates the conclusions—again tentative—of another short novel of this period, *Family Happiness*,[2] which moves still further on in the search by setting the happily and naturally 'selfish' love of the early months of marriage against a deadening, theoretic kind of self-sacrificing love on the one hand, and a more natural, spontaneous kind of family love between husband and wife, parents and children, on the other.

Though all of these works have a strong element of the autobiographical in them, *Family Happiness*, told by a woman narrator, has the least, and it thus stands outside that line of novels in which a central part is taken by a character close to Tolstoy himself, an aristocratic seeker after the truth of things. Such characters are Olenin in *The Cossacks*, Pierre and Andrey in *War and Peace*, and Levin in *Anna Karenina*; but the line begins with the rather unpromising character of Prince Nekhlyudov in *A Landlord's Morning*, as it is to end with him half a century later in *Resurrection*.

A Landlord's Morning is the nearest thing we have to a continuation of *Childhood, Boyhood and Youth*, in that it recounts the experiences of a young landowner who leaves the University before taking a degree and devotes himself to farming his estate and looking after his serfs, a set of circumstances which parallels part of Tolstoy's own career. The bulk of the story deals with Nekhlyudov's round of visits to various serfs on a Sunday morning, visits which only serve to emphasise the futility of his idealistic efforts to help them. It is the documentary realism with which Tolstoy describes the poverty, cunning and stubborn suspiciousness of the serfs which is its most striking feature (in *Resurrection* Nekhlyudov is to meet similar suspicion of his well meant reforms). At the end of the story, as Nekhlyudov returns with a sense of failure from his round, Tolstoy makes him recall the impulses which a year earlier had led him to make his attempt in the first place: lying in the garden one May morning he had looked for the means to satisfy the feelings, the unshaped impulses, which the Spring morning inspired in him. First woman, then abstract speculation on the laws of being had presented themselves to his imagination as the means to happiness, but each time a 'higher feeling' had told him 'not that', and his search had gone on, until finally

'Without any thoughts or desires, as always happens after intense activity, he lay on his back under a tree and began to gaze at the translucent morning clouds, passing above him across the deep, unending sky. Suddenly, for no reason, tears poured into his eyes, and, God knows how, a definite idea came to him, an idea he held on to with delight, the idea that love and goodness are truth and happiness, the only truth and the only possible happiness in the world. The higher feeling did not say "not that" . . . "What rubbish is all I know, what I believed in, what I loved" he said to himself, "love, self-denial—that is the only true happiness, the only happiness independent of chance!" . . . Applying this idea to all aspects of life, and finding it confirmed there as well as in that inner voice telling him that this was "it", he felt what was for him a new sensation of joyful excitement and delight. "And so, I must do good to be happy" he thought, and his whole future appeared before him, no longer in the abstract, but in the vivid shape of a landowner's life.' (Chapter 18)

In its context, the fidelity with which Tolstoy follows the concurrent development of thought and feeling is impressive, but more so is the mature self-awareness that enables him to place these early aspirations with a firm irony. For not only does Nekhlyudov now have to recognise that his course of action has not brought him the happiness he had expected: it hasn't even done the peasants any good. Later on the same day, reflecting on one of the young serfs he had seen in the course of his visits, he recognises a simpler, more spontaneous and self-sufficient form of happiness, and thinks of it with envy: ' "Splendid" Nekhlyudov whispered to himself; and the thought also came to him: "Why am I not Ilyushka?" ' (Chapter 20)

With this unanswerable question *A Landlord's Morning* ends. The ideal which the vibrantly healthy, unselfconscious Ilyushka represents does not go with self-sacrifice. It is closer, instead to a Rousseauan ideal, and it is the possible Rousseauan solutions to the problem which Tolstoy goes on to explore in *The Cossacks*, replacing Ilyushka with the still more inaccessibly natural, unsophisticated figures of Eroshka, Lukashka and Maryanka. Though Tolstoy had, as we have seen, begun the intended sequel to *Childhood, Boyhood and Youth* with a statement of commitment to Rousseau, it is Olenin in *The Cossacks* who becomes his first really Rousseauan hero, the first wholehearted seeker after a way of life that is not artificial and dishonest, a natural way of life that he hopes to find amongst the Cossacks with whom he lives, and with whom he falls in love.

If, as Rousseau had taught, man was happiest when living most nearly in accord with his own instinctive nature and most in harmony with the natural world around him, it was inevitable that this search should begin with an exploration of the extent to which it was possible for a civilised, sophisticated man of Tolstoy's time to throw off his corrupting education and return to this natural life. For a Russian, it was almost equally inevitable that it should be the Caucasus that was the site for this attempt. Pushkin, Gogol and Lermontov had all presented the area and its inhabitants in a more or less Romantic light, itself influenced by Rousseau's ideas. Tolstoy set out, characteristically, to examine the reality of life among the Cossacks, taking advantage of the two and a half years during which he was stationed in the Caucasus to do so.

His overall strategy was a simple one: to take his naïve but sensitive hero, Olenin, from Moscow society to a Cossack village and to explore the relationship between Olenin and the local inhabitants. In practice the novel presented him with a great deal of difficulty; he worked on it over a period of ten years or so, and was never satisfied with the result, eventually abandoning the longer novel of which it was to be the first part, and turning to a new work, *1805*, which was itself to become the first part of *War and Peace*. The fact that a sequel was intended for *The Cossacks* explains a good deal about it. Olenin's experience in the Caucasus is only the beginning of a longer search for happiness, just as it was for Tolstoy himself. When his *troyka* leaves the village at the end of the novel, Olenin is setting out on a new phase of his life, as well as concluding an old one.

Even allowing for this element of incompleteness in the final version, there was some reason for Tolstoy's dissatisfaction with it, and not only because he had failed to arrive at any really firm conclusions. The problems he faced grew out of the very nature of his theme: on the one hand his central character is a man whose background and education render him ineffectual in the Cossack society, unable to impinge in any very significant way on the lives of those amongst whom we see him living. On the other hand, the Cossacks are presented as simple, natural and unselfconscious: they are people whom the novelist can only describe from the outside, since they have by definition no complex inner life of the kind Tolstoy is so well able to describe. Thus we never have much more than a purely physical sense of the presence of the three main Cossack characters, Eroshka, Lukashka and Maryanka. This presence, especially in the cases of Eroshka and Maryanka, he manages to convey with an immediacy that is truly masterly, but it is all that he can convey, because it is all that there is. The problem is not so much, as John Bayley suggests, that we are uncertain whether we see the real Cossacks or the Cossacks as seen by Olenin.[3] We do see what Tolstoy, at any rate, believed to be the real Cossacks; but we can only see them. We are thus given a central character who can think and feel, but whose capacity for significant action is severely limited, and three important characters who can act, but can scarcely be described as thinking. The reader has, as one might expect, no very convincing sense of the interaction of these four characters, and the result is that for all Tolstoy's detailed realism, there is an uneasy area of unreality at the very centre of the novel. We often feel, as Olenin himself does, that he is living in a kind of dream.

Tolstoy's problem was that at the same time as it promotes a sense of unreality, this lack of interaction between the characters is also the result of one of his fundamental conclusions—that is,

47

that there *can* be no real communication between Olenin and the Cossacks, that they live in different worlds. This is a point obvious enough not to need much critical underlining: Tolstoy reminds us of it frequently, showing, for example, how Olenin's attempts to dress like a Cossack still leave him looking like a Russian soldier in disguise. It is something Olenin himself comes to realise, accepting for a time the role of stranger living amongst the Cossacks, rather than trying to become one of them. It is his love for Maryanka that forces him to abandon this detached position, only to find that his first impression had been right, and that she was not simply unattracted to him, but inaccessible.

Put thus simply, the whole novel might seem to involve a refutation of Rousseau's ideas. In fact it does not: it involves a modification of them to accommodate the realities of the situation in which Olenin finds himself. When he leaves Moscow, he is consciously quitting what he sees as a corrupt and corrupting society in order to begin a new and purer life in a more natural state, a state which he sees vaguely in terms of the Romantic version of the Caucasus presented by the Russian poets. It is to be a new life of heroism and love, 'a life in which there would be no more mistakes, no remorse, and certainly only happiness'. Tolstoy is indulgently ironic at Olenin's expense in these opening pages, stressing his youth and naïveté along with the unreality of his dreams. We are invited to share a feeling of pleasure in, and superiority over, the young man's hopes. But those hopes were the young Tolstoy's also, and the irony diminishes sharply when Olenin gets his first view of the Caucasus:

> 'The fast movement of the *troyka* along the straight path made the mountains seem to be running along the horizon, their rosy peaks gleaming in the rising sun. At first, the mountains only surprised Olenin, and then gladdened him; but as he gazed more and more at the receding chain of snowy mountains, apparently not rising out of the other, black mountains, but directly from the plain, he began gradually to assimilate that beauty and to *feel* the mountains. From that moment, all that he saw, all that he thought, all that he felt, acquired a new, austerely majestic character like the mountains. All his Moscow reminiscences, shame and repentance, all his commonplace dreams about the Caucasus, all disappeared and returned no more. "Now it has begun" a solemn voice seemed to say to him.' (Chapter 3)

There is still an element of irony in the solemn voice which speaks to Olenin. But his experience is a serious, if not a solemn one, a moment of spiritual awakening after which he is no longer the same naïve young man whom we saw in the early pages. The way in which the majesty of the mountains gives rise to a new way of seeing the world is reminiscent not only of Rousseau, but of Tolstoy's own description of his sensations when looking at the mountains at Clarens. Olenin is already beginning to learn, and he is doing so along broadly Rousseauan lines, a fact that we should bear in mind all the time that we witness his failure to make himself into a carefree, unselfconscious Cossack.

Tolstoy leaves Olenin at this point to give us a more objective account of the area into which he is travelling. The objectivity is set over against Olenin's expectations, of course, but also against that whole Romantic tradition which conditioned Olenin's view. Against the Caucasus of Pushkin, Lermontov and Marlinsky, we have a more sparely realistic version which marvellously combines the accuracy of the geographer or the social historian with a primitive epic grandeur which may be consciously Homeric, since Tolstoy had been much impressed by reading the *Iliad* at just this time.[4] From general description he moves on to the singularly unromantic marriage negotiations between the mothers of Maryanka and Lukashka, and thence to the cordon and the appearance of Eroshka, after Olenin the most substantial character in the novel.

Eroshka, we know, was based on the extraordinary ninety-year-old Cossack Epishka, with whom Tolstoy lived for a time during his service in the Caucasus. However accurate the portrait may have been, the Eroshka of the novel is unmistakably, and rather surprisingly, real, never becoming a cipher for a Rousseauan noble savage. He is, though, the supremely natural man, not only outside Olenin's sophisticated world, but even outside the more simple, natural society of the Cossacks themselves. Within the limits dictated by his simplicity, his lack of introspective self-awareness, Eroshka is in every sense a massive character. He suffers, perhaps more than any other Tolstoyan character, from translation: not only does he undergo the indignity in English of being called 'Daddy' Eroshka or even 'Gaffer' Eroshka (the Russian *dyadya* has no such awkwardly literary overtones), but his speech is almost impossible to translate without losing its idiomatic quality. It is terse and slightly archaic; perhaps its nearest equivalent in the English novel is the use of dialect in *Wuthering Heights*, in George Eliot or in Lawrence. It is, at any rate, important for the English reader to be aware that his archaisms do not run to such things as 'Oh, I am a wag' or 'there's a good chap', though it is difficult in translation to avoid this kind of coyness.

Eroshka is the man Olenin would have to become if he were able to throw off all his inhibitions, all his self-consciousness, indeed, all his past life. He is the supreme example of that spontaneous life that Tolstoy and Rousseau so admired. From the very moment of his introduction, the impossibility of this ever happening is quite clear. More importantly, we come to question its very desirability, not because of Eroshka's drunkenness and apparent amorality, but because however happy he may be (and this itself is called into question), the life of the spontaneous natural man seems here a severely limited one. Eroshka is truly at home and happy only when he is in the forest, and he feels a greater respect for the animals he hunts than for the men with whom he lives. In his essential self-sufficiency he could be based on a sentence from *Émile* where Rousseau writes: 'The natural man lives for himself; he is the unit, the whole, dependent only on himself and on his like.' (p. 7) Whether this is so or not, Eroshka is a version—one version—of Rousseau's natural man, placed in the context of a real, not a philosophical, life. He follows the promptings of his feelings in all respects, explaining his philosophy to Olenin in the two central speeches which are summarised by the statement that 'God created everything for the delight of man. There is no sin in any part of it.' Thus Eroshka takes, or has taken, whatever he wanted from life, regardless of the consequences for himself or others. He is saved from any serious condemnation on the part of Olenin, Tolstoy or the reader by his essential innocence and lack of hypocrisy. Even when we find him lying to Lukashka about Olenin, or are shown how apparently calculated is his friendship for the latter, his actions remain innocent; they are of and for the moment, and have for him no moral implications. He lives according to his own philosophy, a philosophy centred entirely on himself.

If we ask, though, whether we prefer Eroshka's life and standards to those of Olenin, we find ourselves faced with the problem that was to follow Tolstoy through *War and Peace* and *Anna Karenina*: the problem of whether it is better to be simple, unselfconscious and happy, or to be selfconscious, to have a larger view of what happiness might involve, and therefore to find it more difficult to achieve. Many years later, Tolstoy was to tell Gorky and Chekhov that he had never been happy, because he had never lived simply for himself,[5] and he always envied the kind of self-sufficiency he saw in the Cossacks or the peasants. But he was always, as a novelist, honest enough to face the fact that the sophisticated man was sophisticated, however difficult that made life for him. Olenin cannot simply become another Eroshka or Lukashka, he cannot shed his 'habit of constant moral analysis' any more than Tolstoy could. But if this is a disadvantage in the particular situation in which he finds himself, it is also a strength in that it opens for him wider horizons than Eroshka or Lukashka could ever know. Indeed, even within *The Cossacks* Olenin finds for himself a kind of happiness that is incomprehensible to those around him. The philosophy of self-sacrifice which he formulates on his solitary trip to the forest is one that he questions strongly later, but it is not an empty one, and Tolstoy was to return to it frequently throughout his life. Through it Olenin achieves a *modus vivendi* with his environment that is only destroyed when he tries to marry Maryanka instead of accepting, as he should, her remoteness from himself and his whole way of life.

The passage in which Olenin formulates his new philosophy comes in one of the finest and most characteristically Tolstoyan chapters in the novel. Out shooting in the hot, humid forest, covered with mosquitoes which have tormented him for so long that they have come to seem a necessary part of the charm of his surroundings, hot, tired and happy, with seven pheasants hanging from his belt, he lies down in a thicket where the previous day a stag had lain:

'And suddenly he was overcome by such a strange feeling of groundless happiness and love for everything that, after his old childhood habit, he began crossing himself and thanking someone. Suddenly, with extraordinary clarity the thought came into his head, "Here am I, Dmitri Olenin, such a distinct being from the rest, now lying all alone, God knows where, on the spot where a stag used to live, an old, beautiful stag, who perhaps had never seen a man, a spot where no human being has ever sat or thought

C

in this way. I sit, and around me stand young and old trees, and one of them is festooned with wild grape vines; around me pheasants are moving, chasing each other and perhaps scenting their dead brothers." He felt his pheasants, examined them, and wiped the warm blood off his hand onto his coat. "Perhaps the jackals can scent them and are sneaking away in another direction with dissatisfied faces; around me, flying among the leaves that seem to them like enormous islands, mosquitoes are hanging in the air and buzzing: one, two, three, four, a hundred, a thousand, a million mosquitoes, and all of them buzz something or other around me, and each one of them is just such a Dmitri Olenin, distinct from the others, as I am." . . . And it became clear to him that he was not at all a Russian nobleman, a member of Moscow society, the friend and relation of so-and-so and so-and-so, but just such a mosquito or pheasant or stag as those which were now living all around him. "Like them, like Eroshka, I shall live for a while, and die. And he says truly, 'The grass will grow, and that is all.' " ' (Chapter 20)

This is another of those lucidly simple and yet epiphanic moments in Tolstoy where man is in complete harmony with the natural world; it is reminiscent in particular of the passage describing the orchard in *Youth* that was quoted earlier. Under the influence of his surroundings, Olenin moves on to his discovery that 'happiness lies in living for others', and becomes 'glad and excited at having discovered this, as it seemed to him, new truth, and impatiently began to seek someone for whom he could sacrifice himself, for whom he could do good, and love'.

There is still an element of irony here at Olenin's expense, but it is a generous irony directed as much at Olenin's naïveté in thinking that he is the first to have discovered this idea as at the idea itself. More damagingly ironic, though, is the fact that as soon as he gets up and leaves the forest, looking for someone on whom to practise self-sacrifice, he gets lost, and has to be taken home by Lukashka, the intended beneficiary of his new philosophy. This irony does not dismiss the ethic of self-sacrifice, but it gives the reader serious doubts about it, doubts which are increased later when we find Olenin writing in his diary:

'Many things have I pondered over lately and much have I changed . . . and I have come back to the copybook maxim: The only way to be happy is to love, to love with a self-denying love, to love everybody and everything; to spread a web of love on all sides and catch all who come into it. In this way I caught Vanyusha, old Eroshka, Lukashka and Maryanka.' (Chapter 28)

What disturbs about this is that though he may have caught his serf Vanyusha, he has done so long ago, without either of them knowing it, while the three Cossacks are by no means caught in his web of love. What is curious is that, as we have seen, this passage is a favourite of Tolstoy, adapted—or perhaps misunderstood—from Sterne, and is very close to the one which he entered in his own diary in 1856. We are presumably not, therefore, expected to be altogether dismissive about it: the impression he leaves is one of uncertainty as to how far one can live happily by the rather sterile ethic of self-sacrifice. A few years later, in *War and Peace*, he pursues the idea again, with Pierre finding it unsatisfactory, Sonya living a life that is devoted to self-sacrifice but which is presented as somewhat unnatural and sterile, but with Princess Maria, on the other hand, finding it natural and deeply enriching—though even Maria's self-denial for the sake of her father appears at times in an unfulfilling, unnatural light.

Olenin's discovery in the forest, then, can only bring him a temporary, and therefore, from Tolstoy's point of view, an unsatisfactory answer to the problem: but it is, again, a step on the difficult road he is taking. The real irony is that he makes his doubtful discovery during a moment of true and spontaneous happiness—and that happiness arises out of his momentary sense of his own self-sufficiency and harmony with the natural world around him, a sense which we never see him regain during the rest of his stay, for it is something which by definition cannot be willed. It is a moment that is, like his first view of the mountains, based on that belief in the beneficent influence of nature, and of man's need to be in harmony with it, that Tolstoy shares with Rousseau. And, despite the shortcomings of the theory which he builds on it, the role played by the natural world around him is something Olenin does understand. In the rather clumsily placed letter (it is a little too obviously a convenience for the novelist), which he writes explaining his situation, Olenin relates his growing love for Maryanka with the nature to which she seems so close:

'Perhaps I love nature in her, the embodiment of everything that is beautiful in nature; but I do not love by my own will, some spontaneous force loves her through me; the whole of God's world, the whole of nature presses this love into my soul and says, "Love." I love her not with my mind, not with my imagination, but with my whole being. Loving her, I feel myself an integral part of all God's joyous world.' (Chapter 33)

It is this love that replaces for Olenin his ethic of self-sacrifice; with his recognition that happiness lies in the fulfilment of his love for Maryanka, things become much clearer. He now knows where happiness lies, but as he had recognised earlier, Maryanka's inaccessibility to him makes that love impossible to consummate. By trying to overcome that inaccessibility, Olenin forces matters to a crisis, a crisis to which Lukashka's wounding is only marginally relevant. It is Maryanka's complete failure to understand him, and her final note of contempt, that force him to recognise the truth and leave the village.

What, then, does Olenin learn? First, and most important, is the fact that however desirable a simple life close to nature may be, it cannot be willed on himself by civilised man. Olenin can only admire and envy the Cossacks from a distance, never become one of them. Secondly, there is the discovery that the natural world, here the world of the Caucasian mountains and forests, has its own beneficent moral influence to offer to the man who is open to it; in Olenin's case it awakens new horizons which make his break with his earlier life more clear, and helps answer the serious questioning within him of his reasons for living, the great Tolstoyan question 'in what lies true happiness?'. The answer is one that Tolstoy was never to be wholly certain about, but there seems little doubt that by the end of *The Cossacks* he does not believe it lies in a self-sacrificing love, so much as in the kind of essentially selfish love which Olenin feels for Maryanka—a natural, and not a willed response. He makes Olenin reject self-sacrifice with characteristic gusto: ' "Self-sacrifice—it's all absurdity, nonsense. It's all pride, refuge from deserved unhappiness, salvation from the envy of others' happiness. To live for others, to do good! Why? when in my soul is only love for myself and one desire: to love her and to live her life with her." ' These last words express Olenin's most important discovery, unsuccessful though it may be in this particular context. Through it, he is able to throw off his selfconsciousness, to become as free as Eroshka or Lukashka, though in a wholly different way:

'Not for others, not for Lukashka, I now desire happiness. I do not now love those others. Before I would have told myself that that was wrong. I would have been tormented by questions: What would happen to her, to me, to Lukashka? Now it's all the same to me. I don't live as I like, there is something stronger than me, which directs me. I suffer, but before I was dead, and only now am I alive. Now I'll go to their house and tell them everything.' (Chapter 33)

There is a paradoxical self-sufficiency to be found in love, a self-sufficiency that makes him feel in harmony with himself and the world around him. The answer is essentially the same as that which Tolstoy develops further in *War and Peace*, but which in *The Cossacks* his own uncertainty and his integrity as a novelist prevented him from pursuing any further. What may happen to Olenin when his love is rejected belongs to the next, unwritten part of the novel. But he has at least advanced from the position in which we found him at the beginning, when, in Moscow, he had found it impossible to love anyone. And he has done so by discovering the truth of Rousseau's dictum in *Émile* that 'The only natural passion is self-love or selfishness taken in a wider sense'. (p. 56)

Two shorter works of this period help to illuminate this concept of a selfishness which issues as spontaneity and which leads to a simple, unreflecting happiness for those who possess it, making them loved by those around them in a way that those who have the 'habit of constant moral analysis' can never be. In *Kholstomer: the Story of a Horse*,[6] a splendid *tour de force* on Tolstoy's part in which an old horse recounts its life history to an audience of younger horses, the piebald gelding Kholstomer tells of one of his owners:

' "With the officer of hussars I had the best time of my life.
Although he was the cause of my ruin, although he never loved anything or anyone, I loved him and love him still, for just that reason.
I liked it especially in him that he was handsome, happy, rich, and therefore loved nobody." '

This is the position put at its most extreme. Tolstoy evidently wished to emphasise the point, however, since he repeats it on the following page: 'Master and coachman resembled each other. Neither of them was afraid of anything, or loved anyone but himself, and for that all loved them.' (Chapter 8)

What master and coachman possess is a simple pleasure in being themselves, a *samodovolnost'*, which John Bayley rightly identifies as an important quality in many of Tolstoy's characters.[7] Such 'self-satisfaction' rarely carries with it the kind of limiting complacency we might expect; instead the lack of self-doubt and introspection communicates itself to others, making its owner the object of their involuntary love, as Tolstoy loved his brother Sergey:

> 'I was enraptured by his handsome exterior, his singing—he was always singing—by his drawing, his gaiety, and especially, strange as it may seem to say so, by his spontaneity, by his egoism. I was always conscious of myself, always sensed, mistakenly or not, what other people thought and felt about me, and this spoilt the joy of life for me. Because of that, probably, I particularly loved the opposite in others—spontaneity, egoism.'[8]

The qualities which give a special vitality to Natasha or to Stiva Oblonsky are just those which Tolstoy saw in his brother. Of them it could be said, as he says of Sergey, 'He was what he was, did not hide anything, did not wish to appear anything else.' We are reminded too of Levin: 'He felt that he was himself and did not want to be anyone else.'

The quality itself is, of course, amoral: it is possessed by Anatole Kuragin as well as Oblonsky. But those who possess it, while they possess it, are given a kind of grace which at least partly exempts them from moral censure, as one feels that Anatole is partly exempted in his seduction of Natasha. Their life, like Eroshka's, is the spontaneous life of the body, and follows its own laws. This point is made in another fine story written before *War and Peace*, *The Two Hussars*, in which Tolstoy examines the behaviour of two officers, a father and son, who visit the same town and meet the same people, with a gap of more than twenty years between their respective visits. The father's cavalier behaviour, though it offends the moral standards of the townspeople, is nevertheless attractive to them because it is simple, spontaneous, and at bottom generous. His self-satisfaction is of a kind that communicates itself to others, so that they too feel satisfied with him, as we feel satisfied with Stiva Oblonsky. His son's selfishness, however, is of quite another kind, altogether more calculating and cynical: instead of helping an innocent who had been cheated at cards, as his father had done, the son takes ten roubles off an old woman, the same woman whom, a generation before, his father had seduced in a spirit of wholehearted but transient love which had left her with nothing but happy memories. The son, too, turns to lovemaking, with the woman's daughter (she is an heiress), but in this too he is cynical and hesitant where his father was committed and impetuous. His attempt at seduction is a failure, and he goes off leaving behind him memories of himself which are as unpleasant as those left by his father had been pleasant.

Put thus starkly, it is possible to see how didactic *The Two Hussars* is: it is a celebration of spontaneity, of unselfconscious egoism, its events set up by Tolstoy to enforce the distinction he wants to make between an extreme of *samodovolnost'*, of pleasure in being oneself, on the one hand, and the worst kind of self-conscious, calculating behaviour on the other. Nothing could show more clearly, though, how misleading it can be to assume that the didactic, in Tolstoy or any other writer, is necessarily associated with a failure in art. Simple though its scheme may be, *The Two Hussars* works because form and content correspond. It is only when one of the two becomes disproportionate, when form no longer serves content, that 'didactic' becomes a pejorative term. Tolstoy himself made this point when explaining to Gorky his liking for Maupassant: 'True talent always has two shoulders: one is ethical, the other aesthetic. If the ethical shoulder hitches itself up too high, then the aesthetic shoulder dips down to the same degree, and the talent becomes misshapen.'[9]

Family Happiness, his most substantial work of this period after *The Cossacks*, has seemed too 'ethical' in this way to some, too 'aesthetic' to others, and more or less mediocre to most. None of these judgements seem to me just ones, though they suggest by their variety something of the complexity of this fine and underrated short novel (its form is that of the Russian *povest'*, neither short story nor novel, but something between the two). As its title implies, it continues his investigation of the nature of true happiness within the context of love and marriage—the context in which, at least until the period when he was writing

Anna Karenina, he believed he could find the answers to his questions.

Family Happiness has seemed crudely didactic to some readers largely because of the role played in it by the principal male character, Sergey Mikhaylich, whose attitudes seem at first sight to make him only too clearly an *alter ego* for Tolstoy. His belief that 'happiness is only to be found in living for others' is familiarly Tolstoyan, and it is one which he impresses on his young bride Masha, the narrator of the novel. We have already seen, though, that Tolstoy was by no means confident in this belief, however often he may have returned to it. The other happiness, the strong, unreflecting happiness which does not think in abstract terms of self-sacrifice and principle, but in terms of a more simple and selfish fulfilment is something which he also recognises, recognises as being in its finest forms more potent and more fulfilling than living for others. In Masha's narrative of her growing love for the older Sergey Mikhaylich we see these two elements of happiness—a joyful spontaneity and a belief that she is made more happy by living for others—brought together, and finally, though very uneasily, reconciled.

Sergey Mikhaylich's influence over Masha's ideas and attitudes is, as we would expect, very great: he is, after all, her guardian, and twice her age. He teaches her during their engagement the kind of things we might expect Nekhlyudov or Olenin to teach their prospective brides, and he inevitably emerges as something of a prig in doing so. There are times when his influence, seen through Masha's eyes, seems overwhelming:

> 'When he looked at my face and asked me a question, his very look would draw out of me the answer that he wanted. All my thoughts at that time, all my feelings, were not really mine: they were his thoughts, his feelings, which had suddenly become mine, and passed into my life and illuminated it. Quite unconsciously I was beginning to look at everything with different eyes—at Katya and the servants and Sonya and myself and my occupations.' (Book I., Chapter 2)

Much of Sergey Mikhaylich's influence is no doubt salutary; but what is important, and particularly significant for those who see him simply as Tolstoy's representative, is that Masha is not overwhelmed by that moral influence so much as by the force of her love for him. It is out of this that her happiness arises, a 'passionate happiness in the present' which is far stronger that the happiness she gains during the period—presented with some irony by Tolstoy—when she goes out of her way to find some means of sacrificing herself for others. She accepts his ideas without altogether understanding them because she is enveloped in a self-sufficient and ultimately selfish happiness which, at this early stage, she does not even recognise as love:

> 'Our garden, our woods and fields, that I had known so long, suddenly acquired a new beauty for me. He was not mistaken when he said that there was only one certain happiness in life—to live for others. Then it had seemed strange to me; I did not understand it; but without me being conscious of it, it had entered my heart. He opened up a whole world of happiness in the present, without altering anything in my life, without adding anything, except himself, to every impression. It only needed him for everything that had surrounded me since childhood without saying anything, to begin to speak and press for admittance to my soul, filling it with happiness.' (Book I, Chapter 2)

There is surely an irony intended here in Masha's attribution of happiness to the idea of self-sacrifice in the very same breath as she convinces us that it is that more spontaneous and selfish love for one man that is the real source of her joy, and of any good that may come into her actions. Certainly there is a heavier irony, recognised by both narrator and author, when the subject arises later on:

> 'Only now could I see what he meant when he said that the only true happiness was to be found in living for others, and now I agreed with him completely. I believed that together we would be infinitely happy and untroubled. I looked forward, not to foreign travel or society or display, but to something quite different—a quiet family life in the country, with constant self-sacrifice, constant love for each other, and constant recognition in all things of the kind hand of Providence.' (Book I, Chapter 4)

The subsequent course of the marriage underlines the irony of this: the happiness it produces, both before and after the period of misery and spiritual separation they go through, bears no resemblance to this idealised picture. At first it is the spirit of Masha's love, and not of Sergey Mikhaylich's theories which triumphs:

59

'Our dreams about how our life in the country would be arranged turned out rather differently from what we had expected. But our life was not poorer than our dreams. There was no unremitting toil, no fulfilling of the duty of self-sacrifice and living for others, which I had pictured to myself before we were married: there was on the contrary, an entirely selfish feeling of love for one another, a desire to be loved, unreasoning, constant gaiety, and oblivion of everything else in the world.' (Book II, Chapter 6)

Sergey Mikhaylich is able to share this feeling of complete self-sufficiency, but he cannot, as Masha can, give himself up to it completely. For he, too, has the 'habit of constant moral analysis', so that when Masha chafes at the 'peaceful flow of life' and desires 'excitements and dangers and self-sacrifice for the sake of love', he can only meet her with an exasperating reasonableness. Masha, of course, has to learn to accept—as by the end she has accepted—that loving is not the same thing as falling in love; but she does not have to learn that habit will make emotions cease to be spontaneous, and subordinate them to the 'even, passionless flow of time', as Sergey Mikhaylich's influence directs her. It is he, and not Masha, who must bear much of the responsibility for the misery which both go through before they are able to rescue some degree of happiness from their marriage. Tolstoy is far enough detached from Sergey Mikhaylich to make it clear that he endorses the latter's own verdict in the closing pages:

' "You thought it all out, you thought it out a great deal", I said. "You did not love very much."
We were silent again.
"It's cruel, what you just said, but it's true," he exclaimed, suddenly getting up and beginning to walk about the veranda. "Yes, it's the truth. I was to blame," he added stopping opposite me. "Either I ought not to have allowed myself to love you at all, or loved you more simply." ' (Book II, Chapter 9)

The simpler way is the more spontaneous way, the way that would have resulted in moments of anger and estrangement, but also of renewed love. The final, overriding irony of the novel is the one that is the least noticed of all—that it is Sergey Mikhaylich's own 'self-sacrifice' in allowing her to enter society, in following her with cold and more and more unloving tolerance from Petersburg to Baden Baden that is the cause, not of happiness, but of acute misery for both of them. It is only when they return to the country house which was the scene of their early happiness that Masha can break through the barrier of dead and bitter tolerance with which her husband has surrounded himself. And as she does so, she too finds herself able to accept that the time of passionate feeling has been lost for good, to be replaced by a quiet family happiness in which her husband is not a lover but an 'old friend', and in which her feelings are focused on her children—the most natural, perhaps the only natural form of self-sacrificing love. But if something is saved, something has been lost: we should not allow ourselves to believe that the kind of happiness with which the novel closes is anything but a second-best. Underneath the sometimes rapturous, sometimes bitter simplicity of Masha's narrative, Tolstoy has worked out an ironic condemnation of a theoretical, analysing, self-sacrificing brand of love. Clearly it was not for him a final answer: the man who gave up, years later, his lands, wealth, and copyright on his works, who wrote *What Then Must We Do?*, was more concerned with living for others than with the simple, spontaneous love that Masha represents. But for the time at least his attitudes had become more clear; by 1862 he was himself happily immersed in a new married life in which he looked for more fulfilment than that with which *Family Happiness* deals, a married life out of whose ambience grew *War and Peace* and *Anna Karenina*.

4

War and Peace

However high our opinion may be of the best of Tolstoy's early work, it is difficult not to feel, as one encounters the assured mastery, the apparently simple and effortless comprehensiveness of *War and Peace*, that a transition has been made to a mode of writing that is not simply more accomplished, but different in kind from what has gone before. That impression, though, is one that needs to be looked at carefully if one is to see Tolstoy's career as a novelist in its proper perspective. It is certainly true that the years between the publication of *Family Happiness* in 1859 and the beginning of work on *War and Peace* in 1863 had been among the most eventful in his life: they had seen, above all, the death of his brother Nikolay in 1860, and his marriage to Sonya Behrs in 1862, events which had a radical effect on his character—the former a deeper effect than has always been recognised. The death of Nikolay, whom he loved and respected more than anyone, and the beginning of that family life which he so much desired, and in which he believed true happiness was to be found, can obviously have done no other than make the Tolstoy who began *War and Peace* a different man from the one who had written *Childhood, Boyhood and Youth* and *The Cossacks*, and from this point of view it is indeed reasonable to see *War and Peace* as the beginning of a new phase in his career, the phase in which marriage and the family are celebrated in the two great novels.

Looked at through the perspective of the earlier work, however, *War and Peace* seems not so much a new, more assured departure, as a triumphant summation, a gathering together into one hugely designed whole of all the threads which had gone to make up his early work. The marvellous fidelity to experience and acute psychological insight of *Childhood, Boyhood and Youth*, the exploration of love, true happiness, the family, the values by which men live, with which *The Cossacks, Family Happiness* and many of the shorter works are concerned, the interest in the psychology of bravery, and in the actual as opposed to the ideal conditions of battle, which we find in stories like *The Raid* and in the *Sevastopol Sketches*—all these concerns, existing separately or in uneasy conjunction in his earlier work, are brought together in *War and Peace*. What has happened is not that a new and unmistakably major novelist has suddenly emerged, but that Tolstoy has found the form, the framework, which can embrace all his previously disparate, unformed interests. By a paradox of Tolstoyan proportions, the vast and at first sight formless chronicle of the Napoleonic wars offered precisely the formal discipline his painstaking but expansive genius needed. He was now a master by any standards of the short story or of the short novel, the Russian *povest'*, and we should never make the common mistake of forgetting his sheer technical accomplishment in this or any other literary form save poetry. But such was the many sided quality of Tolstoy's character, such was the honesty and thoroughness of his search for the answers to those fundamental problems which, now and always, continued to trouble him, that the ideal form was for him an expansive one, one in which as omniscient narrator he could project not one but many facets of his protean character, without having to commit himself finally to any one of them. Thus he could gain the kind of objective, artistic control over Pierre, Andrey, Nikolay, Maria or Natasha of which one is never wholly certain in a figure like Olenin: rightly or wrongly, the reader of *The Cossacks* always feels that the transformation of Tolstoy's own experience into the terms of art is incomplete, that he is too close to Olenin to allow him to function with complete success as an independent character. His problems are Tolstoy's problems, his desires Tolstoy's desires, and his failure to find the answers he is searching for is Tolstoy's failure.

This is never felt to be true for a moment of *War and Peace*, even in the cases of the two figures who most clearly represent aspects of his own character, Pierre and Prince Andrey. It is not true because the whole has become larger than any single individual, because Tolstoy has withdrawn to a distance at which, with the inner lives of many characters to handle, and with the various threads of a complex narrative to maintain, the artist and the spiritual autobiographer can co-exist happily together. When Tolstoy does enter the novel, he does so with absolute directness and confidence, interrupting his narrative to address the reader on the subject of history, of war, and the vanity of those who believe they can control the course of events, or even understand them.

The result of this omniscient stance on Tolstoy's part is that outside of these direct philosophical interventions, which in fact form a relatively small proportion of the whole, the overall effect of *War and Peace* is a surprisingly undidactic one. It is partly the starkness with which the digressions on the nature of war and history stand out that has given it its still current reputation of a great didactic novel. But these are, to some extent, small, separable units—Tolstoy himself saw them as such, and was particularly doubtful about the inclusion of the long second part of the Epilogue, the fullest of them. The mainstream of the novel, in which the philosopher of history and the artist are happily combined, is characterised more by its open, explorative nature than by any attempt to project clearly formulated ideas about the way man should or should not live.

This openness is one of the major sources of that strength of Tolstoy's most often cited, and yet never adequately explained, his ability to convey the illusion that his characters are 'real' characters living in a 'real' world. When we look closely at *War and Peace* or *Anna Karenina* it is not difficult to see that the impression of all-embracing reality, of an unrivalled comprehensiveness and inclusiveness *is* an illusion: we have only to invoke the names of Dickens or Balzac, or of his greatest contemporary Dostoyevsky, to recognise how exclusive Tolstoy can be. In contrast to these, for example, he rarely touches on the lives or fortunes of any but the classes he knows and loves—the aristocracy and the peasantry. This exclusiveness was something he defended at length in a draft version of the first volume, saying that he felt the lives of other classes than the nobility to be simply 'boring and monotonous', that he was proud of his aristocratic background, and that he could not believe in 'the noble intellect, the refined taste, or the absolute integrity of a man who picks his nose and whose soul converses with God'.[1] This moment of patrician *hauteur* was wisely rejected from the final version, but it reflects the narrow social range of Tolstoy's interests. Within that range the illusion of completeness and reality is achieved largely through the insight with which he presents a number of very different characters, of whom even the least sympathetic—the Kuragins, with their varying kinds of corruptness, the ruthless Dolokhov, or the opportunist Drubetskoy—are given a concrete existence, a livingness, that can only come from a certain sympathy, and even love, on the author's part. This is particularly evident in the case of Anatole Kuragin, whose attempt to seduce Natasha would make him the major villain of the novel, if Tolstoy were dealing in such things, but whose very selfishness, a simple, unreflecting animal selfishness, though it does not preclude moral judgement by Tolstoy or his reader, is inseparable from a vitality that modifies our condemnation of him.

The range from Anatole to Pierre, from Dolokhov to Andrey, is a vast one morally if not socially, but they never come to represent the simple extremes of villain and hero. Tolstoy, we know, was not fond of 'inventing', and that his characters should be rooted in life, should inhabit a real and not an imagined world, a world he knew, was of immense importance to him. His treatment of Sonya is a good example of the way in which a Tolstoyan character can have the elusiveness, the complexity, of reality, rather than the clearer outlines that we normally meet in even the finest of novelists. Although he suggests, through Natasha, that there is something lacking in Sonya, and something calculated and selfish in her self-sacrifice in freeing Nikolay to marry Princess Maria, this is never felt to be the whole moral picture. Sonya's motivation is partly altruistic as well. She can never be easily categorised by the reader, for she has the indefinite moral outlines of those we meet in our everyday experience, even those we think we know best, but which we rarely find in literature. Tolstoy does not reduce things to more manageable literary proportions in *War and Peace* (unless it be in some of his theoretical passages), because he is too honest, too open to the moral and psychological complexities of any situation. It is largely this combination of sympathetic insight, honesty and openness, that gives us the sense of an all-inclusive, supremely realistic picture of life.

In a draft preface, which was not published, he linked the living quality of his characters both to the larger realism of the narrative—the fact that it has no 'formal' limits—and to the fact that they embody no simple didactic intent. He wanted his characters simply to be, and it was this openness, this concern to avoid imposing any falsifying pattern on the reality of things, that led to the open-ended structure of the novel, starting *in medias res*, and ending with the young Nikolay Bolonksky's dream of 'Glory', the first stirrings of the aspirations of a new generation. 'I cannot' he wrote 'and do not know how to set fixed limits to the characters I have invented.'[2]

These very qualities make it impossible to discuss *War and Peace*, particularly in a small space, without being either very partial in its treatment, or very reductive. Unless, that is to say, one concentrates on a short section or a limited theme, any discussion of *War and Peace* is bound to involve a distortion of it. This is not merely a matter of size—though the length of *War and Peace* and *Anna Karenina* is consequent on Tolstoy's unwillingness to simplify, to fit experience to the form of the novel as it was conceived in his day, and does in itself pose special problems for the critic. It is the organic complexity of the whole, rather than its length, that causes the major problem, and in this respect criticism of Tolstoy's two great novels faces the same dilemma as Shakespearean criticism: with Shakespeare, too, however intelligent the critic, and however readily we may agree with him, we are always conscious that there is much more to be said, that the play has been simplified in some way before it can fit into the confines of the critical essay. All that one can hope to do with either writer is to search pragmatically for the least reductive way of talking about the various parts of the whole.

In Tolstoy's case one method is, I think, suggested by the rejected preface to which reference has just been made. As that preface implies, the most urgent centre of interest in *War and Peace* is not the theory of history, the nature of war or peace, or any of the numerous themes with which it deals in passing. The real centre, that which most generates Tolstoy's creative energies and most impresses itself on the reader, is the exploration and development of character, of the individual sensibility. And it is by the rather unfashionable method of following Tolstoy's exploration of his main characters that the critic can, I believe, best hope to uncover the major lines of development in *War and Peace* with the least possible distortion. The generalised theme, whether it is family happiness, the sources of spiritual regeneration, even the nature of war, finds its convincing realisation only through the experience of his protagonists.

This is true even of many of the passages dealing with the

nature of war, where it might seem that Tolstoy comes nearest to using a character to stand for an idea, rather than allowing the idea to manifest itself through the words and actions of the character. There are, of course, occasions where the former happens: Napoleon and his staff are often felt to be no more than the targets for his irony at the expense of *le grand homme*, and even Kutuzov, who is the most fully realised character amongst those in high command on either side, is at times compromised as a character by Tolstoy's use of him to illustrate a point. When, for example, he tells us that Kutuzov could not say to his generals, when the French were already in retreat, ' "Why this fighting and blocking of the road, this loss of our own men, and inhuman slaughter of the unfortunate? Why all this, when on the way from Moscow to Vyazma a third of their army has melted away without any fighting?" ', we are surely entitled to ask 'Why couldn't he?', the point being, one would have thought, a perfectly reasonable one. Tolstoy's insistence, plausible in many ways, that a commander-in-chief's control over his army is a very limited one is stretched too far in instances such as this, making Kutuzov too obviously a peg on which to hang a theory. Other examples of Kutuzov's awareness of the limitations of his power are made more convincing because they are based in a solidly presented reality of circumstance and character. Perhaps the most devastating of all Kutuzov's (or Tolstoy's) gestures against the military strategists, for example, is his falling asleep at the council of war before Austerlitz, a scene highly implausible in the abstract, but rendered wholly plausible in Tolstoy's presentation of it:

'Kutuzov, in his unbuttoned uniform, with his fat neck bulging out over his collar as if it was escaping, was sitting in a low chair, his old, podgy hands placed symmetrically on the arms, nearly asleep. At the sound of Weyrother's voice he opened his one eye with an effort.

"Yes, yes, if you please, it's already late," he said, and nodding his head he let it drop, and again closed his eye.

If at first the members of the council thought that Kutuzov was pretending to be asleep, the sounds he gave out through his nose during the reading proved that at that moment the business being dealt with by the commander-in-chief was far more serious than a desire to show his contempt for the dispositions or anything else: he was dealing with the business of satisying an irresistible human need: sleep. He really was asleep. Weyrother, with the gesture of a man too busy to lose a single minute, glanced at Kutuzov, and having convinced himself that he really was asleep, took up a paper and in a loud monotonous tone began to read out the dispositions for the coming battle.' (I.iii.12)

As with all Tolstoy's descriptions, Kutuzov is made a real physical presence here by the telling use of detail—the fat neck hanging over the collar, the old, podgy hands, the one eye—rather than by a full description of his appearance. Since we at once recognise him as both human and old, we have no difficulty in believing that he should give way to the 'irresistible human need' for sleep. The bickering of the generals as he sleeps helps justify his action in our eyes, but our belief is not dependent on this; it is dependent on our recognition in Kutuzov of a fully realised character who is neither a peg for Tolstoy's arguments, nor a well-known historical figure, but an old man with a fat neck and podgy hands whose age and experience enable him to see a different order of priorities from those of his generals.

The principle that is operative in Tolstoy's presentation of Kutuzov here is operative in the other 'war' episodes in *War and Peace*. Despite Professor Berlin's eloquent apologia for Tolstoy as a philosopher of history[3] (and there is no question but that we should take him seriously in that role), it is when he is engaged in the creative, explorative examination of human behaviour—that is, when he is most a novelist, rather than a philosopher—that he is at his most persuasive. The more exclusively didactic he becomes about the nature of war and the distortions of the historians, the less convincing he becomes, and the less engaged is the reader. This is not primarily a matter of whether or not we agree with his philosophy: there is much that he offers us that, if contentious, is at any rate highly plausible. His underlying contention that there is no 'science' of history, that historians can offer no adequate explanation of the vast movements of which the Napoleonic campaigns provided the most striking example, because so vast a number of contingencies are operative, is difficult to refute. The smaller propositions consequent on that belief—the argument that neither Napoleon, nor any other general or 'great man' can control the movement of events on or off the battlefield, that the morale of an army is more important than its relative size or equipment, that a small unit acting without any knowledge of its strategic importance can turn the tide of a battle—are all likely sounding arguments. What is important in this context is that Tolstoy is able to present us with concrete examples of such propositions, enacted on a wholly convincing human scale, a scale much wider than that of abstract discussion precisely because we are enmeshed in a complex range of individual responses to a particular situation. One of the best examples of this is the episode of Tushin's battery at the battle of Schon Grabern. (I.ii.15–21)

When we first see Tushin, Tolstoy is at pains to stress his lack of obviously heroic qualities. We see him in a tent, an attractive but slightly ridiculous figure, not only absent from his post but not even wearing his boots. Reprimanded by a pompous staff-officer, in the presence of Prince Andrey, he makes a sympathetic if wholly unmilitary impression on the latter. Tushin's battery occupies the centre and the highest point of the Russian line, and it is there that Andrey goes before the battle begins to try to work out the general position. As he makes notes he hears Tushin once again, and recognises 'the agreeable philosophising voice with pleasure'. But as he listens to the discussion that is going on, Tushin's doubts about a future life are interrupted by the first shot of the battle:

' "Some herb-vodka? Certainly!" said Tushin, "but still, to conceive a future life . . ." He did not finish.

At that moment a whistling was heard in the air; nearer, nearer, faster and louder, louder and faster, and a cannonball, as if it had not finished saying everything that was necessary, smacked into the ground not far from the hut, uprooting the silver birches with superhuman force. The earth seemed to groan at the terrible impact.

At once the little Tushin rushed out of the shed before anyone else, with a pipe in the corner of his mouth; his kind, intelligent face was slightly pale.' (I.ii.16)

Tolstoy stresses Tushin's essential humanity, his mixture of intelligence and simplicity, fear, bravery and kindness. Knowing nothing of him, we still recognise in him a separate individual, and one to whom our sympathies go out as do Andrey's. As the battle gets under way, Bagration and his suite, Andrey among them, ride up to Tushin's battery:

'A small, round-shouldered man, Captain Tushin, ran forward, stumbling over the gun carriage, and not noticing the general, peered out from under his small hand.

"Add two more degrees and it will be just right," he cried in a feeble voice to which he tried to add a dashing note which did not go with his appearance. "Number Two," he squeaked. "Fire Medvedev!"

Bagration called the captain, and Tushin, raising three fingers to his cap, with a bashful and awkward gesture, not so much a military salute as a priest's benediction, came up to the general. Though Tushin's guns had been intended to cannonade the valley, he was firing incendiary balls on the village of Schon Grabern, which rose opposite, and in front of which large masses of French were advancing.

No one had ordered Tushin where to fire or what ammunition to use, but having consulted his sergeant-major Zakharchenko, for whom he had a great respect, he had decided that it would be a good thing to set fire to the village. "Very good!" said Bagration to the officer's report, and began to scrutinise the battlefield extended before him as if he were deliberating over something.' (I.ii.17)

Bagration, it becomes clear to Andrey, is not deliberating, and exerts no control over the battle. Instead, he merely gives his assent to the inevitable, not giving orders but making it seem that whatever happens is part of his strategy. In this he is not without his value, but it is Tushin and not the general who plays the crucial role. As the Russian army is forced to withdraw, his battery is left without support of any kind, and is 'only not taken by the French because the enemy could not conceive of the effrontery of anyone firing from four undefended guns. On the contrary, the energetic activity of this battery led them to suppose that here in the centre were concentrated the main Russian forces, and twice they had attempted to attack this point, and both times they had been driven back by grape-shot from the four isolated guns on the hillock.' (I.ii.20) Tushin succeeds in setting fire to the village, and attracts not only the attacks of the French infantry but a heavy artillery bombardment. The behaviour of the kindly, intelligent Tushin under fire is scrutinised carefully by Tolstoy:

'Owing to the terrible din, the uproar, the need for concentration and activity, Tushin did not experience the slightest unpleasant sense of fear, and the thought that he might be killed or painfully wounded did not enter his head. On the contrary he became more and more elated. It seemed to him that it was already a very long time ago, almost as long as yesterday, when he had first caught sight of the enemy and fired the first shot, and that the scrap of ground he stood on was a well known, familiar place. Though he thought of everything, considered everything, did everything the best of officers could do in his position, he was in a state akin to feverish delirium, or that of a drunken man.

From the deafening sounds of his own guns on every side, from the whistling and thudding of the enemy's cannonballs, from the flushed, sweating faces of the crews bustling round the guns, from the sight of the blood of men and horses, from the little puffs of smoke on the enemy's side (always followed by a ball flying over to hit the earth, a man, a gun, or a horse), from the sight of all these things a fantastic world of his own had established itself in his mind and at that moment afforded him pleasure. The enemy's guns were in his imagination not guns but pipes from which an invisible smoker let out occasional puffs of smoke.' (I.ii.20)

It is in this situation that Andrey finds him when he brings the long delayed order to withdraw. In complete ignorance of any strategic plan, and without orders of any kind, Tushin's four guns have enabled Bagration's army to do what Kutuzov had hoped it would do—hold up the French advance and prevent the main Russian army from being cut off. Not only Tushin, but Bagration's staff and the general himself, are unaware of the importance of the role the battery has played. Rather than a medal, Tushin receives a reprimand for abandoning two guns in a scene which underlines the lack of contact between strategists and soldiers with a powerful, controlled irony. Only Andrey's brusque intervention saves him, and Andrey himself is left disillusioned and depressed: 'it was all so strange, so unlike what he had hoped.'

Tolstoy has made his point, and made it more persuasively than he is ever able to do in his moments of more abstract discussion. Instead of simply being told that a single unit can influence the outcome of a battle in a way out of all proportion to its size, or that the strategists on the staff rarely have knowledge, let alone control, of the events of a battle, we see these propositions acted out in a way that convinces us that on this occasion at least they are true. We can accept them because they are presented with the insight of the great novelist, as part of a complex human scenario in which richly plausible characters as different as Tushin and Andrey stand at the centre. Tushin, we feel, is not simply there to dramatise a didactic point; the paradoxes of his character and the irony of his situation make him a unique figure, for all his implied representative quality. He has an identity of his own which extends beyond the situations in which, briefly, we see him at the centre of events, and it is because of this, because we know him as we know Andrey, that we can accept the truthfulness of Tolstoy's account.

This is essentially the novelist's way of making his point; it is instructive to compare the Tushin episode, indeed the whole account of the battle of Schön Grabern, with Tolstoy's generalisations arising out of the battle of Tarutino, where the philosopher of history is much more obviously present:

> ' "That's how things always are with us, all topsy turvy!" said the Russian officers and generals after the battle of Tarutino, just as people will say now, implying that some fool there is doing things topsy turvy, but that we would not have done so. But people who talk like that either don't know what they are talking about, or knowingly deceive themselves. No battle—Tarutino, Borodino, Austerlitz—no battle ever happens as those who planned it anticipated. That is an essential condition.
>
> A countless number of free forces (since nowhere is man freer than during a battle, where it is a matter of life and death) influence the direction taken by a battle, and this direction can never be known beforehand and never coincides with the direction of any one force.
>
> If many simultaneously and variously directed forces act on a given body, the direction of the movement of that body cannot coincide with any one of those forces; but will always be a mean, the shortest direction, that which in mechanics is represented by the diagonal of a parallelogram of forces.
>
> If in the descriptions of the historians, especially the French, we find that their wars and battles happen according to a previously made plan, the only conclusion that we can draw is that their descriptions are not true.' (IV.ii.7)

Tolstoy is here making much the same points as he is in the earlier episode, indeed the same basic point as he makes about the whole campaign. In the description of the battle of Tarutino, however, we have no real sense of the creative re-enactment of events in a convincingly human context that we do in the battle of Schön Grabern: the characters involved are the generals on either side who, with the exception of Kutuzov, are no more than the victims of Tolstoy's irony at the expense of military strategists and the 'heroes' of the nineteenth-century historian.

In general, therefore, Tolstoy's strategy in his presentation of the 'war' episodes is not basically different from that of the 'peace' episodes. Such passages as that describing Tushin and his battery serve to underline the basic truth that the parts of the narrative which deal with war and peace cannot be separated from each other in the way that some critics have suggested. We do not, that is, have a large 'family' novel along English lines interleaved with an epic-didactic-historical narrative of the Napoleonic wars. The war (as it was Tolstoy's purpose to show) impinges too closely on the lives of all the major characters for it to be in any way separable from the narrative of the family life of the Rostovs, the Bolkonskys or Pierre, as the presence of Prince Andrey in this episode serves to remind us. That family life, the 'real life' of ordinary people as Tolstoy calls it at one point, is essential to his basic argument about the war and the science of history. Not only do we see the careers of Andrey, Pierre, Natasha or Nikolay caught up in those vast, apparently predetermined and involuntary movements of humanity from West to East and from East to West, but they are themselves examples of those millions of 'differentials' with which, he argues, the historian would have to come to terms before he could give an adequate account of those movements. To understand events we need to know as much about the response of such private figures, in whom is reflected the unconscious response of the Russian people, as we do about the public figures who believe they govern a tide which is in fact merely carrying them along on its surface. For this reason, Tolstoy implies, the historical novelist can offer an account that reflects the reality of events much more accurately than the historian can hope to do.

Of these 'private' figures, the figures from 'real life with its essential interests of health, sickness, work, rest, with its interests of thought, science, poetry, music, love, friendship, hatred, passions,' (I.ii.3) it is the Rostovs who stand most obviously at the very centre of the novel. They do so not because they receive the closest attention from Tolstoy—this is reserved for the spiritual quests of Pierre and Andrey—but because of their normative role. The Bolkonskys are not, in this sense, normative: they are outside and somewhat above even the highest society of Moscow or Petersburg. But the Rostovs provide a stable centre to the novel in which, against the background of war, and in contrast to the uncertainties, intellectual and emotional, of Pierre and Andrey, we see the 'essential interests' of 'real life' at their clearest and most typical. In one of his early drafts for the novel, Tolstoy's name for the Rostovs was *Prostoy* (Simple), and simplicity in its best sense—a self-sufficiency, a lack of disabling introspection, an instinctive sense of what is right and what is wrong—is a characteristic which as a family they retain. In this respect they offer a contrast both to the unnatural hypocrisies of society on the one hand, and the more honest but equally unnatural 'habit of constant moral analysis' which we see in Pierre and Andrey on the other.

It is in fact with this set of contrasts that Tolstoy, after much experiment, decided to open his novel: the corrupt society world of Anna Pavlovna's *soirée*, and (for they are really part of that same world) of Dolokhov and Anatole, the disillusionment of Andrey and the confusion of Pierre, are all introduced in the first three chapters, to be followed by the scene in which the Rostovs are described. Significantly, we first see them engaged in a family celebration—the name-day of Natasha and her mother—in which the polite visitors who call to offer their congratulations appear, to us if not to them, as intruders. It is the naturalness and spontaneity, particularly of Count Rostov and Natasha, which most impress the reader, here, and set the tone for Tolstoy's presentation of the family throughout. Within this family circle only the somewhat cold and 'unnatural' Vera, who is to leave it to marry the complacent *arriviste*, Berg, and the niece Sonya, lack the characteristic Rostov qualities of simplicity, openness, and above all a *samodovolnost'*, a pleasure in being themselves and nobody else, of which we have already seen the importance in Tolstoy's earlier work. It is an interesting comment on his genius for presenting these qualities in his characters that although we never have any clear physical picture of the old count and countess, Natasha or Nikolay, we are much more immediately aware of them as vital physical presences than we are of Sonya, who is described in some detail, or the 'handsome' Vera, whose combination of outward beauty and inner emptiness corresponds in a minor, much less vicious way, to that of Hélène, just as Berg corresponds in a lesser way to Boris Drubetskoy.

Natasha is the figure who most clearly embodies the Rostov qualities of spontaneity and good-natured egoism, standing at the centre of the family group as the family stands at the centre of the novel; but it is difficult to separate her possession of these qualities from the collective possession of the whole family, in each of whom they take slightly different forms. The geniality and naïve appetite for life of the old count, the intuitive wisdom of the countess, the directness and honesty of Nikolay, are all variations of it. But though one feels that for much of the novel the atmosphere of the Rostov household is, for all its emphasis on youth and gaiety, dictated by the old count, it is to the younger generation that Tolstoy turns his closest attention.

By the very nature of the qualities that make them so sympathetic, the Rostov children don't possess the kind of complex inner life that we see in Pierre or the Bolkonskys. Nevertheless, Natasha and Nikolay, in particular, develop a great deal in the course of the novel, from the innocence and exuberance of the opening chapters to the settled married life in which we see them both at the close. Of the two, it is Nikolay who is felt to have changed least over this long period: his development, considerable though it is, has an inevitability about it that is dictated by his forthright and simple nature, a nature which makes him the most stable of the major characters in the novel. One is reminded of Tolstoy's words near the end of his life—'as I was at five, so I am now'. The Nikolay whom we see in his 'baptism of fire' on the bridge at Ens (I.ii.8) or in the justly famous hunting scene (II.iv.3–6) is essentially the same man as the successful Tolstoyan landowner we see in the Epilogue: 'He could not have said what constituted his standard of what he should or should not do; but the standard was firm and inflexible in his soul.' (Ep.i.7) This instinctive knowledge is something that the more intelligent Pierre comes to only after his experiences as a prisoner of war. For Nikolay, as for Natasha, Petya and their parents, it is something innate, not a matter of conventionally-measured intelligence, nor even of a finer moral conscience, but of natural instinct.

It is Nikolay's willingness to be guided by his instincts and not by his reason that enables him to save Princess Maria from the mutinous peasants at Bogucharovo, where his action in confronting the crowd alone seems dangerously illogical, and yet is precisely what is needed:

> ' "I'll give them military force ... I'll 'over-resist' them," uttered Nikolay mechanically, breathless with irrational animal fury and the need to vent it. Without considering what he would do he moved unthinkingly, with a quick, resolute step, towards the crowd. And the nearer he drew to it, the more Alpatych felt that this unreasonable action might bring good results. The peasants in the crowd felt the same when they saw his quick, firm walk and resolute, frowning face.' (III.2.14)

The natural 'rightness' of Nikolay's response to a situation serves Tolstoy well in the battle scenes of *War and Peace*, where the reader is willing to accept, without being explicitly told so, that his feelings have a strongly normative quality about them. The chase and capture of the young French officer, and Nikolay's bewildered awareness of having done something guilty, despite the fact that he had acted with courage and propriety according to the criteria of those around him, is one example of this.

At first the excitement of the charge is like that of the hunt. Only at the moment of impact of human on human does the reality of war come sharply home to Nikolay: he has hunted and wounded a man against whom he feels no personal animosity, and who as he hops around with one foot caught in his stirrup looks up at him in terror from a face which 'was not suited to a battlefield, was not the face of an enemy, but a most simple, homely face'. (III.i.15) Nikolay himself cannot account for the 'vaguely disagreeable feeling of moral nausea' which haunts him, but the reader is never in any doubt about the essential rightness and naturalness of his response. The same is true in the more frequently quoted episode of his own wounding at the battle of Schon Grabern, where he is the quarry, not the hunter, and where the same emphasis on a battle as made up of the wholly unnatural, unmotivated assaults of one individual human being on another comes out in Nikolay's incredulity that the Frenchmen should want to kill *him*. '*Me*, whom everyone is so fond of.'

This intuitive rightness of response is seen at other important points in the novel—in Nikolay's scepticism about Natasha's engagement to Prince Andrey, which he shares with the rest of his family, or in his bewilderment at the respect and friendship shown to Napoleon by the Russians at Tilsit. But his 'naturalness' is most fully and lovingly celebrated by Tolstoy in one of the greatest pastoral scenes in all literature, that of the hunt in the second book. The scene takes in more than Nikolay, of course: it is a celebration of the harmony of the whole Rostov family with the natural world into which they fit so easily (it is significant that a distant relative whom they call 'Uncle' should appear, epitomising the simplest and most wholesome of country lives). It is a celebration, too, of the undeniable elation of the hunt, with its paradoxical mixture of love for the whole living world, and the singleminded aim of killing one part of that world. In the end, with its vibrancy of detail, its loving depiction of physical reality, it is a celebration of nature and the springs of life itself. But it is Nikolay who is at the centre of this scene, and it is right that he should be so, for it is precisely here, in the world of spontaneous, unreflecting physical action, in which man and nature are in most intimate contact, that he is most at home, most himself (Dostoyevsky, to whom pastoral was alien, and who had no conception of such a simple naturalness, found Nikolay merely dull and insignificant).

No single extract from Tolstoy's account of the hunt can convey this relationship of Nikolay to the events in which we see him so completely immersed. The four chapters which he devotes to it are a complete and indivisible whole, and that seemingly effortless capacity to render a world in which we seem to have not a description of an event but the living event itself is seen at its clearest here, where all is detail, but no detail is superfluous or laboured. In it, Nikolay takes what seems his inevitable part, the part of the man whose natural affinities are with the Russian land and the peasants who people it. It is obviously his destiny to become that successful farmer who instinctively loves ' "our Russian people" and their way of life with all the strength of his soul' whom we see in the Epilogue.

The great pastoral scene of the hunt is followed by a more domestic but still very Russian pastoral which, if quieter in tone is scarcely less telling in its overall effect. This is the scene at the house of 'Uncle' (*Dadyushka*) in which Natasha, rather than

Nikolay, is the central figure. Again one feels that it is life itself that is being celebrated through Natasha's vitality and her delighted response to the idyllic world of 'Uncle' and Anisya Fedorovna, a celebration that culminates in the Russian dance which comes so easily to her:

> 'Where, how and when had this young countess, educated by an *émigrée* French governess, drunk in that spirit from the Russian air she breathed, from where did she get that manner which the *pas de châle* should long ago have effaced? But the spirit and the manner were the very ones, inimitable, unteachable, Russian, which "Uncle" had expected of her. As soon as she had stood up and smiled triumphantly, proudly, and with a sly merriment, the momentary fear that had seized Nikolay and all those present, the fear that she might not do it right, disappeared, and they were already admiring her.' (II.iv.7)

In this setting, we feel, it is impossible for Natasha *not* to do the right thing: she, as no other character in Tolstoy (unless it is Hadji Murat) has that essentially aristocratic quality of total and unreflecting confidence in the rightness of whatever she does which he so admired and envied. Even more than Nikolay she embodies the Rostov qualities of naturalness, intuitive judgement and sheer enjoyment of being herself and no one else. Her favourite mood is 'love of, and delight in, herself', and more than once Tolstoy conveys her self-satisfaction to us with great precision:

> 'She could not get to sleep for a long time. She kept thinking that no one could ever understand all that she understood and all that was in her.
>
> "Sonya?" she thought, looking at that curled up, sleeping kitten with her enormous plait of hair. "No how could she? She's virtuous. She fell in love with Nikolay and doesn't want to know anything more. Mamma, even she doesn't understand. It's wonderful how clever I am and how . . . charming she is," she went on, talking of herself in the third person, and imagining that some very wise man, the wisest and best of men, was talking about her. "Everything, everything is in her" this man continued. "Unusually clever, charming . . . and then pretty, unusually pretty, and agile—she swims and rides splendidly, and her voice! One can truly say it's a wonderful voice!" ' (II.iii.13)

It is a measure of the skill with which Tolstoy can body forth all the charm and vitality, the sense of life brimming over, in such passages as this that we never feel inclined to regard Natasha's *samodovolnost'* as a form of unwarranted complacency or conceit. It is, however, a frankly and naturally selfish quality, of a kind that he appears to endorse in the contrast he sets up between Natasha and Sonya, whose at first sight admirable ethic of self-sacrifice he presents as a somewhat hollow virtue, based on a lack of that 'egoism' (Natasha's word) which is so strong a characteristic of her adopted family.

Natasha does not go in for self-sacrifice, either of Sonya's or of Princess Maria's more wholehearted kind: instead she acts on her whims, instincts and appetites, be they large or small, and on all but one occasion they serve her well. The exception is, of course, the episode of her attempted seduction by Anatole Kuragin, an episode to which Tolstoy once referred as the 'key-point' of the novel.[4]

One can see many reasons, apart from its physical position in the novel (it comes at the end of the second book), why he should have felt the seduction scene to be so central. It is certainly the most crucial single event in Natasha's life, and, since she stands so much at the centre of the Rostov family, whose members in turn are so central in the scheme of the novel, it follows that what is crucial for her is crucial for the novel as a whole. That the event does indeed have such an importance can be seen from its consequences: it affects the lives, and the very characters, of Natasha, Pierre and Andrey in the most far-reaching ways, turning Andrey back towards that preoccupation with death, and rejection of life, which Natasha had temporarily stilled in him, leaving Natasha herself a more bruised but a more mature figure, a woman rather than a naïve girl, and leading Pierre to his spiritually liberating declaration of his love for her.

Tolstoy may have seen the seduction episode as central in a further sense, however, a sense suggested by the passage already quoted describing Natasha's dance. The contrast that he implies there between the instinctive knowledge of the 'natural' Russian dance and the superficial layer of 'artificial' French education that one might have expected to have effaced it is for him a serious moral one. It runs as a *leitmotif* throughout *War and Peace*, reflected on a massive scale in the war itself, and in the personal contrasts between Napoleon and Kutuzov, Natasha and Hélène,

Mademoiselle Bourienne and Princess Maria, and on numerous other occasions. In its most basic form it is not simply a contrast between French and Russian, but between the artificial and the natural, and thus, for Tolstoy, between the true and the false, good and evil. Natasha stands throughout, of course, on the side of what is natural and therefore true: but on the occasion of her seduction, Tolstoy goes to great lengths to show her as having been disorientated by her sudden exposure to the alien world of the false and artificial, represented in its most extreme and yet most powerfully alluring form by the Kuragins and the opera. At first the opera seems 'grotesque' to Natasha after her life in the country, 'so grotesquely artificial and unnatural that she at first felt ashamed for the actors, then amused at them'; but we gradually see her, in her already disturbed state of mind (she is waiting for Andrey's return, and has just had her painful interview with Princess Maria and been insulted by the old prince) falling into a 'state of intoxication' in which everything around her seems not false, but, ironically, 'simple and natural'. In this world of inverted values Anatole's attentions, promoted by his sister, do not seem offensive to her: Anatole (who is himself in many ways a 'natural' man perverted by his corrupt environment) talks to her 'boldly and naturally', though such a circumstance is for Natasha anything but a natural one, and she returns to her box feeling that this is the real, natural world, that the opera is no longer artificial and grotesque, and that her life in the country and her engagement to Andrey belong to a remote past.

By laying this sort of stress on the artificiality of the society to which Natasha is exposed, by emphasising the inversion of values, so that what seems natural is artificial and what seems artificial is natural, Tolstoy prepares us for the seduction scene where, still being led by her impulses, Natasha has yet lost for the moment that instinctive sense of what is right and what is wrong that has guided her in the past. The whole episode serves as a very powerful focus of the basic Tolstoyan theme of the power of society to corrupt the good, natural, innocent instincts of man.

After the seduction episode Natasha's old self-confidence and enjoyment in being herself return only after a good deal of remorse and physical suffering. When it does return, her spontaneity is tempered by a thoughtfulness, a tact and maturity, which were absent before, but which enable her to cope with Petya's death (the event which most of all brings her back to life), and with nursing the dying Andrey. She is able, too, to understand something of the latter's attitude towards death, and to value the qualities of Pierre and Maria, in a way that she would not have done before. The change in her, once her depression and illness is over, helps to prepare us for the very much greater change we see in the Epilogue where, after seven years of marriage, she appears as a 'robust mother' whose 'features were more defined and had an expression of peaceful softness and serenity'. (Ep.I.10)

Whether it helps us to accept that change as something convincing and apparently inevitable, though, is another matter. There is a sharper discontinuity between the Natasha we see in the Epilogue and her previous self than there is in the cases of any of the other characters whom we see there. Nikolay, Maria, Pierre, Sonya and the old countess are all consistent and even predictable projections of their former selves. Tolstoy insists that Natasha's development into a wife and mother totally preoccupied with family affairs is also predictable, and perhaps it is: it is possible to accept that that 'too much of something' which her mother had seen in her as a girl has found its outlet and fulfilment in her intense maternal emotions. But there remains the suggestion that there is something programmatic about the Natasha of the Epilogue, that she has been reduced to a type, her values and attitudes willed on her by Tolstoy so that she can act as a norm, not as she had done before, but in the more damagingly didactic sense of that word. It is not so much that her development is not a possible one, but that one feels that such considerations as consistency were not uppermost in Tolstoy's mind. What he wished to do was present us with his ideal version of womanhood, and Natasha, who has been in many respects an ideal (but a very real ideal) of girlhood, is inevitably his vehicle.

The slightly false didactic note that is struck by the presentation of Natasha's family happiness is made more obvious by its contrast with that of Nikolay and Maria, who are both much more clearly consistent with their former selves, and whose relationship is described by Tolstoy without that programmatic zeal that he employs for Natasha and Pierre. It is the latter who provoke the heavy-handed insistence that 'the aim of marriage is the family', but the former pair who are more likely to convince us that this is so.

Elsewhere in the novel, Tolstoy's handling of Natasha is supremely sure: she stands for the vital, the instinctive, the natural, but, with all her charm and vivacity she is always a clearly defined individual, uniquely there in the novel, never a cipher through whom he can present an ideal. She is the successor to Pushkin's Tatyana, the precursor of Kitty in *Anna Karenina* and of Pasternak's Lara in her intuitive wisdom and (what is almost synonymous for all three writers) her closeness to the pulse of 'mother Russia,' but like those other heroines, she is pre-eminently herself, a presence in the novel of whom the reader is always aware, even when—as in much of the last two books—she takes no direct part in the action.

That this is so is partly due to the response to her of the two major male characters, Pierre and Andrey. It is a commonplace, and no more or less accurate than most such commonplaces, that Tolstoy gives the illusion of life to his characters partly by describing the responses of others to them. But in this case it is not a matter of a simple response, as it is, for instance, in the famous paragraph that introduces Princess Lise: 'Old men and dull dispirited young men, after being with her and talking to her for a time felt as if they were becoming like her. Whoever talked with her and saw at every word her bright smile and the constant gleaming of her teeth felt that he was in a specially amiable mood that day.' (I.i.2) The response of Pierre and Andrey to Natasha is, as here, a response to health and vitality, but it is not a merely transient one. Natasha becomes a permanent factor in their lives, and in doing so becomes still more a central, pivotal figure for the novel.

To say this is not to say that Natasha herself represents the final, living answer to the spiritual quests of either Andrey or Pierre, as is sometimes suggested. This is true of Andrey in particular: though his love for Natasha both before and after her seduction is a singularly important part of his spiritual experience, it is in the end a love of quite another kind, inimical to his love for Natasha, that comes to seem, to him at least, the answer to his doubts and unhappiness. He first discovers this 'principle of eternal love' for all mankind as he lies in the

operating tent after Borodino, and sees his enemy, Anatole
Kuragin, suffering under the surgeon's hands:

> 'Now he remembered the connection that existed between him
> and this man, who was gazing dully at him through the tears that
> filled his swollen eyes. Prince Andrey remembered everything,
> and ecstatic pity and love for this man filled his happy heart.
> Prince Andrey could no longer restrain himself, and wept
> tender loving tears for mankind, for himself, and for its errors and
> his own.
> "Compassion, love for our brothers, for those who love us; love
> for those who hate us, love of our enemies, yes, that love which
> Princess Maria taught and which I did not understand: that is
> why I was sorry to lose my life, that is what remained for me had
> I lived. But it's too late. I know it." ' (III.ii.37)

Andrey comes to experience this kind of generalised love, love
for all mankind, rather than for a particular person, only when
he is in the closest proximity to death. It becomes clear to him
at Borodino, but he has already had some insight into it in his
epiphanic experience on the battlefield at Austerlitz, when the
'high, infinite sky' into which he looks as he lies wounded tells
him of 'the insignificance of everything I understand, and the
greatness of something incomprehensible and all-important'.
(I.iii.19) What that something is he finally learns only when he
is really dying, and recognises that that love he had felt for
Anatole, which had given him such happiness, is in fact an
aspect of God, and that to die simply means 'for me, a particle
of love, to return to the general and eternal source' of all love.
This prefigures very closely the much later doctrines of *What I
Believe* and *The Kingdom of God is Within You*. Here, Tolstoy emphasises the extent to which this love is bound up with death—
is, in fact, an emotion hostile to all that Natasha stands for, and
incompatible with the love that Andrey has felt for her:

> 'During the hours of suffering, solitude and semi-delirium that
> he spent after he was wounded, the more he penetrated into this
> principle of eternal love that had been newly revealed to him, the
> more he unconsciously detached himself from earthly life. And the
> more he was filled by this principle of love, the more he renounced
> life, and the more completely he destroyed that dreadful barrier
> which, when we have no such love, stands between life and death.

When during that first period he remembered that he would have to die, he said to himself: "Well, what of it? So much the better!" (IV.i.16)

The question of Tolstoy's attitude towards Andrey's concept of eternal love is, as this passage suggests, a delicate and complex one. Although that concept so clearly anticipates much that he himself was to preach later, and even anticipates certain aspects of Pierre's experience later in the novel, it would be a mistake to assume that it has here his wholehearted endorsement. Tolstoy was certainly not at this stage prepared to view the prospect of 'detaching himself from earthly life' with any kind of equanimity, and the effect here is much more of an exploration of a possible attitude towards death than of a didactic illustration of how we ought to feel. 'Eternal love' here is something that is clearly opposed to life, and to what one feels to be the more creative concept of love represented by Andrey's relationship to Natasha. When the latter begins to nurse him, Andrey feels that 'love for a particular woman crept unnoticed into his heart and once more bound him to life', and it is only after his 'last spiritual struggle between life and death, in which death gained the victory' that the generalised 'eternal love' for all mankind regains control. After this struggle, the 'awakening into death', Tolstoy, as if involuntarily, presents Andrey as peculiarly cold and repellent, emphasising the bloodless whiteness of his skin, and the callousness of his attitude towards those around him; he refers to the 'terrible [strashny] moral symptoms' which Natasha recognises. Altogether, there is something deadly about Andrey in a pejorative sense in these final scenes, for all the sympathy and insight with which Tolstoy enables us to see and understand the feelings of the dying man. Tolstoy is at this stage, one feels, passionately involved with Andrey's attitude towards love and death, without being able to endorse it. He undoubtedly projects through Andrey many of his own feelings, even aspirations, but as Lawrence recognised 'As a true artist he worshipped . . . every manifestation of pure, spontaneous, passionate life, life kindled to vividness',[5] and at this stage of his life death did not press on him so strongly as to make him reject that life in the way that a wholehearted endorsement of Andrey's experience would involve. Nothing could show more clearly, though, the way in which the doctrines of the older

Tolstoy are a development of one aspect of his outlook which was there from a very early stage.

As one looks back over Andrey's life from the point of view of his death one can in fact see it almost in its entirety as a struggle between the polarities of life and death, with death a predestined victor. It is true that all Tolstoy's 'seekers', all those characters through whom he projects some aspect of his own continuing quest for meaning and truth, are prompted in their search by their awareness of the inevitability of death, an end which seemed to Tolstoy to render meaningless all that had gone before it. His very feeling for life was the more acute because of this awareness, just as his horror of death was intensified by the abundance of life in him. But no other of Tolstoy's heroes has the special relationship to death that Prince Andrey has. During his description of Andrey's death, Tolstoy talks of 'that remorseless, eternal, distant, unknown, the presence of which he had never ceased to feel throughout his whole life', and the reader assents at once that an aura of death, an other-worldliness, has hung over Andrey from the beginning—not his sister's awareness, but something more disabling, more nihilistic than her simple piety.

Thus, when we first see him, bored and disillusioned, Andrey tells Pierre that his life is over—that he has been trapped by his marriage in a kind of living death, his 'part played out'. His slightly naïve fantasies before Austerlitz, dreams of a Napoleonic glory to be won, if necessary, at the expense of all those he holds dearest, are really a desperate attempt to escape this sense that, for him, everything is finished. Instead of the satisfaction he expects, his brief moment of glory at Austerlitz leaves him with the memory of the infinite sky, and a concomitant awareness of the insignificance of that very Napoleon whom he had so admired. On his return to Bald Hills, with a new understanding of the importance of an outgoing love in his life, he arrives in time to see the little princess, whom, whatever her failings, he has treated badly since their marriage, die in childbirth. Later he explains his reactions to this event to Pierre in their discussion on the ferry. It is Lise's death, not philosophical argument, that has led him to look beyond life, into death, and to see something there:

' "What convinces is when you see a being dear to you, bound to you, before whom you were guilty and hoped to make it right" (Prince Andrey's voice shook and he turned away), "and suddenly that being suffers and is tormented and ceases to exist . . . Why? It cannot be that there is no answer! And I believe there is . . . That's what convinces, that's what has convinced me," said Prince Andrey.

"Well, yes, yes," said Pierre, "isn't that the very thing I'm saying?"

"No. I only say that it is not argument that convinces one of the necessity of a future life, but this: when you go hand in hand with a person, and suddenly that person vanishes *there, into nowhere*, and you yourself stop at this abyss, and look into it. And I have looked in . . ." ' (II.ii.12)

The important point here is the stress on Andrey's insight through Lise's death into another world, that 'remorseless, eternal, distant, unknown' world that he knows to lie beyond death. It is a world that comes, for him, to stand over against life, a life for which he has lost all appetite since Lise's death. The life he now lives, retired from the army and concentrating on building at Bogucharovo, is based wholly on negatives, as he tells Pierre. He speaks in French, a language which Tolstoy often uses in the novel to indicate an element of unnatural coldness and artificiality (here Andrey echoes Joseph de Maistre):

' "Je ne connais dans la vie que maux bien reels: c'est le remord et la maladie. Il n'est de bien que l'absence de ces maux. To live for myself, so as to avoid those two evils: that is my whole philosophy now." ' (II.ii.11)

A little later he tells Pierre: ' "I'm alive, and that is not my fault, so I must live till my death as best I can, without harming anyone." '

Andrey's denial of life, and his consequent preoccupation with death and what lies beyond it, is stressed by Tolstoy throughout this period of his life. The cold precision of his language (interlaced with French) and the detached efficiency with which he manages his estates, underline it. But it is the growing similarity we begin to notice between Andrey and his father, whose proud and embittered rationalism is itself a form of spiritual death, that drives the point home most forcibly.

This life-denying state is shaken by Andrey's first encounter with the young Natasha on his visit to Otradnoye. That visit is framed, as it were, by the rather ostentatiously symbolic transformation of the old and apparently dead oak which he sees before he goes to Otradnoye, and which he sees again 'wholly transformed, spreading out a canopy of sappy, dark green foliage' on his return. As Andrey looks at the oak he too is 'seized by an irrational, spring-time feeling of joy and renewal' which we recognise to be closely related to his experience at Otradnoye, where after overhearing Natasha's moonlight conversation with Sonya 'In his soul there suddenly arose such an unexpected turmoil of youthful thoughts and hopes, contrary to everything in his life, that, feeling unable to explain this condition to himself, he fell asleep at once'. (II.iii.2)

From this point on, we recognise Natasha as the embodiment of the forces which pull Andrey back towards life: meeting her again at the ball, he feels himself 'revived and rejuvenated' after dancing with her. After the ball, he can no longer concentrate on the political reforms into which he had thrown himself, and the politician Speransky, with his 'precise, mirthless laughter' is seen in what is, for Tolstoy, the true light of all such rational, liberal reformers—as a man partially dead, unable to see the irrelevance of his reforms to the important issues of life. We tend to feel this is a perversity on Tolstoy's part, but it is worth noting that Andrey's question 'Can it all make me any happier or better?', the question which 'suddenly destroyed all the interest [he] had felt in the impending reforms', is strikingly similar to that asked by that decidedly liberal reformer John Stuart Mill, who records in his *Autobiography* how a sudden insight into the spiritual emptiness of Benthamite Utilitarianism left him in a state of aimless bewilderment. Mill had no obvious answer to his dilemma, but in Andrey's case the question is both provoked and answered by Natasha, in whom he 'was conscious of a strange world, completely foreign to him, and brimful of joys unknown to him, a foreign world that in the Otradnoye avenue and at the window on that moonlit night had so disconcerted him'. (II.iii.19)

Natasha draws him into this world, the world of essential life, but Andrey can never quite become a harmonious part of it. It is their sense that Andrey belongs to a world alien to theirs that makes the Rostovs fear as well as respect him, and makes the countess in particular feel that there is 'something unnatural and dreadful' in the impending marriage. What is so alien to the Rostovs is not so much Andrey's powerful intelligence or high social standing (they might be pleased that Natasha should have made 'one of the best matches in Russia'), but his continual awareness of death and the world that, for him, lies beyond it: that eternal presence hangs over Andrey even when he is stirred into new life by his love for Natasha. As he listens to her singing, he has 'a sudden, vivid sense of the terrible contrast between something infinitely great and illimitable within him, and something limited and material that he, and even she, was'. That 'something infinitely great and illimitable', though for the moment it seems to co-exist with his love for Natasha, can, as we understand later, only lead him away from her and the life that she promises. The 'terrible contrast' between it and Natasha, between the spiritual and the physical, is the basis of a dualism that is to become much clearer in Tolstoy's later work. Here it is an expression of that struggle between life and death in Andrey, in which death is the inevitable winner. It is because he is so acutely aware of the possibilities of life without ever being able, as his sister is able, to live in a state of harmonious acceptance of the claims of both worlds, that he emerges as a tragic figure.

On the eve of the battle of Borodino, Andrey looks back over his past life from the point of view of death, a death he expects to meet the next day: 'And from the height of this perception all that had previously tormented and preoccupied him suddenly became illumined by a cold white light without shadows, without perspective, without distinction of outline.' (III.ii.24) In this light of death, so similar to that in which Anna Karenina makes her last drive to the station, all his past life seems very clear, its problems and aspirations merely false images, rendered meaningless by the great fact of death. Although, as we have seen, he is again drawn back to life by Natasha, whose nursing of him might in this sense be seen as a symbolic activity, this 'cold white light' of death is the one in which he eventually dies; only through it does he find love, relief and truth.

Andrey's quest and the answers at which he arrives are perhaps the most desperate and extreme of those of all Tolstoy's 'seekers'. His 'awakening into death' denies the importance of much that Tolstoy at this time believed in passionately—love for a particular person, family happiness, the joy of spontaneous natural life. But he undoubtedly represents a powerful side of Tolstoy's searching, restless personality, and one which was to grow into the dominant part of it. In *War and Peace*, however, Andrey's character and values are placed by their comparison with those of Pierre, Natasha or Maria, to none of whom does the opposition between life and death, between the body and the spirit, present itself as starkly as it does to Andrey, or as it was to do to the older Tolstoy.

If Andrey's preoccupation with death, as well as his aristocratic *hauteur*, certainly correspond to important elements in the massively complex and paradoxical character of his creator, we rightly tend to see Pierre as a projection of other aspects of his character, equally 'Tolstoyan' in his search for truth, for the meaning of life. He stands clearly opposed to his friend Andrey in many ways: he is humble where Andrey is proud, warmly impulsive where Andrey is reserved, credulous where Andrey is cynical. The differences between them are bodied forth by Tolstoy in their physical difference—the small, neat figure of Andrey contrasting sharply with the heavy, shambling, untidy Pierre, of whose physical characteristics (the large hands, the spectacles, the corpulence, and the unusual strength) we are made more aware than in the case of any other figure in the novel. Pierre is most notably different from Prince Andrey, however, in his lack of will, his lack of the ability to translate intention into action. Whereas Andrey has, in Tolstoy's own words, 'a practical tenacity which Pierre lacked', we see the latter from the outset as a figure drifting amiably, but with a fundamental unhappiness, from one situation to another. Quite unable to take either the practical decisions demanded of him by the society around him, or the moral decisions necessitated by his own unease at the life he leads, he is manipulated with extraordinary ease by such people as Anna Mikhaylovna or Prince Vasily. Though there is something of the holy fool in Pierre, with his naïve honesty and openness, and his dislike of the hypocrisies of society, it is clear that his malleability in the hands of that society is a serious weakness, leading him as it does to the loveless and unhappy marriage with Hélène, and the duel with Dolokhov. That duel marks a crisis in Pierre's career, since it is only after he has been drawn into it that he is driven to act more positively—to separate from Hélène and take stock of his situation. Only during this period, after the duel, does he really become engrossed by the great Tolstoyan questions, ' "What is bad? What is good? What should one love and what hate? What is life for, and what am I? What force directs it all?" ' (II.ii.1), questions that follow him through the novel, as they followed Tolstoy through his whole career. That the answers which Freemasonry, through the admittedly impressive figure of Bazdeyev, promises to these questions should arouse such enthusiasm in him is a measure of both his continuing naïveté and his desperate hunger for an answer. Tolstoy shows Pierre as still lacking in a will of his own, and being too quickly convinced by Bazdeyev at their meeting in the post-station: he submits to him 'involuntarily' (*nevol'no*), and it is appropriate that the initiation ceremony should involve his being led blindfold into the movement.

The Masonic movement takes up a considerable part of Pierre's career as we see it in the novel, and its presence there requires some explanation. Tolstoy's original plan had been to write a novel based on the aftermath of the Decembrist plot of 1825, a reformist plot which had close connections with the Masonic movement, and it is natural that Pierre, who retains many of the characteristics of Tolstoy's Decembrist hero, should be a Mason. In the political climate of the 1860s, when he was writing *War and Peace*, it would have been extremely difficult for him to explore in any detail the relationship of the Masons to political change in Russia, and the only real indications remaining of the social-reformist aspects of the movement are Pierre's unsuccessful speech to the Petersburg Masons (II.iii.7) and his own fruitless efforts to improve the lot of his serfs. But, though he felt they were 'fools', Tolstoy sympathised with many of the social aims of the Masons, and more importantly with their moral—as opposed to mystical—teaching. Thus he makes Pierre associate Masonry with 'God, death, love, the brotherhood of man', a complete if rather vague summary of his own preoccupations.

That Pierre should seize on Freemasonry as a source of spiritual knowledge and regeneration is not, then, unreasonable: but it is always clear to the reader, from the induction ceremony onwards, that it cannot, by its very nature, provide him with the answers to his questions. For, as we discover, those questions are of a kind that have to be answered out of his own, personal experience, and not by the revealed mysteries of a sect. For a time the movement seems to have given Pierre the answers, or at least to have promised them. On the ferry with Andrey he is confident in his knowledge of what is good and what is bad, and his enthusiasm, if not his actual ideas, helps to re-open spiritual and emotional horizons for Andrey. But the 'regeneration' is never profound enough to last for long, and it collapses in the face of Bazdeyev's death, Hélène's callous infidelity, and, most important of all, the engagement of Andrey to Natasha. After this event, Tolstoy says, 'Pierre, without any obvious cause, suddenly felt it impossible to go on living as before'. The tormenting questions return, only to be desperately avoided:

'Moments of despair, melancholy, and disgust with life no longer descended on him, but the malady that had formerly been expressed in such acute attacks was driven inwards and never left him for a moment. "What for? Why? What is happening in the world?" he asked himself in perplexity several times a day, involuntarily beginning to inquire into the meaning of the phenomena of life; but knowing by experience that there were no answers to these questions, he tried hurriedly to turn away from them, and took up a book, or hurried to the club, or to Apollon Nikolayevich to gossip about the affairs of the town.' (II.v.1)

As with the duel, it is again a crisis that is needed to drive Pierre out of this state: this time, it is his involuntary involvement in the aftermath of Anatole's attempted seduction of Natasha. As in the earlier episode, so now, Pierre reacts with a simple, unreflecting anger against the Kuragin family, frightening Anatole with his strength as he had previously frightened Hélène. This emergence of the instinctive man from beneath the layers of spiritual indecision is suggestive, but its most important manifestation comes a little later, when Pierre, to his own amazement, finds himself declaring his love for Natasha. As so often in Tolstoy, the image of the high, expansive sky is used to convey the emotional effect of a liberating and joyful discovery, an event of immense spiritual scope; as he leaves the Rostovs'

'At the entrance to the Arbatsky Square a huge expanse of dark, starry sky opened before Pierre's eyes. Almost in the centre of the sky, above Prechistensky Boulevard, surrounded and sprinkled on every side with stars, but differing from them all by its closeness to the earth, its white light, and its long uplifted tail, hung the enormous, brilliant comet of the year 1812, the same comet which was said to portend all kinds of terrors and the end of the world. But in Pierre this bright star with its long luminous tail aroused no feeling of terror. On the contrary, Pierre gazed joyfully, with eyes moist with tears, at this bright star which, having travelled on its parabolic line with inconceivable speed through immeasurable space, suddenly, like an arrow piercing the earth, remained fixed in a chosen spot in the black sky, vigorously holding its tail erect, shining, and playing with its white light amongst countless other glittering stars. It seemed to Pierre that this star fully responded to what was in his own softened and uplifted soul, now blossoming into new life.' (II.v.22)

This is the beginning of a genuine regeneration in Pierre, one that is more solidly based than that offered by Bazdeyev, because based on a spontaneous, unreflecting love. From this time the great questions about the purpose of life no longer press on him, because his life at least has a purpose in his love for Natasha: now, 'the problem of the vanity and absurdity of all earthly things that had incessantly tormented him, ceased to present itself. That terrible question "Why?" "What for?" which till then had come to him in the middle of every occupation, was now replaced, not by another question, and not by a reply to the former question, but by *her* image.' (III.i.19) As to Andrey, but more lastingly, Natasha brings new life, and a new kind of wisdom, to Pierre. For Tolstoy, we know, the solution was not to be a lasting one; but in the terms of the novel, it is sufficient. Nearly a century later, Tolstoy's greatest successor sees Lara as playing almost exactly the same role in the life of Zhivago: 'Later, I have often tried to name and define the enchantment of which you sowed the seeds in me—that gradually fading light and dying sound which have spread throughout the whole of my being and have become to me the means of understanding everything else in the world through you.'[6] From now onwards, whether he knows it or not, Pierre 'understands everything else in the world' through Natasha. Although for the moment he is not free to marry her, or even to hope that he may do so, this awareness of love is the stone on which his subsequent career rests.

That career, of course, takes in a great deal of fresh and disturbing experience: the battle of Borodino, the burning of Moscow, the ludicrous attempt to assassinate Napoleon which ends, ironically, in Pierre's rescuing a child, and, most decisive of all, his capture and imprisonment by the French. All this consolidates, as it were, the strength which he has initially derived from his love for Natasha, developing his new found stability, and helping him towards a new philosophy through the person of Platon Karatayev, who, along with Natasha, Andrey, and to a lesser extent Bazdeyev, is one of the major influences in his quest for the truth.

After Borodino, Tolstoy shows Pierre's thoughts turning towards the common people, seeing in their uncomplaining submission to whatever may occur a spiritual wisdom and strength which he feels to be lacking in himself. He carries away from the battlefield an 'overwhelming sensation of his own nothingness and falsity in comparison with the truth, simplicity and strength of that class of people who had impressed themselves on his soul under the name *they*'. (III.iii.27) In particular, '*they*' gain strength from their total acceptance of death: they have no fear of death, accepting it as part of God's order. Platon Karatayev is the embodiment of this peasant wisdom, 'an unfathomable, rounded, eternal personification of the spirit of simplicity and truth', who, in his story of the falsely condemned merchant, sees death as a sign of God's forgiveness. There is undoubtedly a certain awkwardness in Tolstoy's presentation of Karatayev: he is an obviously idealised figure amongst so many real ones, introduced to guide Pierre towards that wisdom of acceptance, that embracing of life in its entirety, which he does indeed gain. But if Karatayev himself is a slightly unreal figure, it does not follow that Pierre's response to him, and to the whole experience of the imprisonment and the retreat, is also unreal and idealised. Tolstoy avoids striking a crudely didactic note because one feels that even here his attitude is still the explorative, open one of the great novelist. Karatayev, like Andrey, may prefigure much that we are to find in the later, more didactic work, but Tolstoy's narrative gives us a sequence of events that elicits a wholly credible response from Pierre, and the effect is of the novelist working out just what Pierre's reactions might be, rather than putting the desired reactions first and organising the narrative of events to fit them.

What Pierre learns most of all from Karatayev and the rest is really no more than what Natasha or Nikolay has always known instinctively: that man has an innate moral sense, a sense that operates when he lives in harmony with his own nature and that of the world around him, and that that sense comes from a God who is present in him and in everything around him. As Pierre phrases it in a dream, ' "Life is everything. Life is God. Everything changes and moves, and that movement is God." ' (IV.iii.15) It is only after he has come to this wholehearted acceptance of life that his doubts about its aim disappear, and he can return to marry Natasha. And it is on the affirmative note of that marriage, the note that might be summarised in the phrase 'Life is everything', that the great novel comes to its close.

5
Anna Karenina

Despite the thoroughly optimistic note on which *War and Peace* closes, the belief that 'life is everything', the years that follow its completion show an intensification of that spiritual anguish always latent in Tolstoy's complex, paradoxical character. The very success—both artistic and material—of *War and Peace* may well have helped to cause the depression that followed its appearance, by bringing out all his more ascetic instincts. In *War and Peace* he had celebrated the idea of family happiness, apparently exalting the life of the body as opposed to the life of the spirit, in a way that had satisfied many of his readers, but which plainly did not satisfy himself. His whole treatment of Andrey's career and death shows how far the novel was from being the simple celebration of the physical life, the life of the body, which many readers still take it to be. The problems which had haunted Andrey and Pierre, the problems of the meaning of life, of death, and of the nature of moral responsibility, continued to haunt Tolstoy during and after the completion of the novel. It was never conceived by him, of course, as a final, all-embracing answer to such problems—the very nature of its greatness, like that of *Anna Karenina*, lies in an expansiveness which resists the temptation to come to falsely reductive conclusions. It remains true, however, that the prevailing emphasis of the novel, its underlying philosophy, has more to do with the Rostovs than with Andrey, setting the instinctive over against the rational, the intuitive knowledge of the body against the abstract knowledge of the mind, and finding happiness and the 'purpose of life' in the simple pursuits of family life.

Tolstoy could not rest satisfied with such conclusions as these during the years following *War and Peace*. Indeed, as early as January, 1867, two years before the novel was completed, he had written to his friend Samarin a letter which emphasises his sense of spiritual loneliness and dissatisfaction:

'up to now—I shall soon be forty—I have loved truth more than anything; I do not despair of finding it, and I am still searching and searching. At times, and precisely this year more than ever before, I have failed to raise a corner of the curtain to take a peep there—but I am alone, and it is hard and terrible, and it seems that I have lost my way.'[1]

The depression which was consequent on this state of uncertainty, and which is reflected in both Andrey and Pierre, was to intensify over the next few years until we see in the state of mind of Levin at the end of *Anna Karenina* a much greater, even suicidal despair, which is again a reflection of Tolstoy's own position. 'Painfully out of harmony with himself', Levin has problems that are more dangerously urgent than are those of Andrey or Pierre: ' "Without knowing what I am about, and why I am here, it is not possible to live. But I cannot know that, and therefore cannot live," he said to himself.' (VIII.9)

In the same novel, Anna herself reflects, more distantly, another aspect of his position at this time—the loneliness of which he was becoming aware: despite his success he was, as a consequence of his beliefs, cutting himself off more and more from that social class to which he belonged by birth and instinct. Like Anna, he was facing the inevitable prospect of living outside society, in that loneliness which despite the adulation and the disciples, Gorky was to recognise in him over thirty years later. What he says of himself to Samarin might have been spoken by Anna herself: 'I'm alone, and it is hard and terrible, and it seems that I have lost my way.' As in *War and Peace*, so in *Anna Karenina*, his art was to be a close reflection of the flux of his own experience, the ongoing, tortuous and often inconsistent movement of his life and ideas.

Though the germs of *Anna Karenina* were apparently in Tolstoy's mind in 1870, when his wife recorded that he was thinking of a novel about an adulterous woman who was to be represented as 'not guilty but merely pitiful', he did not in fact begin work on it until 1873. The intervening years were filled by reading— Schopenhauer in particular provoking an enthusiasm he was later to disavow—by learning and reading Greek, by an abortive attempt at a novel on Peter the Great, and by the resumption of his practical and theoretical interest in education. His *ABC Book*, which he compiled and published at this time, involved him in, among other things, the translation of folk tales, and the composition of a number of original fables, including 'A Prisoner in the Caucasus' and 'God Sees the Truth but Waits'. This book was for Tolstoy a matter of great, and probably of therapeutic, importance; it was, he claimed, the most important single work of his life, and one to which he had given more care and attention than to anything else he had done. The simple, lucid fables it contains reflect his reading of Greek as well as an immense amount of folk literature, and anticipate the style of much of his later work: but the book itself met with predictable hostility from educational theorists, though a shorter version published in 1875—while he was in the middle of work on *Anna Karenina*—had much greater success.

The transition from the selfconscious simplicity of the fables in the *ABC Book* to the high art of *Anna Karenina*, with its much greater awareness of moral complexity and its concomitantly greater complexity of structure, is an enormous one. There is, though, an important link between the fables and *Anna Karenina* which helps us to understand the considerable differences which, despite their similarity in so many ways, exist between the latter and *War and Peace*. In such a fable as 'God Sees the Truth but Waits', events are so shaped by the writer as to take on a particular moral significance: Tolstoy is not explicity didactic, but, as in all parable, the reader himself is left to interpret the meaning of the narrative from the pattern the writer has given it. Carefully organised though it is in other respects, in *War and Peace* his technique is to avoid any such clear shaping of events into significant patterns: he may, and frequently does, interpret the significance of what has passed, but the narrative itself carries few such symbolic or parabolic meanings; things seem simply to happen with the same lack of order as they do in our everyday experience. In this, it is very different from *Anna Karenina*, which, though it has the character of parable only in the crudest outlines of Anna's career and not in its essentials, does have a very rich symbolic structure, a structure which depends on the same kind of careful manipulation of events by the author. The rich texture of literal, detailed reality of *Anna Karenina* tends to obscure this shaping process on Tolstoy's part, symbol and allegory becoming so firmly embedded in a matrix of literal experience that they may often work on the reader without his being conscious of them; but whether or not we give

97

them explicit recognition, they are there in abundance, adding a new dimension to Tolstoy's art.

An example of such symbolism at work is to be found in the episode (I.21), in which Vronsky calls at Oblonsky's house late in the evening. Anna, who is staying there, is on her way to her room to fetch a photograph of her son, and stands on the landing looking down at Vronsky at the foot of the stairs. As she does so 'a strange feeling of satisfaction mixed with fear' suddenly stirs in her heart. As far as the simple narrative goes, the episode is a comparatively trivial one, but Tolstoy gives it considerable weight, emphasising its effect on the household in general, and Anna in particular. He does so because beneath its literal significance is a symbolic statement of Anna's predicament: at the bottom of the stairs, figuratively as well as literally for Anna, is Vronsky, while upstairs is her son. Anna is at the centre, pulled between the two and still able at this point to go either way. Both Anna on her landing, and Vronsky, who refuses to come into the house, are suddenly and momentarily glimpsed as outsiders in relation to the 'especially happy and pleasant family conversation around the Oblonsky's tea-table', an exclusion which prefigures their later rejection by society, and which helps to explain the irrational fear which both experience for a moment. On the surface we have witnessed an episode, and a relatively small one, in the growing relationship between Anna and Vronsky; on a symbolic level, and without necessarily being conscious of the fact as we read, we have been taken to the very heart of Anna's dilemma.

There is nothing like this in *War and Peace*: on the rare occasions when Tolstoy uses a symbol there—as in the case of Andrey's oak tree—it tends to be slightly obtrusive, jarring with the wholly unsymbolic texture of the narrative. In *Anna Karenina*, on the other hand, such symbols recur frequently, and seem wholly in place, an essential part of the overall pattern of the novel in which we become accustomed to the presence of two levels of meaning, the symbolic or allegoric reinforcing the literal meaning, and rarely conflicting with it. Thus when Anna frowns—' "as if she were screwing up her eyes at her own life so as not to see it all," Dolly thought'—we take it as the real habit of a real woman, as we do, say, the little Princess Lise's habit of drawing up her upper lip, while at the same time, without the least detriment to that realism, we take full cognisance of the symbolic significance which Dolly summarises for us so simply.

Although John Bayley sees the tendency towards 'symbolic schematisation' as a danger,[2] Tolstoy is, I think, quite remarkably sure in his use of it. Only in the case of the storm which howls around Anna as Vronsky makes his declaration to her on the station platform (I.30) does one feel that the complementary balance of symbol and realism has been lost. At this admittedly most climactic of moments, that storm has too much of the air of a stage-property about it for us to accept it happily. Its symbolism for Anna, as the wind threatens to 'carry her off', is too obviously contrived for us to be able to see it at the same time as a real storm, existing independently of the predicament of Anna and Vronsky.

The balance, which is missing here, between the literal and the symbolic status of the narrative is an essential one for Tolstoy, as it must be for any novelist whose technique is fundamentally a realistic one. The reader must be able to accept both levels of meaning, as he can, for example, in the subtly penetrating allegory of the locked garden gate in *Mansfield Park*, where the symbolism, for all its central importance for the novel, is securely embedded in the coolly realistic narrative. Such a balance is, I believe, found in the most obvious and the most controversial of the symbolic episodes in *Anna Karenina*, that of the steeplechase. Joyce Cary and others have argued that the allegory here jars, despite Tolstoy's realistic description, having 'an effect not congruent with the situation of the moment, involving characters we have accepted as actual in an actual world'.[3] Barbara Hardy, on the other hand, in a fine essay on *Anna Karenina*, has maintained that the literal meaning of the episode is paramount, that it is 'part of the natural flow of events, and symbolic only in the way in which events are symbolic in life, in their typicality which is only part of their nature and function'.[4] Both these views seem to me to be partial ones, over-emphasising opposing sides of what is, as in the *Mansfield Park* episode, a delicate balance between the 'natural flow of events' and their wider symbolic significance for the novel. For, despite Professor Hardy's persuasive argument, we can hardly avoid recognising that symbolic significance, even if we did not have the evidence of the earlier drafts to confirm that it was very much in Tolstoy's mind (there Anna and the mare are both given the same name, and the allegory is more crudely present).

99

At the same time, her argument bears witness to the powerful self-sufficiency of the narrative on a purely literal level—it is a convincingly, indeed excitingly real steeplechase, involving the real death of a living and not an allegorical horse. But the horse is also a beautiful and sensitive female animal whom Vronsky rides with exhilaration and a sense of danger, only to destroy her by a fault as seemingly trivial as his careless answer to Anna's note. We cannot—nor is there any reason why we should want to—escape the fact that the death of the mare portends the death of Anna, and not only because it is somehow 'typical' of Vronsky. Cary, I think, sees the two levels of meaning as conflicting partly because he wants to make the allegory too precise; his account of its intended meaning—'a premonition of [Anna's] fate when she too is unable to serve his will'—reflects an unacceptable account of Vronsky's relationship to Anna; nor is that relationship a matter of 'the wilful impatient egotism of the man and the patient feminine devotion of his victim', although both are accurate enough if applied to Vronsky and the mare. Allegory does not demand clear one-to-one correspondences even in the hands of Spenser, and it certainly does so much less in the nineteenth-century novel. It is enough that we should recognise the fact that Vronsky loves the beautiful mare and yet rides it to its destruction, and that we should see in this a portent of his and Anna's careers. Taken thus, there is nothing damaging in our responding to the episode precisely as Cary says we do: 'We are checked at once so that we stop and look again and ask, "Is this Vronsky and the mare or an allegory of Vronsky and Anna, of Tolstoy's society male and his unhappy female?".' The answer is surely that it can be and is both, and that as we read and re-read *Anna Karenina* we are continually 'stopping and looking again', sorting different levels of meaning, seeing not just symbols, but hints or prophecies fulfilled, contrasts and parallels of theme and structure, without it ever destroying our sense of that compelling realism of which Tolstoy is a master.

The element of self-conscious artistry, the shaping of events that such symbolism involves, is evident too in these last mentioned aspects of the novel to a greater extent than in *War and Peace*. *War and Peace* has, of course, its structure of parallel and contrast—apart from the major ones, one thinks of such smaller touches as the juxtaposition of Andrey's evening at the Rostovs' and the Bergs' frigid evening party—but, rich though it is, it seems a relatively casual structuring when compared to that of *Anna Karenina*. The major contrast on which *Anna Karenina* is based, that between the fate of Anna and Vronsky on the one hand, and Levin and Kitty on the other, itself predicates a whole series of lesser parallels and contrasts between the two relationships: there is, for example, the very suggestive difference between Levin's angry jealousy of the plump, amiable and amorous Veslovsky, and Vronsky's bland tolerance of the attention he pays to Anna. There is the larger contrast between the country life led by Levin and Kitty, and that led by Vronsky and Anna, where the sense of the rootedness of the former's existence, its stability and naturalness, is set over against the expensive newness and the latent instability of life on Vronsky's model estate. Levin's house is also a home, while Vronsky's, as Dolly perceives, is more like an expensive hotel in which Anna herself is merely a guest.

There are numerous further points of comparison between the two couples as the two stories continue to complement each other, but by no means all the parallels and contrasts in the novel arise out of this interwoven pattern. There is also, for instance, the contrast between Kitty's forced charity at Soden, and her genuine and intuitively knowledgeable compassion for the dying Nikolay Levin; there is that between the clear but deadly form of religion in which Karenin takes refuge from his troubles, and the vague, uncertain, but fundamentally life-centred faith towards which Levin struggles as an answer to his. Then there are the more generalised, typically Tolstoyan contrasts between the town and the country, between Moscow and Petersburg, between the old, traditionally Russian ways represented by Levin, the older nobility and the peasants, and the new, progressive ways, represented by Koznyshev, Sviazhky, and by such Western innovations as the railways, which are associated not only with the fall and death of Anna, but with the corrupt new order in general—the order that keeps 'Prince Oblonsky, a descendant of Rurik . . . waiting two hours in a Jew's waiting room' in order to get a highly paid sinecure on a railway board. Most important of all, perhaps, particularly in view of its implications for Anna, there is the continuing contrast between mind and heart, reason and instinct, abstract and intuitive knowledge, that is carried over from *War and Peace*.

The clearest focus for these latter oppositions is found in the relationship of Levin to his half-brother Koznyshev, though—in another typical instance of parallelism of structure—they are seen almost as clearly in that between Kitty and Varenka. We first encounter the contrast when Levin listens to the conversation between Koznyshev and the professor of philosophy, and discovers that their arguments always avoid what seem to him the obvious and crucial problems, the problems that really bear on life:

> 'he noticed that they connected the scientific problems with the spiritual, and several times almost reached the latter, but just as they came near the main problem, as it seemed to him, they straight away made a hurried retreat, and again plunged deeper into the sphere of fine sub-divisions, reservations, quotations, hints, and references to authorities, and he found it difficult to understand what they were talking about.' (I.7)

Alienated by this evasive rationalism, Levin decides not, after all, to ask Koznyshev's advice about his intention to propose to Kitty, feeling rather unfairly that 'his brother would not look at it as he would want him to', that he would not understand anything as irrational as love.

Koznyshev, as Levin comes to realise, is a man wedded to reason just because that which is instinctive in him is dead or dormant. His concern for the peasants as a class, which Tolstoy contrasts to Levin's natural understanding and sympathy, is a purely rational thing, springing from the mind and not from the heart, as Tolstoy felt was the case with so many of his liberal contemporaries:

> 'Constantine Levin looked on his brother as a man of great intellect and education, noble in the highest sense of that word, and endowed with the ability to work for the common good. But in the depth of his soul, the older he grew and the better he knew his brother, the more and more often it came into his mind that this ability to work for the common good—of which he felt himself entirely destitute—might not be a virtue, but on the contrary a lack of something—not a lack of good honest noble desires and tastes, but a lack of the power of living, of what is called heart, of the aspiration that makes a man choose one out of all the innumerable paths of life that present themselves, and desire that alone. The more he knew his brother, the more he noticed that even he, and many other workers for the common good, were not

led to this love for the common good by their hearts, but because they had decided in their minds that to occupy themselves with it was a good thing, and for that reason alone they did it. Levin was strengthened in this conviction by noticing that his brother did not take the question of the common good, or of the immortality of the soul, any more to heart than a game of chess, or the ingenious construction of some new machine.' (III.1)

Only a few pages earlier, we have seen Kitty being forced to arrive at a similar conclusion with regard to Varenka, whose dutiful nursing of the various invalids at the spa had so impressed her. The return of Kitty's father—'simple, sensible, right-feeling' as Arnold calls him—helps bring to a head her realisation that there is something false in her imitation of Varenka's behaviour. Kitty herself is not yet prepared to criticise the latter, but her concise summary leaves us in no doubt that Varenka, like Koznyshev, is lacking in 'the power of living': ' "I can't live except by my heart, but you live by principles. I have loved you quite simply, but you, probably, only in order to save me, to teach me." ' (II.35) When Koznyshev and Varenka come together later in the novel, they are attracted to each other, both recognising how well suited they are, but both feel a certain relief when the irrational, inexplicable, and dangerous—love—fails to materialise. Levin had already predicted as much:

' "You think he can't fall in love, then?' said Kitty, putting his thoughts into her own words.
"Not exactly that he can't fall in love," Levin answered with a smile, "but he has none of that weakness which is necessary . . ." ' (VI.3)

Clearly for Tolstoy it is not weakness in Levin that has led to his love for Kitty, nor is it a corresponding strength in Koznyshev that enables him to avoid such an entanglement: it is rather a lack of that 'power of living, of what is called heart', which both Levin and Kitty possess in such large measure, a lack which leads Koznyshev and Varenka to discuss the varieties of mushrooms instead of marriage.

One could point to many more instances of this kind to support the contention that Tolstoy was nowhere more concerned with form, with the conscious shaping of events into meaningful patterns, than in *Anna Karenina*. For all its expansiveness it is a finely wrought thing, and one which should quash any Jamesian doubts about Tolstoy's mastery of form. He himself justly took 'pride in its architecture—the vaults are so put together that it's not even possible to see where the keystone is', he wrote, 'and this is what I most tried to bring about. The structural bonds do not rest on the plot, and not on the relationships (the acquaintance) of the characters, but on the internal bonding [*svyaz'*].'[5]

In a letter to his close friend, the critic Strakhov, he again refers to this view of the novel's structure, talking about its 'linking' (*stsepleniye*), and associating it with his triumphant success in dealing with his relatively clear-cut ideas on marriage, and the rewards and obligations of family life, without falsifying the moral complexity which such apparently simple concepts may take on in actual experience:

> 'In everything, almost in everything that I wrote, I was guided by the need to collect ideas, linked to each other, for expressing myself, but each idea expressed in words on its own loses its meaning, is terribly reduced, when it is taken alone out of that linkage in which it is found. The linking itself is built not (I think) by ideas, but by something else, and to express the basis of this linkage directly in words is not possible in any way. It can only be done indirectly—by words describing images, actions and situations.'[6]

The danger that 'ideas' might take over and 'reduce' the novel —that is, present experience in a falsely simplified form—was a particularly acute one. The major themes of adultery and its consequences, of the broken marriage contrasted to the happy one, must inevitably have tended to pull the novelist in the direction of simple black/white distinctions. Symbols, parallels, contrasts—all that we think of as part of the artist's shaping of his novel—could very easily have reinforced such a tendency, in the way that they do in the short fables and parables. As the letter to Strakhov claims, however, they in fact do the opposite, placing what might, if baldly stated, seem crude moral judgements, in that context of complicated moral experience which enables us to recognise both their justice and their reality. R. P. Blackmur goes so far as to say that Tolstoy was not concerned with moral judgement in the novel, that 'he wanted only the mimesis of morality as a central experience'.[7] One sees what he meant, but it is a little too precious: for Tolstoy's concern is always a moral one, one of a kind that inevitably entails judgement. But Blackmur's statement does draw attention to the subtlety and sympathy of that judgement, to the fact that the novel recognises no black or white, but only the infinite gradations that come between them. Like the painting on which the artist Mikhaylov works with such commitment, the world of *Anna Karenina* comes alive before our eyes 'with all the inexpressible complexity of everything that lives'.

The introduction of Mikhaylov, the type of the artist, into the novel is a highly significant one, bearing witness as it does to the intensity of Tolstoy's interest in the creative process while he was working on *Anna Karenina*. Mikhaylov serves to remind us of the artifice involved in presenting that 'inexpressible complexity', of the fact that the novel is anything but a 'piece of life' in the simple sense in which Arnold used that phrase. But he reminds us, too, that Tolstoy's kind of art, what Dr Leavis calls rightly 'the highest kind of creativity',[8] is one in which artifice—'technique' as Vronsky calls it—cannot be spoken of in isolation from content. Mikhaylov, in fact, doesn't understand what is meant by 'technique':

> 'He knew that by this word was understood a mechanical capacity to paint and draw, entirely independent of the subject. He had often noticed . . . that technique was set against inner quality, as if it was possible to paint well something that was bad. He knew that much attention and care were needed when removing the wrappings not to damage the work itself, and that all wrappings must be removed; but the art of painting, the technique did not exist . . . And the most experienced and artistic technical painter could not paint anything with mechanical ability alone, if the outlines of the subject did not first reveal itself to him.' (V.11)

This is more accurate as a description of the way the writer works than of the way the painter does (Mikhaylov sounds, in general, like a very bad painter); it is, in fact, the way Tolstoy worked, allowing the novel to develop as its own internal logic demanded, 'removing the wrappings', but refusing to impose preconceived or simplified solutions. Any shaping of events, any formal structuring, must have at the very least the negative quality of not violating that internal logic: we have to feel that the characters are free moral agents, and not the puppets at the end of Tolstoy's strings. He himself expressed as much when, in the letter to Strakhov already mentioned, he went on to describe how, long after the chapter about Vronsky accepting a different role after seeing Karenin's forgiveness of Anna during her illness had been written, he began 'to correct it, and wholly unexpectedly for me, but indubitably Vronsky went away and shot himself. Now in the sequel it appears that this had an organic necessity.' Elsewhere he makes a similar assertion about the inevitability of Anna's suicide. Such was for him the process of 'removing the wrappings' of his novel.

What this means is that our sense of the careful structuring of the novel, though we may delight in it for its own sake, is in the end secondary to our sense of its vast mimetic scope and complexity, the supreme honesty with which it records not what should have been, not what was wished, but what we come to feel *would* have been. Thus it is that we see Karenin emerge, with all the unpredictability of reality, from his shell of bitter pride and repressed feeling, to be genuinely ennobled for a time by his charity towards Anna and his love for her child: but that charity does not last or develop, as in any lesser novelist it might have done. It turns instead into a selfish, self-deceiving and even vindictive form of refuge. No more than any other major character in the novel does Karenin fit a preconceived pattern. He is a living, and therefore complicated human being who cannot be pigeon-holed.

The same openness and honesty that we see here in Tolstoy's treatment of character is also evident in his treatment of the major themes of marriage and the family. Here, too, he is willing to allow the complex moral reality of the situation priority over preconceived ideas. D. H. Lawrence, of course, accused Tolstoy of doing precisely the opposite, of driving Anna towards suicide, and Vronsky towards an abject and pitiable state, because he willed it so, because he hated and envied the spontaneous life and passion of these characters he had created: 'Tolstoy has a perverse pleasure in making the later Vronsky abject and pitiable: because Tolstoy so meanly envied the healthy passionate male in the young Vronsky.' So, Lawrence argues, Tolstoy 'puts his thumb in the scale' of the novel, and gives it a false conclusion.[9]

Certainly it was central to Tolstoy's plans that Anna and

Vronsky would both suffer as a result of their actions—whatever uncertainties and variations the early drafts show, they show none about that, and to this extent we might agree that he willed their fate on them. But such a skeletal account cannot be taken as evidence of any kind of distortion: to find that we would have to look not at an abstract of the novel, but at its inner logic—and there, it seems to me, it is very difficult to find. What Lawrence did, understandably enough in view of the parallel Anna and Vronsky presented to his and Frieda's situation, was precisely what Tolstoy refuses to do, to abstract and distort, to ignore all the subtle moral complexity of the situation as Tolstoy presents it, and deduce a cruder, antipathetic morality from the bare outline of events, and from what he knew of Tolstoy's later attitude towards sex. It is as if Lawrence the reader was putting his thumb in the scale: only thus could he have seen *Anna Karenina* as a merely social tragedy, in which Anna is killed by her cowardice in the face of society's disapproval, and not by her own cumulative sense of guilt, her awareness that the relationship founded on passion and the abandonment of her son had carried in itself from the very outset, and regardless of society's attitude, the seeds of its own destruction.

We can probably, if we wish, deduce from the novel, as well as from outside it, what Tolstoy's general moral position is: we can surmise that his answer, if pressed, would probably have been that Anna should have stayed with Karenin, however much repression of her own vital instincts this might have involved. She should have stayed not to placate society and save Karenin from scandal, nor to fulfil a legal promise, but because the concept of the family is something more important than the powerful, passionate love she feels for Vronsky. It is for this reason that the marriage vows, emphasised in the account of Kitty and Levin's marriage service, are so important; through Anna's own relationship with Serezha, through Dolly's experience with Stiva and her children, and later through Levin's and Kitty's, we can see that for Tolstoy this is so.

But it is important to recognise that Tolstoy isn't asking or answering this question, not at least in the simplified form in which he might have posed and answered it later. *Anna Karenina* is simply not that kind of novel: it is one in which, as Lawrence's anger at the outcome testifies, there is much to be said for Anna's departure (we may recall that Tolstoy was in the end willing to leave his own family, if for different reasons), one in which the 'happy' marriage of Kitty and Levin is by no means a neat counterpoise to the 'unhappy' relationships of Anna and Karenin or Anna and Vronsky. Although in its conception it may well have been something like this, an extension of the conclusions about family happiness found in the Epilogue to *War and Peace*, in execution it takes on an openness towards moral experience, a recognition of its complexity, that makes it anything but this. Tolstoy is notably willing to let doubts enter on both sides of the question, so that Anna can be 'unpardonably happy' and Levin acutely, even suicidally depressed, while that fear of sexual passion, which we know was to possess him more and more, till it issued in the bitter distortions of *The Kreutzer Sonata*, and which we might expect to distort this novel, is scarcely ever felt to be interfering with its proper balance. The later Tolstoy was too often prone to reject the unmanageable truth of things in favour of a simplified version which could be made to conform to equally simple moral absolutes. The great novels do the opposite: they testify to the immense complexity and particularity of moral experience, accepting as truth nothing that has not been proved on the pulse of actual life, a life in which the simpler moral absolutes are so unreliable that Stiva Oblonsky, who stands to be condemned on several counts—his adultery, his neglect of Dolly and his children, his profligacy at their expense—survives all such potential judgements more or less unscathed, by virtue of that amoral *samodovolnost'*, that complacent blend of innocence and physical well-being, which he exudes. If Tolstoy does invite us to condemn Oblonsky, it is not so much on such grounds as these, as because of his willingness to serve the forces that are destroying the old Russia: more real corruption seems evident in his calculated, and not at all innocent decision to seek a commercial post, to become the first of his family not to work, if he worked at all, in the service of the state, than in his sexual adventures or his neglect of his family.

Anna's moral dilemma, many times more acute than anything her brother is capable of experiencing, is likewise not a clear-cut matter for the reader. We cannot, because Tolstoy doesn't allow us to, take a simple stand either on the side the older Tolstoy would probably have taken, or on the opposite side Lawrence was to take. It is understanding and sympathy, the love that he once said a novelist must have for all his characters, and not an insidious condemnation, that is paramount in Tolstoy's treatment of Anna. As we follow the gradual stages of her 'fall', we are not at first aware of it as a fall, so much as a growing intensification in Anna of the process of living. Her love for Vronsky is a quickening of the life within her, the life that has been repressed by her loveless marriage to Karenin, and which when we first see her is made evident in that 'subdued anima-tion', the 'excess of something' which 'over-filled her whole being, so that it expressed itself against her will, now in her smile, now in the light in her eyes'. (I.18) This is that 'too much of something' which Natasha and Kitty have as well, and which Sonya or Varenka lack. It is an excess of vitality that should find release in marriage and motherhood, and after some mis-adventure it does so for Natasha and Kitty. But for Anna it has not and clearly never can: when it takes the form of a passionate love for Vronsky we cannot but feel that it is a force that is in it-self good, a fulfilment for Anna that we have not the right to deny her. But, as Tolstoy's art so wonderfully conveys, that very fulfilment also involves an opposing intensification of Anna's moral life: that too, we must remember, has been complacently dormant during the years of her marriage to Karenin, and it, too, is awakened and brought into full play by her feelings for Vronsky. The more we learn about it, the more we realise that her life with Karenin has depended on the suppression of the moral voice that would have told her of its falsity, of the fact that she could not love him. The moral awakening, the bringing to life of her conscience, is both consequent on, and yet in conflict with, the awakening of her love for Vronsky; but, whatever tragic consequences it may have, we cannot help but see the quickening of Anna's moral life as another gain, and this sense of Anna's being brought new life in two quite different ways is something that counts very strongly in our judgement of her actions.

This being so, we might expect that our judgement of Karenin, the man who has so stifled the life in Anna, and who is as Dr Leavis says 'a purely "social" being, ego-bound, self-important, without any spontaneity of life in him and unable to be anything but offended and made uncomfortable by spon-taneity of life in others',[10] to be a simple matter. But, of course, it is not: even before we see his readiness, when he believes Anna to be dying, to forgive both her and Vronsky, and before we see his altogether sincere love for Anna's baby, Tolstoy presents his bewilderment and suffering in a way that arouses at least a degree of sympathy for him without making him answer any the less to Leavis's description, or to Anna's own bitter account: 'They do not know how for eight years he has been smothering my life, smothering everything that was alive in me, that not once did he think that I was a live woman who needed love. They do not know how at every step he hurt me and remained self-satisfied.' (III.16) Karenin is not set up by Tolstoy with the obvious animus Lawrence shows for Clifford Chatterley, or for Rico Carrington in *St Mawr;* he lets us see enough genuine suffering on his part as he reacts in bewilderment at 'being confronted with life' for the first time for it to mitigate our judgement of him.

Despite this, though, despite even his temporarily transfiguring love for Anna's baby, that judgement must still remain a damning one. In his case, as Leavis says, '*tout comprendre* is not *tout pardonner*', and if it was only Karenin who was to be considered, then Anna's departure, marriage vows or not, would not present the reader with a truly serious moral dilemma. In such a context, Lawrence's 'Nobody in the world is anything but delighted when Vronsky gets Anna Karenina'[11] could be allowed to stand. But Karenin is not the only person affected by Anna's departure: she also leaves her son behind, and more than any other factor it is her abandonment of Serezha, who has been the focus till now of her power to love, that counts in her own—and the reader's—sense of her guilt. In leaving him she is betraying that which is in Tolstoy's eyes both function of and fulfilment for any woman: the role of mother. If we recall the emphasis laid on motherhood in the Russian cultural tradition, and the particularly emphatic development by Tolstoy of the ideal of motherhood in *Childhood, Boyhood and Youth, Family Happiness* and *War and Peace,* we can understand why the part played by Serezha is so crucial in the delicate moral scheme of *Anna Karenina.* But even without knowledge of this background, the novel itself, in its presentation of Anna's struggle, is clear and convincing enough for it to be difficult to see anything but a willed blindness in Lawrence's apparent refusal to take this aspect of it into consideration. Though Serezha himself is not a particularly prominent character, we are again and again being reminded of his existence. His presence in the novel mostly takes the negative form of a significant *absence* from Anna's life after her departure, whether in the dilettante emptiness of Italy or on Vronsky's estate: we are reminded of him directly by Anna's and Oblonsky's important meetings with him, and indirectly (and poignantly) by such things as the expensively furnished nursery in which Dolly sees Anna's baby by Vronsky, the baby which she is unable to love because, we feel, Serezha still dominates her conscience in a way that engrosses all her maternal love.

The moral dilemma with which Serezha presents Anna (though not, we should notice, Vronsky) is necessarily at its most acute earlier in the novel when she is facing the inevitable choice between him and Vronsky, a choice so impossible for her that she simply avoids thinking about it:

> ' "Yes" she continued, "to make myself your mistress and ruin everything . . ."'
> She again wanted to say "son," but could not utter the word.
> Vronsky could not understand how she, with her strong, honest nature, could endure this state of deception and not wish to leave it; but he did not guess that the main cause lay in that word "son" which she could not utter. When she thought about her son and his future relations with the mother who had left his father, she became so terrified at what she had done, that she did not reason, but, like a woman, tried to comfort herself by specious reasoning and words in order that everything should be left as before, and so that it was possible to forget the dreadful question of what would happen to her son.' (II.23)

That 'like a woman' is a little disturbing, but whether or not we agree with Tolstoy's belief in the essential nature and role of woman, there is surely no doubt that for this particular woman he is right in laying the stress that he does on her relationship with her son, and the impossibility of the choice between him and Vronsky. Here, indeed, we are at the very centre of Anna's tragedy. Her fate is tragic because the two forces at work in her innermost being—her need for the masculine love which Karenin has never been able to give her, and her maternal love for Serezha—are set in irreconcilable conflict. Whichever way Anna might go, it must involve the suppression of one of these instinctive and powerful forces. In fact, we scarcely see her as confronted with a clear moment of choice, as we rarely do with any of Tolstoy's characters. Instead, Anna's growing attachment to Vronsky is presented as a thing gradual and inevitable, the apparent inevitability making her situation all the more tragic. Anna is trapped by her fate as surely as Macbeth or Hamlet is, and though Serezha is, in a telling analogy, the compass by which Anna knows she is diverging from the proper course, even that analogy is used by Tolstoy to suggest her absolute helplessness to alter course; Serezha's presence, he says:

> 'evoked in Vronsky and in Anna a feeling similar to the feeling of a sailor, who sees by his compass that the course along which he is rapidly moving diverges widely from the right one, but knows that it is not in his power to stop the movement, that every moment takes him further and further from the right course, but that to acknowledge the divergence to himself is tantamount to acknowledging that he is lost.' (II.22)

'The right course' makes Tolstoy's general judgement clear enough; but set powerfully over against it is the old image of the ship that is driven helplessly by the wind, set on a wrong course and quite unable to stop.

That the passionate love which drives her and Vronsky on this course is not in the end enough to compensate for what has been lost, that it is impossible for them to live, as Lawrence wished them to, 'in the pride of their sincere passion', is obvious from the start—though again one must insist that this does not involve a crude imposition of the didactic will on Tolstoy's part. What we have in Anna's relationship with Vronsky is a compelling and wholly convincing account of the insufficiency of such love as the only basis of a lasting relationship. In normal circumstances, as we see in the case of Levin and Kitty, love between husband and wife gains new dimensions, and new strengths, in the context of the family as a whole. Levin's early romantic love for Kitty moderates into his love for the mother of his children: indeed, Levin, like Tolstoy, loves the idea of his future family before he loves Kitty. Elsewhere, too, Tolstoy often insists on the difference between romantic love and the less ecstatic but more solid love relationship which sustains marriage —one thinks, for example of both Andrey's and Pierre's relationship with Natasha in *War and Peace*, or that of Masha and Sergey Mikhaylich in *Family Happiness*. But not only can Anna not move from her initial love for Vronsky to this kind of family centred relationship; she actually has the destruction of such a relationship, albeit a decidedly limited one, weighing heavily on her conscience.

In such a situation it is inevitable that she should remain insecure, her liaison with Vronsky depending on the artificial prolongation of the initial passionate, romantic attraction. Unlike Natasha, who gives up trying to appear attractive once she is married to Pierre, Anna must go on dressing up and making up to show herself to the best advantage. Indeed, it becomes so much second nature to her that for no good reason she involuntarily tries to make Levin fall in love with her on the one occasion that they actually meet. Always trying to tie Vronsky to her in this way, she makes the kinds of demands on his attention that are only sustainable in the first, ecstatic period of love; demands that Vronsky, less exclusively dependent on her love than she on his, cannot but resent, until he has reached a state in which he thinks of their relationship as 'this dismal, burdensome love to which he must return'. Anna herself diagnoses their situation in that terrible piercing light which reveals so much to her as she drives to the station on her way to her suicide—the only way out of her predicament:

' "My love becomes ever more passionate and more self-regarding, but his dwindles and dwindles, and that is why we are separating," she thought. "And there is no help for it. For me everything is in him alone, and I need him to give himself up to me more and more. And he wants more and more to move away from me. Before our union we really drew towards each other, but now we are irresistibly moving apart. And it cannot be changed. He tells me I am unreasonably jealous, and I tell myself that I am unreasonably jealous; but it isn't true. I am not jealous, but dissatisfied. But . . ." She opened her mouth, and shifted her position in the carriage, agitated by a sudden thought which came to her. "If I could be anything but his mistress, passionately loving nothing but his caresses; but I can't and don't want to be anything else. And through this desire I awake disgust in him, and he anger in me, and it cannot be otherwise." ' (VII.30)

So she is driven by the insidious logic of her situation to play her highest card in the struggle to retain Vronsky's love—her own death, 'the only means of restoring love for her to his heart, of punishing him, and of gaining victory in that battle which an evil force that had moved into her heart was waging against him'. (VII.26)

We do not feel inclined to blame Vronsky for Anna's suicide: given her nature and her values it is something we can see with hindsight to have been close to inevitable. Indeed, we can admire a good deal in Vronsky's behaviour: his honesty and sincerity, which impress Levin when they meet at Kitty's; his commendable unwillingness to be satisfied with a society liaison with Anna; his understanding tolerance of her fits of unwarranted jealousy and hostility; his unquestioned loyalty to her, and his refusal to hold against her his loss of a possibly distinguished army or public career. To call him a 'stallion in uniform' as did a friend of Dostoyevsky, or 'less a man than a sensual force inhabiting a man' as did R. P. Blackmur is clearly to underrate him.[12] Even Kitty's father, on whom we might usually rely, is wrong when he sees him as just another 'Petersburg fop' in comparison to Levin.

It is true, though, that there is a fatal lack in Vronsky of those particular qualities which might have saved Anna. For all his honesty and loyalty he is unable to provide her with any substitute for that stable family life which she has forgone. We see him trying to do this on his estate, but to Dolly, to the reader, and evidently to Anna herself the attempt is false to his nature, giving us merely an empty, expensive parody of the real thing. Vronsky himself, it is important to note, 'had never known family life': he is, as Levin bluntly puts it, ' "A man whose father crawled up from nothing by intrigues, and whose mother was involved with God knows who" '. What we see of his family, through his mother and brother, confirms the accuracy of Levin's bitter account: deprived of a solid family background, his aristocratic status of a new and dubious kind, he has grown up in a world which makes him regard 'the family, and especially the husband, as something alien, hostile, and above all ridiculous', and which does nothing to make him remotely aware of what is lacking in him. On the contrary, as Tolstoy shows, the society in which he moves is one whose values are entirely antipathetic to those which Levin represents. In the eyes of that society Vronsky knows that 'the role of the unhappy lover of a girl, or of any single woman, might be ridiculous; but the role of a man pursuing a married woman, and making it the aim of his life to seduce her into adultery at any cost, this role had in it something beautiful and dignified and could never be ridiculous'. (II.4) The jealous husband is the legitimate butt of contemptuous amusement—as in the affair of the offended Titular Counsellor whose wife has been pursued by Vronsky's fellow officers—and the family a mere formal institution.

Vronsky is better than his code, and grows to recognise its inadequacies, especially in the face of Karenin's forgiveness of Anna. But the signal point is that living by his code as he does, he can find nothing to stop him from trying to seduce Anna in the first place, or to enable him to give her at least the passable semblance of a secure family life after he has done so. In the end, if blame must be apportioned, much of it must go not to Vronsky himself, but to the society that has made him, essentially a good man, what he is, a man in whom, despite all his single-minded passion, we sense a lack of that 'power of heart' that is so strong in Levin—and in Anna.

The opposition of Levin to Vronsky is an obvious part of Tolstoy's scheme. Though in his isolation from the normal run Levin is also set in contrast with many others—notably Karenin, Oblonsky, and his brother Koznyshev—it is the contrast between him and Vronsky that the logic of the novel, both in structure and feeling, places uppermost. That contrast is not a simple matter of polar opposition—Anna, we recall, sees in Levin 'that common trait which had caused Kitty to fall in love with them both'—but Levin does stand for much that Vronsky can neither achieve nor understand. His concern for family life, his deeply engrained loyalty to his parental home and land, his instinctive empathy with the peasants, are all foreign to Vronsky.

Tolstoy presents these values as especially Russian ones in retreat before encroaching Western European liberalism and scientific materialism, the 'progress' of the railways, the elections and the law courts, and no doubt he is right to some extent. But they are not exclusively Russian: they can equally well be seen in their essentials as representative of the best kind of conservative, patrician outlook in any country, at any time. Two passages in particular bring out this patrician aspect of

E

Levin's character; one is the moving and sensitive evocation of all that his home means to him when he returns from Moscow after being rejected by Kitty, and finds that he regains much of his former composure in the familiar surroundings:

> 'when he got out at his station and recognised his one-eyed coachman Ignat with the collar of his *kaftan* turned up, when he saw his carpeted sledge in the dim light falling from the station windows, his horses with their plaited tails in their harness with its rings and tassels, when Ignat, while the luggage was still being put into the sledge, began telling him the village news, about the arrival of the contractor, and about Pava having calved, he felt that bit by bit the confusion was clearing itself and his shame and dissatisfaction with himself were passing. He felt this at the mere sight of Ignat and the horses; but when he put on the sheepskin coat that had been brought for him, and, snugly wrapped up, had seated himself in the sledge and driven off, thinking about the orders he would give in the village, and when he glanced at the side horse, once a saddle horse, but overridden, a spirited horse from the Don, he began to understand what had happened to him quite differently. He felt that he was himself and did not want to be anyone else.' (I.26)

Only Tolstoy, we might note in passing, would or could choose to make a one-eyed coachman in a dim light truly welcoming and comforting. But the significance of this passage, and the following chapters, is that they bring home to us the full charm and strength of one of the prime motivating forces in Levin's life, a force only slightly less strong than his love for Kitty—indeed it is inseparable from that love, since he can see no context for it except here, in 'the world in which his father and mother had lived and died'. Only here is he truly himself; in other contexts, in Moscow or Petersburg, or at the elections, he is uneasy, uncertain of himself and of his values. Here, the Tolstoyan *samodovolnost'* returns to tell him instinctively what is right and what is wrong.

The other passage, which brings out the patrician Levin more explicitly, has already been quoted in the first chapter, but is important enough to bear repetition at slightly greater length. Levin bitterly attacks Oblonsky's description of Vronsky as a 'perfect aristocrat', asking

  ' "what is Vronsky's or anyone else's aristocracy that I should be slighted because of it? You consider Vronsky an aristocrat. I don't. A man whose father crawled up from nothing by intrigues, and whose mother was involved with God knows who . . . No, excuse me, but I consider myself and people like me aristocrats: people who can point back to three or four honourable genera- tions of their families, all having a high standard of education (talent and brains—that's a different matter), and who have never cringed before anyone, but lived as my father and grand- father lived. And I know many like that . . . We are the aristo- crats, and not those who can only exist by the handouts of the powerful ones of this world, and who can be bought for a piece of silver." ' (II.17)

Such justifiable pride in his background is one of the main pillars of Levin's identity, as it was of Tolstoy's, and this speech alone is enough to remind us of how much of himself he put into Levin, just as it is also suggestive of how right Gorky and others were to see much of the radicalism, the resentment of authority, and the so-called Christian anarchism, of the old Tolstoy as an expression of this patrician pride and independence, rather than of any more truly democratic inclination.[13] John Bayley rightly makes the point that one of Levin's most important functions in *Anna Karenina* is to free us from the confines of the conventional novel, into which the story of Anna and Vronsky would have fitted comfortably enough, by taking us once more into the realms of Tolstoyan spiritual autobiography.[14] It is largely through him that *Anna Karenina* opens out to become another part of that 'enormous diary' which Merezhkovsky saw the whole of Tolstoy's work as forming. Of all the Tolstoyan seekers after truth, Levin is the most dogged and the closest to his creator. For many readers, indeed, both the doggedness and the closeness are too great: Turgenev was only one of many who have found Levin too egoistical a figure, serious and self- absorbed to the point of being merely boring, while for Mirsky, he was in his close identification with Tolstoy a figure out of place in an otherwise more distanced, objective novel, an un- fortunate throwback to such earlier *alter egos* as Olenin.[15] In fact Levin both loses and gains by his closeness to Tolstoy: he loses some of that distancing that makes of Pierre and Andrey more balanced, less single-minded, less completely egoistical beings, but he gains along with his Tolstoyan egoism a concomitant in- tensity of purpose, an urgent self-absorption that draws the reader into an interested complicity in his quest. It is this urgency and sincerity which save Levin from the charge of being a boringly self-centred crank, immersed in his own problems to the exclusion of all others: his may be a chaotic soul, as Dostoyevsky said it was, but it is certainly not (as he also said it was) a sauntering idle one.[16]

The problems which so absorb Levin are close to those which trouble Andrey and Pierre in *War and Peace*—problems posed above all by death, and the shadow of meaninglessness which it seems to cast over life. He differs from these two, however, in that without realising it he has from the outset an instinctive knowledge of the answers to his questions. In this he is, like Tolstoy himself, something of a compound of Pierre and Nikolay Rostov, a man who like Nikolay has an innate moral sense which tells him quite clearly what is right and what is wrong in any given situation, and who yet, like Pierre, torments himself with the search for an abstract, philosophical basis on which to erect such a morality. This is why so much of Levin's spiritual struggle seems like a heroic milling in the void, or, to use a Tolstoyan analogy, like a cogwheel that turns round and round without engaging with anything. His questions about the aim and meaning of his life are sincere—they are Tolstoy's own questions also—but the novel makes them seem irrelevant when it convinces us that he already knows by instinct rather than by reason that 'marriage is the chief thing in life, on which the whole happiness of life depends'. This is not the whole story, of course; but the important point is that the Levin whom we see bounding up the stairs to Oblonsky's office in the opening pages of the novel is a man who clearly *has* a purpose and meaning in life which he has not arrived at by reason or introspection, but by his quite spontaneous love for Kitty.

This means that Levin's rejection by Kitty necessarily involves a loss of his sense of meaning and purpose, a loss from which his return home and immersion in farming can only partly shield him. The problems which now confront him more acutely seem for a brief period to be answerable by developing his relationship with the peasants: the idyllic mowing episode, followed by that of the haymaking on his sister's estate, leads him to consider a complete renunciation of his old life, 'to change his wearisome, empty and artificial personal life for that pure, delightful life of common toil', just as Tolstoy wished to do himself. Tolstoy the novelist, however, sees the falseness of this aspiration more clearly than did Tolstoy the prophet. After Levin has spent the night lying on a haycock working out his new life along lines of which the Tolstoy of *A Confession* would approve, he catches a brief glimpse of Kitty as she passes in the coach. As he does so, 'He remembered with disgust his dreams of marriage to a peasant girl. There alone, in that coach rapidly going away from him on the other side of the road, there alone was the possibility of an answer to that riddle which had been weighing on him so tormentingly of late.' (III.12)

Nowhere could one find a clearer example of Tolstoy's honesty as a novelist: the teacher in him would certainly have liked to be able to reduce Levin's problems to a level at which they could be answered by a formula of the kind Levin has been meditating. He was at this point in the process of doing just that for himself. But neither Levin's problems nor his own can be answered by solutions based on abstract theories. It is once again intuitive knowledge, the spontaneous response, which is the right one, marriage to Kitty at once appearing as the only possible solution. The peasant way of life is, it is true, not an altogether abstract alternative for Levin: it exerts a very real, non-theoretical attraction, as the mowing episode in particular makes clear to us, and the suggestion of a tension between the 'delightful life of common toil' and the claims of the family remains there throughout the novel. In the novel, though, the rationalisation, the idea of becoming a peasant on theoretical grounds, is shown to be false in a way that it is not in Tolstoy's later prose. To work with the peasants, to enjoy their company and their wisdom, is a different matter from persuading oneself that one should join them.

Levin's genuine empathy with the peasants is, curiously enough, an aspect of his patrician outlook, as it was of Tolstoy's. The old landowning aristocracy and the peasants form a natural conservative alliance, based on work, land and custom, against the new, urban, middle-class intelligentsia which Tolstoy so despised. ' "Our work," ' says the old landowner to whom Levin talks at the new, spuriously democratic elections, ' "is not done here, at the elections, but at home. There is a class instinct as to what should and what should not be done. Then, take the peasants; I see it in them too: if you take a good peasant, he will always try to rent as much land as possible.

However bad the land, still he goes on ploughing it. Also without profit. Simply loss."

"Just like us' said Levin." ' (VI.29)

The problem of *how* he should live is, for Levin, intimately related to the problem of death, with its attendant question of *why* he should live. It is through his brother Nikolay that he first becomes truly aware of his own mortality, and the sudden dawning of that awareness, as Tolstoy describes it, is one of the most terrible and powerful passages in the novel. Levin lies awake listening to his brother's tubercular cough, and as he does so

'Death, the inevitable end of everything, presented itself to him for the first time with irresistible force. And that death which was here in his dear brother, waking up moaning and calling indiscriminately on God or the devil, was not quite so far away as it had seemed before. It was in himself too—he felt it. If not today, then tomorrow, if not tomorrow, then in thirty years, was it not all the same? But what this inevitable death was, he not only did not know, not only had never considered, but could not and dared not consider.

"I work, I want to do something, but I had forgotten that it all ends, that . . . death."

He sat on his bed in the dark, folded his arms round his knees and thought, holding in his breath from the mental effort. But the more he strained his mind, the clearer it became to him that it was undoubtedly so, that he had really forgotten and overlooked one little circumstance in life—that death will come, and everything will end, that it was not even worth beginning anything, and that there was no help for it. Yes, it was terrible but true.

"But I am still alive. Well then, what to do, what to do?" he said despairingly. He lit a candle, got up carefully and went to the mirror and began to look at his face and hair. Yes, there were grey hairs on his temples. He opened his mouth. His back teeth were beginning to decay. He bared his muscular arms. Yes, he was very strong. But Nikolenka who was breathing there with the remains of his lungs had also had a healthy body once. And suddenly he remembered how as children they used to go to bed together, and only waited till Theodore Bogdanich went out to throw pillows at each other and laugh, laugh irrepressibly, so that even the fear of Theodore Bogdanich could not stop that overflowing bubbling consciousness of the happiness of life.' (III.31)

The access of Levin's awareness of mortality is made irresistibly real for the reader partly by the lucid simplicity with which Tolstoy follows its development, and partly by the strong sense he gives us of the opposing vitality, the physical existence of Levin, whether sitting on the bed thinking, examining his own healthy body, or, most tellingly of all, remembering his childhood. Again and again throughout his life, death was to present itself with the same kind of urgency to Tolstoy, without any truly acceptable answer to the problem ever emerging. For Levin, however, there is at least a partial answer, and again it is connected with Kitty. After the harrowing description of the death of Nikolay, surely in its mixture of precision and compassion one of the most moving of all such scenes in literature (Blackmur rightly calls the death 'the most innocent and mature in all fiction'),[17] Levin is saved from despair by Kitty and by his love for her. He still doesn't have any rational answer to the problem of death, but he has instead an irrational faith in the possibility of life existing alongside it:

> 'The sight of his brother and the nearness of death renewed in Levin's soul that feeling of horror before the inscrutability, the nearness and the inevitability of death which had seized him on that autumn evening when his brother had visited him. That feeling was now even stronger than before; he felt even less able than before to understand the meaning of death, and its inevitability appeared even more terrible to him; but now thanks to his wife's nearness, that feeling did not bring him to despair: in spite of death he felt the necessity of living and loving. He felt that love had saved him and would save him from despair, and that that love under the threat of despair became even stronger and purer.' (V.20)

Under this influence, the influence of mutual love between himself and Kitty, Levin knows how to live and knows why he lives. His problem continues to be that he thinks he doesn't know: again and again we find that real life, life as he actually lives it, is in conflict with his abstract thoughts about it. When he leaves off thinking, he knows the answers to his problems. This is most apparent in the later pages of the novel, where Levin's search through the philosophers for some clue to the meaning of life reduces him to a nearly suicidal despair: 'When Levin thought about what he was and why he lived, he could find no answer and was driven to despair; but when he left off asking himself about it, it was as if he knew both what he was and why he lived, for he acted and lived unfalteringly and definitely—recently still more unfalteringly than before'. (VII.10)

The despair that leads him to hide the cord and avoid carrying a gun (as Tolstoy himself did at this time) does not emerge in the novel as a real threat to his marriage, as is often suggested, though it is an acknowledgement of its insufficiency as a sole source of meaning in his life. The important point is that in the novel we see, in a way that we do not see in Tolstoy's non-fictional writing that followed *Anna Karenina*, that it is a despair brought on by asking the wrong kinds of question and demanding a rational answer where none exists. Because of this, Levin's depression never really undermines his instinctive belief in the importance of family life. Like Pierre after his experiences as a prisoner, Levin finds that he has an unerring knowledge of right and wrong, for which he can give no rational account: 'Thinking about it led him into doubts and hindered him from seeing what was necessary and what was not. But when he did not think, but lived, he felt at all times in his soul the presence of an infallible judge deciding which of two possible actions was the better and which the worse: and as soon as he did what he should not have done, he immediately felt this'. (VIII.10)

Like Pierre, Levin has to learn to recognise the sufficiency of this innate moral knowledge, to cease to ask for a rational system to justify it. He has to learn the truth of W. B. Yeats's dictum that 'man can embody truth, but he cannot know it'.[18] This is in effect what he learns from the peasant whose commonplace words strike him as such a revelation:

' "Well, you see, people are different; one man lives only for his own needs—take Mityuka who only stuffs his belly, but Fokanich is an honest old man. He lives for his soul. He remembers God."
"How does he remember God? How does he live for his soul?" Levin almost cried out.
"You know how, rightly, in a godly way . . ." ' (VIII.11)

The words mean so much to Levin because they release in him a flood of thoughts which lead him to recognise that he does possess an innate moral sense, that his 'knowledge of what is good and what is bad' is not something acquired by thought or education: 'it was given to me as to all, *given* because I could not take it from anywhere.' This is the essence of Levin's new found, tentative 'faith'—it is not a mystical experience, but neither is it, as Tolstoy is at pains to emphasise, a conclusion that can be arrived at by reason alone. The knowledge of good and evil is something given, and if it is given, then it must be given by God. The process is logical enough to satisfy the rationalist in Levin, and, for the moment, in Tolstoy, and to answer for a time at least the questions about why and how he should go on living. Later Tolstoy was to seek a more clear cut, more rationalised, answer, and in doing so to simplify much of the complexity of his experience. But the greatness of *Anna Karenina*, as much in its treatment of Levin's spiritual quest as of Anna's adultery, lies in its refusal to do this. It offers us what is perhaps the best example in all literature of Lawrence's contention that 'The novel is the highest example of subtle inter-relatedness that man has discovered. Everything is true in its own time, place, circumstance, and untrue out of its own time, place, circumstance. If you try to nail anything down, in the novel, either it kills the novel, or the novel gets up and walks away with the nail.'[19] Lawrence felt that Tolstoy was trying to nail things down; but he was not, he was exploring with an openness to moral experience that is found in only the greatest art, and which ensures that morality in *Anna Karenina* remains what it should be, that delicate, forever changing balance between the author and his circumambient universe which Lawrence defined so well.

6

The religious crisis: *A Confession*

During the years in which he was working on the later books of *Anna Karenina*, Tolstoy entered on what was to prove the most profound, the most sustained and the most agonising spiritual crisis of his life. The questions which tormented him were not new: they were the problems of how and why he should live which had troubled him throughout his adult life, and which directly or indirectly had entered into everything he had written up to this point. It was in these years of the late 1870s, though, that the problems intensified for him in such a way that they demanded some more definite answer than he had been able to give before. The final mysteries of life and death had now to give way before the remorseless, rationalist urge to see things clearly and see them whole. To surrender to the stream of life, to say 'you cannot understand the meaning of life, so don't think about it but live', was no longer enough: the meaning of life, and above all of death, had to be accounted for once and for all. *A Confession*, begun in 1879, was the first and by far the most powerful of a sequence of books and pamphlets in which Tolstoy tried to forge for himself a clear and final answer to the questions 'how?' and 'why?'

In turning to *A Confession* one turns to some extent from the concerns of literary criticism to those of biography. But this book marks such a pivotal point in Tolstoy's career, that without coming to terms with it we cannot hope to reach a real understanding of his work either before or after it was written. Besides which, spiritual autobiography is so central to Tolstoy's greatness as a novelist that his spiritual biography is not something the critic can or should hope to eschew, and *A Confession*, for all its many faults, is the most succinct and revealing link we have between the actual, historical figure of Lev Nikolayevich Tolstoy and the man as he appears through his novels.

To read *A Confession* is to realise just how close Tolstoy's experience could be to that of his central characters. The religious crisis which we see Levin undergo in *Anna Karenina* corresponds very closely to that which Tolstoy describes in *A Confession*: the sense of an absence, and of a 'want of clearness' in the soul, the clash between reason and an instinctive faith, the periods of acute despair, even the removal of the potential instruments of suicide, are all common to Tolstoy and Levin. The faith towards which Levin is moving at the close of *Anna Karenina*, based on the faith of the peasants and not of the intellectuals, is also close to that to which Tolstoy was moving (though it is, I think, largely hindsight, a confusing of art with biography, which leads critics to see in Levin's faith a serious threat to the values of marriage and the family which the novel celebrates). It is not only Levin whom we can recognise re-emerging in *A Confession*: so far is the crisis of the 1870s from being the expression of new doubts or new answers, that we are frequently liable to feel that we are reading the thoughts of Andrey, Pierre, or even Olenin.

Still, it is Levin who is closest of all to the Tolstoy who speaks with such trenchant directness in *A Confession*. Indeed, at times it seems the kind of book that Levin might have written had he been able. And in this we have a clue to the source of much that is wrong with it. For Levin is, like Tolstoy's other *alter egos*, not Tolstoy, but a character in a novel, a character who is placed with all his limitations, as well as his strengths, within the context of a much wider, more complex reality than he himself is able to perceive. He is not a Zhivago figure, nor even a Prince Andrey: there are a host of things which his creator can understand which are closed to him. We don't, in the novel, object to Levin's obsessions, his self-absorption, his blindness to other ways of thinking and feeling, because we see that he is at heart a good man struggling to find his way with what honesty and sincerity he can in a world that has lost its old clarity and simplicity. We judge him within the overall context of the novel, and if Vronsky, Koznyshev or Oblonsky regards him as an eccentric, we are likely to agree, but to feel that nevertheless he has the advantage over them in most respects. But we don't therefore have to accept him as a sage, or to feel that if instead of his book on agriculture he were to turn to a description of his spiritual struggle it would carry a really authoritative weight. We expect from Tolstoy himself something much richer than Levin's version of his religious experience might be. In *A Confession*, it is at times as if Tolstoy had become that single aspect of his character that is Levin, and not the great novelist who can understand, besides Levin, the inner workings of Anna, Vronsky, Karenin or Oblonsky. Instead of the openness and expansive honesty of the great novelist, we have for the first time in Tolstoy a determined narrowing of vision, a desire to see only part of the truth so that it may be made more manageable: a prose medium of wonderful and incisive simplicity is seen too frequently, here, and even more in the later religious work, at the service of a vision that is willing to twist experience to fit an argument—to do, in fact, what Tolstoy the novelist has up to this point characteristically refused to do.

That *A Confession* remains nevertheless a work of considerable power and persuasiveness there is no question (though it seems to me to fall well short of the point where it may be compared favourably with Augustine's *Confessions*, as Professor Christian does, or be set alongside Job and Ecclesiastes, as Mirsky suggests).[1] It is true that it suffers more than most of Tolstoy's work in translation, since no English translation at least can capture the colloquial and yet dignified simplicity of the vocabulary he uses, a vocabulary owing much to the Russian Bible, but remaining very much a live, idiomatic medium. But Aylmer Maude's translation is tactful and intelligent as always, and, as Mirsky says, conveys at least the 'oratorical movement' of the original, the effects which depend on logic and figures of rhetoric rather than on the texture of the language itself. Mirsky is one of many who reserve very high praise indeed for *A Confession*, rightly emphasising its craftsmanship, and calling it 'in some ways his greatest artistic work'.[2] In a limited sense he is right: but he himself suggests how limited when he emphasises the way in which 'it is *constructed*, and constructed with supreme skill and precision' to serve a certain end. In fact, *A Confession* is effective as the greatest oratory is effective, but not as the greatest art is—not, at least, if we take as our pattern for such art either *Anna Karenina* or *King Lear*. For it involves, as 'constructed' suggests, the calculated imposition of Tolstoy's will on his experience in a way that is antipathetic to the explorative openness we find in Shakespeare or the Tolstoy of the two major novels. Indeed, it recounts the very process of that limiting imposition taking place—for that is surely what Tolstoy's conversion as he describes it amounts to in the end, a circumvention of crisis by the inventing of a rational faith, and of a God, which will suit his requirements, answer his needs.

A quarter of a century earlier he had noted in his diary the birth of an idea to which he felt capable of dedicating his whole life, 'the founding of a new religion . . . the religion of Christ, but cleansed of dogma and mystery, a practical religion, not promising future bliss but giving bliss on earth'.[3] The idea took a long time to develop, but its spirit is essentially that which we find in *A Confession* and the subsequent religious writings: in them Tolstoy is constructing his new and 'practical' religion, rejecting anything in existing Christian doctrine that does not answer to the demands of his reason. In *A Confession* he may reasonably be said to be creating his own God; having done so, he was to go on to rewrite the Gospels to make them coincide with his own interpretation of what they should have been, rejecting what he called 'useless passages', and regarding anything he was not already inclined to believe as a textual or doctrinal corruption of Christ's original teaching. The deep seated, almost Luciferian egoism which is present in so much of his work and his life was never so clearly displayed as in his search for humility and faith, and to read his religious works from *A Confession* onwards is to recognise the justice of Gorky's comment on his relationship with God:

> 'In his diary which he gave me to read, I was struck by a strange aphorism: "God is my desire."
>
> Today, on returning him the book, I asked him what it meant.
>
> "An unfinished thought," he said, glancing at the page and screwing up his eyes. "I must have wanted to say: 'God is my desire to know Him.' . . . No, not that . . ." He began to laugh, and, rolling up the book into a tube, he put it into the big pocket of his blouse. With God he has very suspicious relations; they sometimes remind me of the relation of "two bears in one den." '[4]

As it happens, Tolstoy's rejected explanation was not such an inaccurate summary of the attitude to God that we find in *A Confession*. Ultimately this search for a clear conception of God can be seen as an attempt at a final working out of that conflict between reason and intuition, which runs through so much of his writing. In *War and Peace* and *Anna Karenina* he had celebrated intuitive knowledge above abstract reason; there, his simpler heroes and heroines know instinctively what is right and what is wrong, without having to have a clear philosophical base for their knowledge. But when Tolstoy's thinking charac-

ters come to recognise such innate moral knowledge in themselves, their rationalisation of it is always slightly evasive;
Nikolay Rostov, Natasha and Kitty don't need to explain their
knowledge of good and evil to themselves or to us. But Pierre
and Levin do, partly because it is a fresh discovery for them,
and partly because they are, inescapably, thinkers. In fact, their
explanations are based on a notably vague theology: we may
feel that we understand the experience, because Tolstoy presents its emotional concomitants so persuasively. But it would
be difficult to put Pierre's or Levin's apprehension of God into
clear philosophical terms, because Tolstoy himself is so uncertain. It is thus that reason is given fairly short shrift in his
account of their religious experience: ' "The law of loving
others" ' thinks Levin to himself ' "could not be discovered by
reason, because it is unreasonable." ' (VIII.12) Significantly,
Tolstoy was to feel the opposite to be true after he had written
A Confession: then he was able to convince himself that such
things as the law of non-resistance were so simple and clear that
he would have worked them out for himself if Christ and his
doctrine had never existed. He was too much of a rationalist to
accept for good the vague theology he had given to Pierre and
Levin: only when his belief had a firm ground of reason could
he feel secure in it, and A Confession was the first and most important step in that direction.

Why he should have felt so strong a compulsion to move in
that direction, why the need for an explanation in religious
rather than materialist terms was so pressing, is largely accounted for by the obsession with death which we see running
through all his work. As he grew older the question of how to
live, the problem of happiness, gave way more and more to the
question of why, the problem of death. The prospect of a complete annihilation as the inevitable end of all that he might
achieve was an agonising one: that he was simply moving towards death seemed to him to rob all that he did of meaning
and value, to make a cruel joke of his life, a life which he saw
above all as a struggle towards meaning and truth. If there was
no other end than death to his activities as artist, father, landowner, teacher, then it was better not to struggle. The vision of
a terrible pointlessness is seen again and again in his diaries,
letters, stories and novels, and in the pages of A Confession, and
it is in the latter that it finds its most stark and concentrated ex-

pression, as he describes how the questions 'What is it for? What does it lead to?' drove him to the very edge of suicide:

> 'My mental condition presented itself to me thus: my life is some kind of stupid and evil joke played on me by someone . . . it seemed to me that there, somewhere, is someone who is now amusing himself by watching how I have lived for a whole thirty or forty years: lived learning, developing, growing in body and mind, and how now, having with a mature mind reached that summit of life from which it all lay open before me, how I stand on that summit like an arch-fool, understanding clearly that there is nothing in life, was not and will not be.' (Chapter 4)

The agony of annihilation was so terrible for Tolstoy partly because, as this passage suggests, life had given him so much, not only in his birth and material success, but in his enormous vitality. He was so much more alive than most men that death was all the greater an enemy: what it took from him would be more than it took from others. His pride and egoism were aspects of this vitality: that he, Lev Nikolayevich Tolstoy, should cease to exist seemed absurd and terrible, all the more so because the search for meaning and significance, for the purpose of it all, had become his *raison d'être*. Thus it is that more and more in the years before *A Confession* his remorseless rationalism returned him to the question 'why?', worrying the problem like a tenacious dog, and again and again coming to the same, terrifying conclusion: that life had no meaning in the face of death, that even his boundless energies and appetites could not give it such a meaning, that it was simply a cruel joke, and that the only worthy way of escape was not to submit to the joke, but to stop living—to commit suicide. Tolstoy's respect in *A Confession* for those who, finding themselves in such a position, do have the courage to kill themselves casts an interesting light on Anna's suicide. For Anna's clear vision of life as she drives to the station, the book she reads 'filled with anxieties, deceptions, grief, and evil', is very close to that view of life as a cruel joke which Tolstoy holds to be the logical view of anyone who has no faith. Not only do we come to understand better the respect with which he viewed Anna's suicide, but it seems likely that he put into the utter nihilism of her newly enlightened vision something of his own most desperately bleak moments at this time.

Without underrating this despair—indeed, it is impossible to do so when we look at Anna, or at Levin's fears that he may kill himself—it seems doubtful if suicide was ever quite so close for Tolstoy as *A Confession* maintains. The 'irresistible power' which drew him away from life seems to have been matched by that instinctive belief in life which was, after all, the ultimate cause of his troubles. And in the end it is that force of life that wins in *A Confession*, though only at a great cost to itself. It drives him to construct a rational religion that will enable him to go on living, but in the process the old, generous vitality, the love that is not based on principle or theory, is itself forced into a rational straitjacket, from which it is only to emerge in flashes in the later work, and only finally to reassert itself in the posthumously published *Hadji Murat*.

Though it was the major factor, the need to come to terms with death was not the only motive that drove Tolstoy towards his new faith. Another was undoubtedly that strong sense of guilt which pursued him from his earliest years, and which emerges most clearly in the diary entries of his early manhood. In those diaries we find a frequently repeated pattern of confessions of prurience of one kind or another, followed by remorse, a new and firm resolution to live a life of moral purity and simplicity, and a repetition of the same sins, the whole cycle often taking place in the space of a day or two. What these diary entries bear witness to is not hypocrisy of any kind, but a struggle between immensely strong appetites. The desire for an ascetic life, a life of absolute moral purity, was very great in Tolstoy, but so too were other desires, particularly sexual ones, which worked in the opposite direction. At times the spectacle of Tolstoy *agonistes* is a truly moving one; at others it can become comic, as when he tries to persuade himself that he is pleased he has caught syphilis: 'Yesterday, at the thought that my nose might fall in, I imagined what an enormous and beneficial impulse this would give me in the direction of moral development.'[5]

This strong conflict in the young Tolstoy was only temporarily quieted by marriage, which helped to order not only his sexual appetite, but also those other excesses, particularly gambling, to which he was prone (the sums he lost at cards during these early years were enormous, and had to be met by such desperate measures as selling serfs and land). With his wife to guard him, his growing family to provide for, and his estates to manage, Tolstoy was given, as it were, a high plateau of some fifteen years in which his genius could flower without his hyperactive conscience bringing him too close to the edge of despair. But though a long respite, it was still a temporary one; the very success it brought him helped to add new dimensions to his sense of guilt, as he came to see himself more and more as a parasite on society, a purveyor of entertainment for the rich few who, like himself, lived at the expense of the work and sufferings of countless thousands of others, to whom his novels were so irrelevant as to be meaningless. So to his strong sense of sexual guilt, no longer assuaged by the idea that it was legitimatised by marriage, was added one of social guilt, and a desire to humble himself in the eyes of the world, to atone for the birth and privileges he felt he had enjoyed so irresponsibly.

These then were the major forces driving him towards his 'conversion', the forces underlying the account given in *A Confession*. Tolstoy begins there by setting out briefly the course of his life up to the time when the crisis arrived: he describes the early decay of his boyhood Christianity, 'as is usual among people of our level of education', and the way in which his innate desire for moral perfection was deflected by the ways of the world into a desire to perfect himself in lesser ways—to be physically and mentally stronger than other men, and thus to become 'more famous, more important and richer than others'. It is here that one first notes that deliberate over-simplification of experience that is to recur too often in the subsequent pages. For the desire for moral perfection never did disappear in the way he suggests: the diaries and the earlier stories and novels provide unanswerable evidence that it remained very much alive during this period of youth and early manhood.

He goes on to summarise these years in a way that distorts the reality still more. Searching for the striking, paradoxical effect, as well as indulging in the exaggeration of past sins common to all converts, he writes:

'I cannot think about those years without horror, loathing and heartache. I used to kill men in war and challenge men to duels in order to kill them, lose at cards, consume the labour of the peasants, punish them, debauch and deceive. Lies, robbery, adultery of all kinds, drunkenness, violence, murder ... There was no crime I did not commit, and for all that my contemporaries praised me, and considered and still consider me to be a comparatively moral man.' (Chapter 2)

His contemporaries, of course, were quite right, and it is sad to see the man whose concern was always to find the truth, whose greatest work is characterised by its refusal to distort experience in order to fit his requirements, indulging in this ostentatious self-humiliation by way of half-truths. The picture of Tolstoy as a drunken, adulterous robber is a ludicrous one, whatever logical justification there may be for it, just as is his account of his early work as a writer. He began to write, he says, 'from vanity, covetousness and pride', in order to get 'fame and money', and for the sake of this it was necessary to 'hide the good and display the evil'. This description covers *Childhood, Boyhood and Youth*, the *Sevastopol Sketches*, the beginnings of *The Cossacks*, and shorter pieces like *The Raid* or *A Landlord's Morning*, any one of which would serve to show the inaccuracy of his account of both his motives and his execution.

Tolstoy is no more just to his literary contemporaries, the writers amongst whom he moved during the next few years. Like him, he says, their 'real innermost reasoning was . . . to get as much money and praise as possible', to which end they had developed the attractive theory that they were the teachers of mankind, although they had no idea what it was they were teaching, and were almost all 'bad, worthless in character, much inferior to those whom I had met in my former dissipated and military life'. This covers such men as Turgenev, Goncharov, Nekrasov, and Fet. As elsewhere, there is no doubt a glimmering of truth in what he says, but again it is obvious that there is also a wilful blindness to other aspects of these men's characters, and their work, that makes the whole account a viciously distorting one. It gives Tolstoy a platform from which he launches a splendid attack on 'progress' as a faith, but its manifest unfairness undercuts much of the force which that attack would otherwise have.

The same distorting treatment of his experience is evident in the rest of his autobiographical account: after his marriage, for example, he devoted himself to writing 'as a way of improving my material position and of stifling in my soul any questions as to the meaning of my own life or life in general'. And yet it is of the essence of *War and Peace* and *Anna Karenina* that they explore rather than stifle such questions, so that his statement that he wrote 'teaching what was for me the only truth, that one should live so as to have the best for oneself and one's family' is quite unacceptable as a summary of either novel.

It was towards the end of this period that Tolstoy moved into the crisis already described, in which 'before occupying myself with my Samara estate, the education of my son, or the writing of a book, I had to know why I was going to do it. While I did not know why, I could do nothing and could not live.' For an answer, he turned to the two spheres of human knowledge that seemed most likely to offer it—to what he calls the 'experimental' and 'abstract' sciences, by which he means physical science and philosophy respectively. The former, as he well knew before he asked, could return no answer at all, while philosophy, though it returned a kind of answer, only confirmed the conclusion that he himself had already reached: that life is indeed an evil, and that death is the logical way out. He quotes a decidedly selective group—the Buddha, Socrates, Schopenhauer and Ecclesiastes—to support his contention that this is the conclusion of all 'real philosophy'. But though his reason, thus supported by other thinkers, led him to the point where suicide was the next logical step, something held him back, 'something which I can only call a consciousness of life'.

Looking away from the philosophers, away from his own, educated class in general, he thought he saw in the common people, the 'enormous masses of . . . simple, unlearned and poor people who have lived and are living', a sense of the meaningfulness of life. They, and not the idle parasitic rich who rode on their backs, were the people who had the answers to his questions. With the entry of the common people (they are actually only marginally relevant to the logical argument, but highly relevant biographically) that note of wilful distortion and blindness to the complex reality of things again enters *A Confession*. One doubts (and Gorky's observations help bear this out) whether Tolstoy ever wholly believed that 'with rare exceptions' all those many millions of people who had lived the simple life of the peasant could both understand the question that so tormented him, and 'reply to it with extraordinary clarity'. There is an intellectual dishonesty in this, as great as there is in his perverse contention that the whole of his adult life had been useless, 'senseless and evil', destructive of life in himself and others. His exaltation of physical labour at the expense of his art is a form of *trahison des clercs* that grows out of his strong, and largely unjustified, sense of social guilt, together with what he himself calls his 'strange physical love . . . for the real working people'; but whatever its sources, we cannot help recognising it as a betrayal of that clear-sighted search for truth to which he had dedicated himself.

Seeing the contentment that the faith of the common people appeared to bring them, Tolstoy would if he could have moved at once towards it: but his reason could not allow him to accept it. He had reached an *impasse* to which, since he could not abandon his reason, there was only one solution—faith must become reasonable: 'Either that which I called rational was not so rational as I thought, or that which seemed to me irrational was not so irrational as I thought.' Predictably, both propositions are found to be true: reasoning had taken a false route in that it had tried to find an answer to a question about the relationship between the finite and the infinite in terms only of the finite: 'I asked: "What is the meaning of my life, beyond time, beyond cause, beyond space?" And I replied to the question: "What is the meaning of my life within time, cause and space?" And it came out that, after long efforts of thought, the answer I reached was: "None." ' (Chapter 9) Only faith could supply the answers, however irrational they might seem at first, because only faith introduced 'into every answer a relation between the finite and the infinite'. Thus Tolstoy reaches a point where faith, while seemingly irrational in itself, is made necessary by a process of reasoning. By adopting some kind of faith, as long as it did not demand a direct denial of his reason, he could provide himself with the answers to his questions about the meaning of life, he could 'apply reason to explain it'.

The search for such a faith was, as he says, a long and hard one. Predictably, the faith towards which he was most drawn, and was at first most able to accept, was that of the peasants; but at the same time as he extols their faith, he makes it clear that it could never be wholly his own, however much he might wish it so. What he believes he has learnt from the peasants is that no faith, no awareness of a meaning and purpose in life, can exist unless the life itself is lived 'usefully'—that is, in materially useful labour, such as that of the peasant. The immense labour involved in writing *War and Peace* and *Anna Karenina* is not, it is implied, at all useful—it is merely a part of that parasitic and indulgent life-style of the privileged few who can naturally have no faith because their life is 'meaningless and evil'.

It is on the basis of this dubious perception that Tolstoy moves towards the real climax of *A Confession*, his recognition of the existence of God. Reason still plays a considerable part in his search for belief in a God, for it is most certainly a search, and a desperate one, rather than something which comes to him easily. He argues fairly conventionally from the need for a First Cause, only to find himself checked by his own counter-arguments. Whenever he is able to believe for a moment that God might exist, he discovers that his load of spiritual anguish is lifted; but as soon as he decides once again that there is no God, gloom and the prospect of suicide return: 'Not twice or three times, but tens and hundreds of times, I reached those states, first joy and animation, then despair and the consciousness of the impossibility of living.' It is thus that he comes to his conversion, surely the most tentative and rationalised of all famous conversions:

> 'But then I turned to look at myself, at what was going on in me, and I remembered all those deaths and reanimations that went on within me hundreds of times. I remembered that I lived then only when I believed in God. As it was before, so it was now; I said to myself: I need only to be able to be aware of God to live; I need only to forget Him, or disbelieve Him, and I die. What are these animations and deaths? I do not live when I lose belief in the existence of God. I should long ago have killed myself if I had not had a dim hope of finding Him. I live, really live, only when I feel Him and seek Him. "So what more do I seek?" exclaimed a voice within me. "So this is He. He is that without which it is impossible to live. To know God and to live is one and the same thing. God is life.
> "Live seeking God, and then you will not live without God." And stronger than ever before all within me and around me lit up, and this light did not again abandon me.' (Chapter 12)

The 'voice within me' is very much the voice of reason and will, and not of revelation. The apprehension of God is tentative indeed, but it is one Tolstoy could not afford to give up. It gave him the essential key, after which the fashioning of a rationally acceptable ethical and religious system based on Christian principles became possible. Above all it gave a meaning to what seemed otherwise a meaningless existence. For all the distorting arguing that has preceded it, for all that it involves the rejection of so much of life, it still represents an assertion of life, as Tolstoy tacitly acknowledges. He had gone through a crisis in which he had seen into the emptiness, absurdity and triviality of human existence with a clarity as painful as that of any twentieth-century explorer of the absurd, and he had refused to accept the finality of that vision. In *A Confession* he is forging for himself a way to go on living precisely because the 'force of life' in him could not in the end give way to his logical rejection of life as meaningless. In making life meaningful, though, he also simplifies it, denying it much of that complexity, the apprehension of which is so essential to his greatest work. From now on, his work was to take a different tone, as he judged his experience in the cold and simple light of his new faith.

Almost all of his later fiction is illuminated by one form or another of that ruthlessly simplifying light; sometimes it takes the form of a devastating intensity of vision that cuts away all the deceptions, the false values and irrelevant half-truths by which man bolsters up his life, as in *The Death of Ivan Ilyich* or *Master and Man;* sometimes it has a coldly relentless, documentary objectivity about it, as in *Resurrection*; and sometimes it becomes obsessive and reductive, as in *The Kreutzer Sonata*. Always, though, it plays on the corruptions and vanities of human existence with a terrible lucidity that is quite different from the lucidity of *War and Peace* or *Anna Karenina*. Tolstoy still 'makes it strange': but the eye which still sees everyday experience with an incomparable originality and freshness, as though it had never been seen in that way before, is no longer directed by that wide-ranging, apparently involuntary love for whatever comes under its gaze. What Thomas Mann called 'the mighty sense-appeal of Tolstoy's art'[6] is sharply diminished. There is no longer a place for a Stiva Oblonsky, nor even for a Natasha Rostova, in the work that follows *A Confession*. Only in *Hadji Murat*, so significantly unlike all the rest of his late work, does one feel that the vision is again directed by that amoral love of both body and soul which is so vital to the earlier work, and of which he had once written in his notebook: 'the first condition of a writer's popularity ... is the love with which he treats all his characters.' Elsewhere, Tolstoy's newly-forged Christianity emerges, as far as his art goes, in a paradoxical detachment, a lack of that kind of love.

7
The fruits of conversion

The work which grows most obviously out of *A Confession* is that series of books, pamphlets, Biblical studies and translations, of which the most important are *What Then Must We Do?*, *The Kingdom of God is Within You*, *What I Believe*, and *What is Art?*, in which Tolstoy works out more fully the implications of his new beliefs, developing them philosophically, and considering their practical application in relation to social reform and to art. A great deal of his time and effort was spent, in the years between 1880 and his death in 1910, in propagating his beliefs in ways more direct than prose fiction. It is with the novelist, however, that this study is concerned, and a proper consideration of Tolstoy the social, religious or aesthetic philosopher belongs elsewhere, as does an account of his late dramatic writing, and of the terrible tensions which his attempt to live out his new faith raised within his own family. What is important from the point of view of the literary critic is that amidst all the diversions and distractions, and despite his rejection of almost all his earlier work as worthless, he continued to find in prose fiction the most profound and the most effective medium for the exploration of the crisis he had described in *A Confession*. Much as he wished at times to renounce art, he never ceased to be first of all a great artist, one to whom, as to Lawrence, the novel was 'the highest form of human expression so far attained'.

Out of the spiritual crisis of the late 1870s, and testifying more decisively, if less directly, than his non-fiction to its importance for him, there comes a considerable sequence of stories and novels which may be said to deal in some way or other with the theme of conversion—with a crisis which leads towards the rejection of the inverted values and empty assumptions of the higher classes of society, and which involves the discovery of a new world of more stable spiritual values. In fact, it is possible to see all of Tolstoy's work after *A Confession*, with the notable exception of *Hadji Murat*, as related to some aspect of the conversion experience he describes there.

This is most obviously true of such things as *Resurrection* or *The*

Death of Ivan Ilyich, but it is true also of the masterly parabolic stories like *How Much Land Does a Man Need?*, which James Joyce felt to be 'the greatest story that the literature of the world knows'.[1] This is only one of a large number of short stories aimed at a popular audience which Tolstoy wrote in the years following *A Confession*: in them he strips narrative detail to its barest minimum, avoiding what now seemed to him a trivial indulgence in detailed description, and concentrates his art with stringent economy on the communication of the moral lesson which is the *raison d'être* of each story. To speak of communicating a moral lesson, however, is to run the risk of misrepresenting the essential nature of these stories: in fact, the bareness of the narrative, Tolstoy's reliance on the method of parable rather than explication, saves them from becoming merely didactic *exempla*. Though their didacticism could scarcely be clearer, Tolstoy himself enters them much less than one would expect. They do not preach, but merely tell, and in the telling take on at their best a hard clarity of a kind that one associates with the finest folk art, and which goes some way to substantiate Joyce's admiration of one of the best of them.

The relationship which these parabolic stories bear to Tolstoy's own crisis is clear, but tangential: they grow out of it in the sense that they set out to teach to a popular audience certain moral and religious truths which had become more clear to him since his conversion. Though they only occasionally deal with conversion itself, both their content and their form are dependent on the experience recounted in *A Confession*: they teach a rejection of material values, a subjugation of the physical and limited body to the spiritual and divine in man (what is called in *The Kingdom of God is Within You* his 'reasonable consciousness'), through a studiously 'universal' art that does not aim to please a small parasitic upper class, but which is intended to reach those great masses for whom, in Tolstoy's view, 'high art' could have no meaning or relevance.

It was, however, on those works in which he continued to address himself to a more sophisticated audience, that his conversion left its most indelible mark. Here, even when he is most objective and distanced, he is dealing with experiences related to his own in a way that is not the case with the popular parables. To do this, he turned once again to the form of the short novel, the Russian *povest'*, neither novel nor short story, which gave him the space he needed to develop his narrative, and yet enabled him to concentrate his focus as intensely as possible on a single issue. Only once, in *Resurrection*, was he to turn again to the form of the longer novel. Apart from this it was in a series of *povesti*—notably *The Death of Ivan Ilyich*, *Master and Man*, *The Kreutzer Sonata*, *The Devil*, and *Father Sergius*—that Tolstoy's conversion was to bear its richest fruits. These all have in common, together with *Resurrection* and the unfinished *Memoirs of a Madman*, the ultimate recognition of the corrupt, empty absurdity, the desperate meaninglessness of a life lived without some sense of a purpose beyond itself, the same recognition that we have seen in *A Confession*. Tolstoy's moral emphasis differs considerably, so that in *The Kreutzer Sonata* and *The Devil*, and to some extent in *Father Sergius*, corruption and temptation are seen primarily in sexual terms: but that desire of the flesh which torments the central figures of these three stories is in reality only the most intense focus for Tolstoy of that more general 'living for the flesh' that we see in the empty and unconsidered materialism by which Ivan Ilyich, Brekhunov in *Master and Man*, or Nekhlyudov in *Resurrection* live before their 'conversion'.

All Tolstoy's lesser work has suffered from the long shadows that are inevitably cast by *War and Peace* and *Anna Karenina*. Just as his earlier writing tends to be read too often as an interesting preparation for the two great novels, so his later work is, even more frequently, seen as a long, sadly obsessive decline from them. The common judgement is a mistaken one: there is certainly nothing comparable to *War and Peace* or *Anna Karenina* in the later work, but then there is only a small handful of novels outside of Tolstoy's own work that can survive that comparison. If we remove it from the shadow of the two major novels, the later work can be seen to have, at its best, a very real greatness of a different kind from what has gone before. Obsessive, polemic, intense as they are, the greatness of these later works lies most of all in a strong development of Tolstoy's old power to clarify without being reductive, to simplify without dishonesty, and (with the exception of *Resurrection*) in their precise focus on a single episode or issue. When he does fail in these later works, it is when he falls over the brink, when he does become reductive or dishonest in his obsessiveness, as in *The Kreutzer Sonata*. At best, the limpid, generous translucency of *War and Peace* is replaced by a hard, searching light—akin to that light in which Anna sees life as she drives to the station, or the cold, clear light which hangs over Petersburg in *Resurrection*, and which in both cases serves to expose the vanity and corruption of the city so mercilessly.

Tolstoy's attitude to his characters changes along with this change in his way of seeing the world. Though one could not mistake the hand of the author, and though most of the central characters continue to reflect some aspect of his own experience, we no longer enter their worlds with the same unquestioning familiarity as we enter those of his earlier characters. Even as we recognise the terrible fact that Ivan Ilyich is every one of us, we yet remain more removed from him than from Andrey, Pierre or Levin, with whom, in all probability, we have less in common. It is as if the cold light plays not only on the vanities of the world, but also on those who come to recognise them as vanities. Even when Tolstoy turns again to an aristocratic 'seeker' as a hero, in *Resurrection*, he remains as detached from him as he is from Ivan Ilyich, and so too does the reader. It is not that these characters become dead ciphers: their experience can be all too real. But, as has been said, they are invested with little or none of that loving sympathy that Tolstoy had once had in abundance for his characters.

Two stories that seem to belong clearly with this group stand nevertheless slightly aside from it—*The Memoirs of a Madman* and *The Devil*, the first because it is a fragment based very closely indeed on Tolstoy's own experience (and in this sense closest of all to *A Confession*), and the second because it deals with temptation and spiritual crisis without taking the next step, as *The Kreutzer Sonata* does, and spelling out the subsequent conversion, the discovery of truth—though the implications are clear enough.

The Memoirs of a Madman indicates just how strongly an irrational apprehension of death, and a concomitant vision of the emptiness of life, could on occasions take hold of Tolstoy. The 'madman' of the story, who is transparently Tolstoy, is visited by occasional attacks of terrible, irrational despair during his childhood. But it is not until he is a happily married man, busy with the shrewd augmentation of his estate, that the 'madness' returns. On a trip to buy a new estate at what he expects will be a bargain price, he is suddenly visited, as Tolstoy had been on just such an occasion, by a quite unmotivated apprehension of death. The fear experienced is evoked with extraordinary immediacy, as every detail of the journey—the bells of the horses' harness, the white walls of the post-house at which he stops—suddenly becomes bereft of innocence in his eyes. Everything seems to point to death, a death from whose presence there is no escape:

'I tried to turn my thoughts to things which had interested me, to the estate I was going to buy, to my wife, but found nothing to cheer me. It had all become nothing. Everything was hidden by a terrible consciousness that my life was ebbing away. I needed sleep. I lay down, but the next moment I jumped up again in terror. A fit of spleen seized me, spleen such as the feeling before one is sick, but spiritual spleen. It was uncanny and dreadful. It seems that death is terrible, but when you remember and think of life, it is your dying life that is terrible. Life and death somehow merged into one another. Something was tearing my soul apart and could not complete the severance. Again I went to look at the sleeping men, and again I tried to sleep. Always the same terror: red, white and square. Something tearing within that yet could not be torn apart. A painful, painfully dry and spiteful feeling, not an atom of kindness, but just a dull and steady spitefulness towards myself and towards that which had made me.'

It is in the claustrophobic atmosphere of post-houses and hotels that this experience first comes to him, when he is away from the security of his home and his settled way of life. There is a masterly combination of the realistic and the symbolic in the way in which Tolstoy presents those hotel rooms, so terrible to the madman, which, depressingly claustrophobic in themselves, become also the symbols of a trapped condition, a limited, empty life. The same situation of a thoroughly credible fear and a symbolic situation is found in the hunting scene, where the madman loses his way in a forest. As he struggles through the snow, the fear of death settles on him more powerfully than ever. The situation is now the opposite of claustrophobic, but again the likelihood of such a feeling coming at such a time (it may be again based on an autobiographical incident) gives a solid, credible basis to the symbolic force the scene also possesses.

It is on this occasion that insight and relief come with the recognition that he must not argue with or reproach God for the way things are ordered, and that it is he himself who is to blame if he cannot accept death. As he recognises this fact, he finds his way out of the forest and on to the road home—though the process does not strike the reader with quite the allegorical patness that such a summary might suggest. But it is a moment of conversion, a conversion that is followed by an obviously hurried and unsatisfactory attempt on Tolstoy's part to finish off the story. The madman's madness at the end consists in his seeing this world from the perspective of a world beyond death, in which injustice, suffering and death are unreal. But the new insight is unconvincing, seems itself unreal, in that it does not grow out of the narrative, but is only willed rather tersely on to the end of it. Even the madness changes its nature, for whereas earlier it had seemed to be something truly irrational, a strange, hyperintense apprehension of death at the most arbitrary moments, now it is a very rational, ironic madness, the madman in fact clearly believing himself to be sane, and the rest of the world mad. It is difficult to see, though, how the story could have been given any convincingly final ending: essentially the report of a series of irrational experiences, it had to remain a fragment, too close, perhaps, to Tolstoy's own experience to be susceptible to the rationalising, rounding-off process that might have turned it into a finished work of art, and he left it unfinished and unpublished at his death.

Tolstoy had trouble too with the ending of *The Devil*, another work only published posthumously, and finally left alternative endings to the story of the struggle of a good man with sexual desires that he cannot master. The story had been suggested to him partly by a local affair, in which a Tula official had killed his peasant mistress, but like *The Memoirs of a Madman* it has a strong autobiographical element in it: he draws on his own experience of temptations of a similar kind, both succumbed to and resisted. It belongs here because it is the story of a struggle between the spirit and the flesh, a struggle set at the very highest pitch of tension, in that only the most violent severance of the physical bond—death—can resolve it. The violent forms which the struggle takes, both here and in *The Kreutzer Sonata* and *Father Sergius*, bear witness to the strength of that sexual appetite which had always tormented Tolstoy, and which since his conversion had done so more than ever. Though renunciation of the flesh seemed to him more and more essential, the powerful attractions presented by the flesh were such that renunciation could only be achieved through a violence permissible in fiction but not in fact. 'Of all the passions' he wrote in *The Kreutzer Sonata*, 'the strongest, cruellest and most stubborn is the sex-passion', and his wife was particularly bitter about the high moral stance taken by the husband whom, she well knew, was by no means, even in his old age, the victor over his libido.

The hero of *The Devil*, Evgeny Irtenyev, is in most respects a model landowner, a man, by conventional standards, of substantial moral integrity. He is scrupulous in the management of his estate, and in the struggle to pay off the debts which, along with that estate, he has inherited from his father. Living unmarried in the country, for some time he eschews the normal patrician solution to the privations of bachelorhood, that of taking a peasant mistress. (Tolstoy had done this on more than one occasion, and his family grew up with the slightly discomfiting knowledge that they had an illegitimate elder half-brother, who is said to have closely resembled his father, working as their coachman.) Eventually Irtenyev, too, succumbs, and takes a peasant mistress 'for the sake of his health'. Tolstoy makes Stepanida, 'barefoot, fresh, firm and handsome', a singularly impressive and credible figure of temptation, never the cipher which Professor Christian suggests she is,[2] but endowed with a considerable physical presence, a matter of crucial importance in our judgement of the sequel. She has, along with her physical qualities, a simple honesty about her position which contrasts favourably with Irtenyev's rather unappealing attempts to justify himself by insisting that she is simply 'necessary for his health' and no more.

When Irtenyev marries, he at once, and as it seems to him easily, breaks off his relationship with Stepanida. His wife, though physically less attractive and less robustly healthy than his mistress, offers him more than he had ever hoped for. In her anticipation of his wishes, her intuitive knowledge of his values and beliefs, she becomes an ideal Tolstoyan wife, able, through her love, to 'penetrate into his soul'. With her, Irtenyev lives happily for just over a year, when he again encounters Stepanida, and finds her power to attract him is undiminished. It now works, however, wholly against his will: his love and regard for his wife make the idea of any renewed liaison with Stepanida morally repulsive. Still, he finds he is drawn towards her with a quite irresistible force of physical desire. Chance, rather than any decisive operation of his will, prevents a renewal of their relationship. A move away for two months, and the birth of a child to his wife, make no difference: the tranquillity he hopes he has found is illusory, shattered at once by renewed sight of Stepanida. The conflict between flesh and spirit, desire and will, is brought now to a desperate head. Seeing he has no defence against the attraction he feels towards Stepanida, and yet unable for a moment to justify his position, Irtenyev's only escape is a violent one: he must kill Stepanida, or his wife, or himself. Tolstoy could not decide which course he preferred his hero to take—one version ends with him simply, and rather lamely, shooting himself. In another, altogether more engaged and interesting, he takes his revolver and, again meeting Stepanida and finding her power over him undiminished, he shoots her and so exorcises the devil that has possessed him.

In either case, as in *The Kreutzer Sonata* (though it is not here a matter of jealousy) sexual passion can be defeated only by violence. If Tolstoy's vision in these later works sometimes seems like an inversion of Lawrence's, it should be remembered, and might have seemed a redeeming feature in Lawrence's eyes, that the mind, the will, self-control, are made to seem almost ludicrously ineffective in the face of the demands made by the body. Certainly there seems little that can stop Irtenyev as he finds himself driven towards his former mistress, who has most of the life in the story, and away from his wife.

The Devil never reaches the heights of *The Kreutzer Sonata*, but neither does it reach its depths; the portrait of Stepanida shows none of that obsessive hatred of the flesh we find in the latter, nor do we find the same extremes of disgust or of over-simplification. Instead of being an assault on sex in or out of marriage, *The Devil* sets a happy and credible married life over against the uncontrollable but equally credible physical passions which threaten to destroy it. It is true that Irtenyev's marriage is built on sand: both his former liaison with Stepanida, and his wife's apparent idolatry of him render it potentially unstable. But though we always see Irtenyev more clearly than his wife does, and though Tolstoy does raise the question as to whether Stepanida is not more truly his wife, neither point is of crucial importance. *The Devil* remains essentially a credible witness to the violent, disruptive power of sexual desire, overriding for Irtenyev every consideration, moral or practical, which stands in the way of its fulfilment. This is why the second ending is so much the more powerful: the insidious mastery of his will which his desire for Stepanida represents is something that has to be destroyed; killing her is an act of symbolic as well as literal significance. To have killed himself would have been to accept a total defeat of the will by the uncontrollable forces of libido; Irtenyev's killing of Stepanida, though neither Tolstoy nor the reader acquiesces in it, represents an effort not to admit such total defeat, to recognise the devil and to exorcise it regardless of the cost to himself or others.

At one point in *The Devil* Irtenyev tries to turn his mind from thoughts of Stepanida by inflicting pain on himself, deliberately holding his finger in the flame of a candle. A precisely similar gesture is made by Father Sergius in the story of that name, but Sergius, like Irtenyev, is driven to more violent means to exorcise the physical temptation posed by the woman—again a convincingly attractive one—who has entered his hermit's cell at night with the intention of seducing him. In an episode whose intensity and matter of fact realism prevent it from toppling over into the ludicrously macabre, Sergius walks past the woman into the porch of his cell, and taking an 'axe in his right hand he laid the forefinger of his left hand on the block, swung the axe and struck with it below the second joint. The finger flew off more easily than a stick of the same thickness would fly off, turned over, and plopped down onto the edge of the block and then on to the floor.' (Chapter 5) This was, presumably, part of that scene which Tolstoy read to Gorky: 'he read it through to the end, and then, raising his head and shutting his eyes, he said distinctly: 'The old man wrote it well, well.'' ' So he did: there are few moments in Tolstoy where a comparable response of surprise and shock is achieved, the surprise making the extravagant violence of the gesture all the more striking. For the time the expedient is successful; but Sergius's self-mutilation, for all its apparent symbolism, is not a castration, an end to all such temptations. It is only a partial victory, one successful battle in the continuing war between spirit and flesh in which Sergius is later to suffer a humiliating defeat, seduced by a far less attractive woman than the one he now manages to resist.

Father Sergius is not, however, simply a story of sexual temptation: it is more complex than *The Devil* in that the desires of the flesh, important though they are, are subsidiary to the more insidious temptation of spiritual pride, one form or another of which follows Sergius throughout his outwardly exemplary career until in the end he finds what Tolstoy offers, not altogether convincingly, as a genuine humility.

As in all of these stories, there is a good deal of Tolstoy himself in Sergius: the high born man who renounces a successful career for a life of self-denial in which he is dogged by temptations both physical and spiritual, by a libido he cannot always control, and an egoism and pride he cannot suppress, is clearly recognisable in outline if not in detail. *Father Sergius* is, in fact, one of the few places in which Tolstoy seems to show a critical self-awareness of his pride; but Sergius differs from Tolstoy in that his renunciation of the world is more clearly based on partly false motives, on a desire to avenge a humiliation to which he can find no other answer—the discovery that his fiancée has been the mistress of the Tsar. It is this that takes the erstwhile Prince Kasatsky away from the life of the court and of his regiment to the ostensibly humbler life of the monastery, a move that only his sister, who is as proud and ambitious as he, can understand:

'She understood that he had become a monk in order to stand above those who wanted to show him that they stood above him. And she understood him correctly. By becoming a monk he showed he despised all that seemed important to others and had seemed so to him at the time he was in the service, and he now ascended a height from which he could look down from above on those people he had formerly envied. But it was not this feeling alone, as his sister Varenka thought, that governed him. There was also in him something else: a genuinely religious feeling which Varenka did not know, which intertwined itself with the feeling of pride and the desire for pre-eminence, also governed him.' (Chapter 2)

The emphasis Tolstoy places on the mixture of motives is important: Sergius is by no means insincere, as the finger-chopping episode confirms. But mixed with his striving towards God

146

is a nearly fatal satisfaction in the admiration of others for his more and more saintly existence. It involves, in fact, a transference of the worldly ambition which had marked him as a young guards officer to the sphere of monastic life. Just as the young Tolstoy had wished to excel at everything he undertook, so does Sergius wish to be recognised as the best, whether as Imperial aide-de-camp or holy recluse. After the finger-chopping episode, in particular, his fame grows, and with it his spiritual pride. Whereas in his early years as a monk, though he felt he was continually failing in his struggles with worldly desires, he did at least struggle, in these riper years of apparent saintliness he becomes more and more complacent:

'Whether he admonished people, or simply blessed them, or prayed for the sick, or advised them how to improve their lives, or listened to the gratitude of those whom he had helped by healing (as they told him) or by precepts, he could not help being pleased by it, and could not be indifferent to the results of his activity, to its influence on people. He thought of himself as a shining light, and the more he felt this, the more he felt a weakening, an extinction of the divine light of truth that shone within him.' (Chapter 7)

He is working more for men than for God, and this is the cause of his downfall. At a time when he is feeling more than usually pleased by the public recognition of his saintliness, a merchant brings his sick daughter to be cured. Sergius has, significantly, just been praying to be cleansed from 'the sin of worldly vanity', a sin to which he realises only too well that he is subject. His 'cleansing' in fact takes the drastic and unlikely form of seduction by the feeble-minded but sensual daughter of the merchant. Unprepared for any spiritual struggle, he falls easily. In the morning, humiliated, he abandons his cell and leaves the monastery with the intention of committing suicide. Instead, a dream directs him to look for his cousin Pashenka, who somehow presents herself to his mind as a means of salvation. He finds his mild, inconspicuous cousin fallen upon hard times, but still modestly resigned, as always, to the blows of fate, supporting her entire household by giving music lessons, and meekly acquiescing in all kinds of drudgery being forced upon her. Pashenka has no sense of her life as a particularly virtuous or holy one; rather the opposite. And this, as Sergius realises, is her

F

salvation, and in the lesson she teaches him, his salvation too:

> ' "Pashenka is that which I ought to have been and was not. I lived for people on the pretext that I lived for God, she lives for God imagining that she lives for people. Yes, one good deed, a cup of water given without thought of reward, is dearer than any benefit I thought I was bestowing on people." ' (Chapter 8)

Like Alyosha Gorshok in the late short story of that name, Pashenka represents an ideal of humility, of unselfconscious goodness, which the proud, ever selfconscious Tolstoy could never attain. For this reason, perhaps, there is an air of unreality, of wish fulfilment, about the final 'conversion' of Father Sergius: he, like Tolstoy, seems too irredeemably proud for his new found humility to take a genuine hold on him, however much he, like Tolstoy, may have wished it to. The concluding pages showing his new life are few and unconvincing, as if Tolstoy could not really imagine what such a life might be like in practice. But the story of the spiritual struggle itself, the insight into the mixed motives of the man who renounces the world for the sake of his soul, the physical and spiritual temptations he faces, is masterly. In the *Reminiscences*, Gorky blames Tolstoy for trying to become a spiritual despot, for wishing to be a martyr, and concludes that he knows this himself—'he knows everything!'[4] Certainly in *Father Sergius* he knows the dangers of such insidious spiritual temptation, and he explores them with much of the old honesty, and with none of the wilful distortion of experience that we find in *A Confession* or, still more clearly, in *The Kreutzer Sonata*.

That *The Kreutzer Sonata* does involve such a distorted view of experience, specifically of sexual experience, few would nowadays be disposed to deny. It is probably equally true that few would deny that Pozdnyshev's nightmarish, fevered narrative has in its later stages an intensity and intelligence about it that compels our utmost respect and attention. This, indeed, is the central problem with which *The Kreutzer Sonata* presents the critic; it is, as it were, broken-backed, with the magnificently handled narrative of the moral decay of a marriage, culminating in jealousy and murder, being introduced by, and partly interwoven with, an obsessively unintelligent, simplistic series of generalisations on the nature (and sources) of sexual passion. The generalisations, which are spoken by Pozdnyshev but which are undoubtedly endorsed by Tolstoy, cannot begin to function as they are intended to, as a serious placing of the significance of Pozdnyshev's terrible story, but neither can they be detached from that story. Extremities of good and bad are inseparably linked in *The Kreutzer Sonata*, in a way for which it is difficult to think of any parallels elsewhere in literature.

That this is so may well be due in a large part to Tolstoy's use of the monologue form for the story. This form was initially dictated by his intention that it should be performed by the actor Andreyev-Burlak, with whom he and the painter Repin had heard a performance of the sonata in Tolstoy's Moscow house. Tolstoy had suggested that each should respond in his own way to the stimulus of the sonata, the first movement of which had always moved him deeply; but Andreyev-Burlak died, Repin never painted his picture, and Tolstoy himself moved a long way from his original conception. The monologue form which he retained, however, had one supremely damaging effect: it deprived him of that degree of objectivity which is necessarily imposed by third-person narrative. It has been pointed out earlier how important the role of omniscient narrator was to the development of a genius such as Tolstoy's, a many sided genius which, if it concentrated on any single aspect of itself, particularly the sexual, tended to become unbalanced and obsessive. In the other late stories of sin and conversion the artistic demands of the third-person narrative save him from blatant didacticism and over-simplification. In *The Kreutzer Sonata* there is no such objectifying agency to stand between the reader and Tolstoy's most extreme views on the viciousness of sexual passion. Instead, the need to persuade, which is inevitably stronger in the monologue, leads him into exaggerations which are still greater than those we find in that other monologue, *A Confession*, and which make the reader associate Pozdnyshev's feverish manner (sustained by frequent drinks of a tea so strong as to suggest a kind of intoxication) with Tolstoy himself. We have in the end no convincing sense of a controlled distance between narrator and author: rather, there is a sense of an unforgivable indulgence on Tolstoy's part, the suspicion that he is using his unbalanced narrator to put forward ideas which he wholly endorses, but which he would not argue with such vehemence and abandon if he had to take direct responsibility for them himself. This may conceivably be defended as a form of self-awareness, an acknowledgement that there is something slightly hysterical about his own attitudes, but it never manifests itself in this way. It is very much a lack of such self-awareness that is communicated overall, and is endorsed by Tolstoy's later defence of the story and its doctrine.

This is not to say that there are not moments when one can agree with Pozdnyshev-Tolstoy: in his attack on the hypocrisies of romantic love, for example, in his statement that the real inequality of woman in the nineteenth century is sexual, not political, or in his belief that ' "real debauchery lies precisely in freeing oneself from moral relations with a woman with whom you have physical intimacy" '. But the overall argument tends always to undercut the assent that one might otherwise give to such propositions as these. Out of context they may be acceptable, even radical and profound: in context, they form part of an unbalanced, obsessive attitude towards sexual relations, which maintains that the whole problem stems from the leisured classes' indulgence in rich foods, which, together with their complete idleness, ' "is nothing but a systematic excitement of desire" '. In this dark world of Pozdnyshev's—and again it should be emphasised that we cannot dissociate Tolstoy from it—intercourse during pregnancy is a major cause of epilepsy and other nervous disorders in women, intercourse is itself unnatural (' "Ask a child, ask an unperverted girl" '), nine out of ten married couples don't believe that marriage involves mutual obligations, and ninety-nine per cent of all marriages follow the same kind of tormenting, vicious course as does his own.

It is this last point that is in a sense the most disturbing. For it might not be too difficult to disregard the more absurd aspects of Tolstoy's argument, and concentrate our attention on the harrowing narrative of the breakdown of Pozdnyshev's own marriage, if it were not for the fact that we are always being made aware of its supposedly representative quality. The only difference between Pozdnyshev and the rest of mankind, it is implied, is that his unhappiness has come to a violent crisis, as a result of which he now sees the truth—that sexual love is itself evil, and the source of nearly all the evil in life. This is the fruit of his 'conversion', the new knowledge brought about by the consequences of his passionate jealousy, and we cannot easily separate the absurd generalisations of the convert from the superbly handled particulars of his story.

If he allowed us to see Pozdnyshev's marriage as the terrible exception that we feel it to be, there is no question but that his story could stand as one of the great triumphs of Tolstoy's career. If Pozdnyshev were truly placed by the author, a critical distance between author and narrator firmly and clearly maintained, then the gradual gathering of narrative pace and intensity could be given the unequivocal praise that would be their due. As an exploration of a marriage without anything but intermittent sexual attraction to hold it together, of 'two egoists quite foreign to each other who wished to get as much pleasure as possible from each other', the story has all the unerring psychological rightness, the insight into complexity of motive and response, that we associate with the very best of Tolstoy. As we see the abyss between Pozdnyshev and his wife gradually widen until it reaches a state in which, with the entrance of the musician Trukhachevsky, a violent outcome seems inevitable, we can believe readily in the particular account, but never in the representative significance Tolstoy attributes to it.

That Trukhachevsky should be a musician, and that music should be involved in the development of the story is, of course, of immense significance: like sex, music had always had a powerfully attractive force for Tolstoy, and like sex it was something he profoundly mistrusted, even at times hated, because it aroused emotions which had no rational end or explanation. Music is a dreadful thing, Pozdnyshev says, because it 'only agitates, and doesn't lead to a conclusion'. Like sexual desire, it involves the release of powerful emotional forces which are not subject to the will, to the control of reason. In both cases the experience is immensely pleasurable, but only justifiable when it has some end, some purpose. Once again we see the old struggle between the rational and irrational, the 'reasonable consciousness' and the physical life of the body, inhabiting the very centre of the story. Pozdnyshev's jealousy and murder of his wife are products of the irrational body, a terrible illustration for Tolstoy of the forces of evil which are released when the emotions are not firmly held in check by what he now saw as the divine, that is the rational, part of man. Jealousy and murder grow out of, and are really at one with, the sexual attraction which brought Pozdnyshev and his wife together in the first place, and which held their marriage together. The alternating periods of sexual love and irrational hatred which they experienced during that time were simply 'the same animal feeling, only at opposite poles'.

It is fitting, then, that music should be the catalyst that accelerates the breakdown of Pozdnyshev's marriage. Trukhachevsky is the purely sensual man, as befits his occupation (it is worth noting the change in attitude when compared to Tolstoy's other peripatetic violinist in *Albert*, written in 1858). Just as his music is a matter of an 'exquisite voluptuousness', so he himself has a voluptuousness which Tolstoy hates now as he had not hated it in Stiva Oblonsky or even in Anatole Kuragin: 'I remember' says Pozdnyshev 'how he crunched the gristle of a cutlet, and how greedily his red lips clung to the glass of wine.' This is Stiva done with malice instead of love. The musical relationship between Trukhachevsky and Pozdnyshev's wife is itself a sensual, sexual one—Tolstoy clearly felt the intercourse between piano and violin in Beethoven's sonata was suggestive of this—and although we never see any explicitly physical contact between the two, the contact between violin and piano, as Tolstoy describes it, is enough to convince us that Pozdnyshev's jealousy is well-founded.[5]

From this point on the narrative grows more detailed, more intense, and yet paradoxically gathers pace. The growth of Pozdnyshev's jealously while away from home, as he remembers the faces of the two as he had seen them when performing the duet, and the description of his hurried return home by coach and train, are dwelt on at length, and the murder itself still more so. John Bayley is relatively unimpressed by Tolstoy's description of the murder,[6] but it seems to me that there is no more striking or convincing use anywhere in his work of his two favourite literary devices, that of 'making it strange' and of convincing us of the reality of a feeling by making it illogical, paradoxical, or simply unexpected, than in the pages describing Pozdnyshev's preparation for the murder and the murder itself. The two devices are seen at work side by side in Pozdnyshev's description of his initial attack:

' "I tore my arm away and threw myself towards him in

silence. His eyes met mine, and he suddenly grew as pale as a sheet to the very lips. His eyes flashed in a peculiar way and, what again I had not expected, he scurried under the piano and out of the door. I wanted to throw myself after him, but a weight hung on my left arm. It was her. I jerked away. She hung on still more heavily and would not let go. This unexpected hindrance, the weight, and her touch which was revolting to me, inflamed me even more. I felt that I was completely mad and must appear terrible, and delighted in it. I swung my left arm with all my strength and hit her straight in the face with my elbow. She screamed and let go of my arm. I wanted to run after him, but remembered it would be ridiculous to run after the lover of one's wife in one's socks; and I did not wish to be ridiculous, I wished to be terrible." ' (Chapter 27)

It is this curious but convincing selfconsciousness of Pozdnyshev, as if the whole episode was brightly and unnaturally illuminated, that is used by Tolstoy to slow down his description of the murder, and thus to 'make it strange'.

The attention to physical detail is a function of this selfconsciousness, of a heightened awareness that makes the event both more real and more terrible than a literary murder can normally be:

' "When people say that they don't remember what they do in a fit of madness—it's rubbish, lies. I remembered everything and did not for a second stop remembering what I was doing. The more strongly I fanned the flames of my madness, the more brightly the light of consciousness burnt in me, so that I could not fail to see everything I was doing. I knew what I was doing every second. I can't say that I knew beforehand what I was going to do, but at the moment when I was doing it, and even, it seems, a little before, I knew what I was doing, as if to make it possible to repent, to be able to tell myself that I could stop. I knew that I was hitting below the ribs, and that the dagger would enter. At the moment I did it, I knew I was doing something terrible, something such as I had never done before, and which would have terrible consequences. But that consciousness flashed past like lightning, and the deed followed immediately on the consciousness. And I realised the deed with extraordinary clearness. I heard, and remember, the momentary resistance of her corset and of something else, and then the plunging of the knife into something soft. She grasped the dagger with her hands, cut them, but did not hold it back." ' (Chapter 27)

In the penultimate sentence here, physical passion reaches its terrible climax, with the stabbing itself seen not just as a consequence of sexual desire, but as itself a kind of rape. Love, jealousy and murder are alike the products of desire, and alike disgusting. And so we are brought full circle, back to the unacceptable implications and statements of the earlier pages. What torments Pozdnyshev after the murder, after the 'moral change' comes over him, is not just the murder, but his whole sex-oriented life, a life whose values and course (except for the murder) he and Tolstoy insist on offering as representative of that of ninety-nine per cent of married couples of the upper classes. Nowhere does Tolstoy insist on Pozdnyshev's abnormality in this respect (his feverish manner is not relevant to this), nowhere does he qualify his absurd over-simplifications, expose the inconsistencies of his argument, or appear to notice the extraordinary egotism which makes of his wife little more than an instrument for his own damnation or salvation. What we see of his wife makes us sympathise wholeheartedly with her, even down to her attraction to Trukhachevsky. But it is symptomatic of Tolstoy's lack of artistic balance throughout, even in the later stages where the narrative is otherwise handled with undeniable mastery, that he himself withholds all sympathy, never ever giving her the tangible physical presence, the vibrant life of the body, that he still allows the objects of temptation in *The Devil* and *Father Sergius*, and making her die in a state of delirious hatred, while her converted and repentant husband emerges as a new man, saved in the sight of God.

Though they too deal with conversion, the accession of illuminating insight as to the true meaning of life and death, the stories of Ivan Ilyich and of the dealer Brekhunov in *Master and Man* are altogether more convincing than is that of Pozdnyshev. Together, they represent the peak of Tolstoy's achievement in this group of stories and novels: more incisive and much more carefully made than the longer but uneven *Resurrection*, only the very different *Hadji Murat* can be put alongside them in an assessment of his work after *Anna Karenina*.

That this is so is doubtless due in part to the fact that sexual temptation is no longer at the centre of the two narratives. It is the emptiness of the whole spectrum of values by which Ivan

Ilyich and Brekhunov live and measure their success that Tolstoy illuminates. But it is at least as important for the regaining of authorial balance that these two stories should both be told in the third person, as that they should not centre on an exclusively sexual corruption. Again in Tolstoy we can see, as so often in Lawrence, how the demands of that narrative mode serve to impose a necessary discipline on the prophet and teacher. It is not that Tolstoy ever gives up being didactic in either story, but that the 'lesson' involved is in each case seen as growing out of a thoroughly credible, particularised context, a real and recognisable world in which Brekhunov and Ivan Ilyich move towards their individual destinies.

It is this sense of particularisation, both of character and context, that separates *Master and Man* from those shorter parabolic stories to which it otherwise bears some resemblance. Both Brekhunov and Nikita, the peasant he employs, are presented as wholly plausible, living figures whose representative significance is secondary to their existence as individual characters. We are thus drawn, as readers, into a much greater involvement with their fates, both moral and physical, than in the simple parables where men tend to be types rather than individuals.

The dealer and innkeeper Brekhunov is a man of considerable complacency and energy, who lives entirely for the business he has built up, and the yet bigger business he is going to build. Although we see him at the outset in the role of a Church elder, it is clear that his religion is simply a matter of propriety, and that material gain is the real mainspring of his existence. So enthusiastic and unquestioning is he in his pursuit of such gain, and so thoroughly pleased with himself at what he has achieved, that there is an almost endearing quality about his particular brand of materialism. For all his willingness to exploit the peasant Nikita, and indeed anyone else with whom he has dealings, he is by no means offered as a thoroughly corrupt man. Rather, he appears as an essentially good-hearted man whose energies have been consistently misapplied. When, at the close, his values have changed drastically, there is not felt to have been any essential change in his nature—he boasts to himself of his achievement at keeping Nikita from freezing with the same kind of relish that he might have congratulated himself earlier on making a good deal (his name is derived from *brekhun*, which has derogatory associations of boasting or bragging). The consistency is important to our acceptance of Brekhunov's conversion as something wholly plausible, an event the seeds of which are already within him.

Nikita is a slightly less satisfactory figure than Brekhunov in that he has about him something of the Tolstoyan stereotype of the good peasant—good natured, submissive, God-fearing and ready to welcome death in the same way as does Natalya Savishna in *Childhood* or Platon Karatayev in *War and Peace*. But he too is real, redeemed from the stereotype by his occasional lapses into drunken violence, a vice which has put him into Brekhunov's grasping but not ill-intentioned hands.

It is these two who set out on the momentous journey through the snowstorm to forestall other dealers in buying a grove of standing timber at what Brekhunov considers will be a bargain price. It is an urgent occasion for him, a considerable potential increase in his fortune, and he is unwilling even to consider the worsening weather as a hindrance. For Nikita the journey is simply another duty laid upon him, an order he obeys willingly enough, though he has little choice but to obey. They are immediately projected into a world almost completely devoid of landmarks, a desolate, snow-covered landscape, which has an obviously symbolic significance in a story of a man spiritually lost in a corrupt world, but whose primary significance is certainly its literal one: it has the same bleak, immediate reality as does the landscape in *The Snow-Storm*, written nearly forty years earlier.

As they wander in this wilderness it is Brekhunov, driven by greed to take the shorter, less well-marked route, whom we see causing them to lose their way, and Nikita whom we see finding it again. The anticipation of his profit makes Brekhunov refuse the hospitality of the old farmer, in whose house they rest after losing their way for the second time. (We see in the latter's family an image of the old agrarian Russia struggling against the new order that Brekhunov and his kind bring with them.) When they get lost for the third and final time, Brekhunov comforts himself, as he settles down to spend the night in the blizzard, with the thought of his money:

'He did not feel like sleeping. He lay and thought: thought only about the one thing that constituted the sole aim, meaning, pleasure and pride of his life—about how much money he had made, and how much he still could make; about how much other people he knew had made and possessed, and how those others had made and were making money, and how he, like them, might still make a lot of money.' (Chapter 6)

The details of the deal he is about to make, of how much he has already improved the property his father left him, and of how he may in time become a millionaire, comfort him for a little while, but such consolations are insidiously undermined by the terrible, unavoidable reality of the storm. Against this background, reduced to being simply a man, his wealth worthless, isolated from society and all he has lived for, Brekhunov's unquestioning confidence in the validity of his ambitions slowly seeps away: 'However much he tried to think about his accounts, his business, and about his reputation and his dignity and wealth, fear took hold of him more and more, and above all his thoughts, and mixed in with all his other thoughts, stood out the thought of why he had not spent the night at Grishkino.' (Chapter 6)

Brekhunov's fear of death grows stronger as the interminable night wears on; it is something against which he has absolutely no defence, unlike Nikita, who is, in the most matter of fact way, ready to accept whatever God may decide is best. Brekhunov finds himself quite alone in the darkness; Nikita does not. It is this that drives Brekhunov to his ignoble and pathetic attempt to escape on the horse, abandoning Nikita whom, he reasons, has nothing much to live for anyway. It is with this attempted escape that the symbolic element in the story intensifies: abandoning his fellow man to his death, the dealer rides in selfishly aimless circles around the snowy wilderness. He has no clear idea of where he is going, but is simply carried along. Twice he believes he sees a village before him, but in each case the object which he thinks is his salvation turns out on closer inspection to be nothing but wormwood. Finally the horse brings him back to Nikita and the sledge in a very different frame of mind.

This brief symbolic passage is crucial to the story as a whole, and Tolstoy's deployment of it is extraordinarily sure. It has a clarity of underlying meaning about it that makes it seem reasonable to call it an allegory in little of Brekhunov's whole life—a life guided by no sure principle, which takes him away from his fellow men, going round in circles in pursuit of ambitions which when they are realised turn out to be wormwood, but a life which in the end is to regain its proper course in returning to love for mankind. But for all its allegorical clarity, the episode never loses for a moment its urgent, literal reality: it is never felt to be an obtrusive digression into a mode at variance with the rest of the story. The wormwood which so frightens Brekhunov when he sees what it is, is real wormwood, just as the storm, the horse and the sledge are all real. As often in *Anna Karenina*, symbolic and realistic narrative are perfectly balanced, reinforcing rather than clashing with each other, so that the change in Brekhunov's attitude when he returns to the sledge is an altogether credible one, rooted in the particular experience and yet given a wider resonance through Tolstoy's allegory.

The change is all the more credible in that Brekhunov's sudden access of love, of a wholly new system of values, is yet seen, as has already been suggested, as wholly in character. It is the determined man of business who decides to save Nikita from freezing to death: 'Vasily Andreyich stood silent and motionless for half a minute, then suddenly, with the same resolution with which he used to strike hands when making a good purchase, he took one step back and tucking up the sleeves of his fur coat began raking the snow off Nikita and out of the sledge with both hands.' (Chapter 9)

As Brekhunov lies on top of Nikita warming him, his pleasure at what he is doing increases, as his fear of death diminishes. In the end, as he dies, there is no fear of death. In his half-conscious condition, sometimes dreaming, sometimes awake, death seems itself joyful, a mingling of identity with Nikita, and a freedom from his own private body and identity. Again Tolstoy's realism is crucial here in helping us accept what might otherwise seem simple Tolstoyan propaganda. Brekhunov's sensations as he dies are so particularised as to belong only to him, and as such the most sceptical reader can accept them as moving and plausible: we can believe in Brekhunov without having to believe in any generalised ethical or religious system, whether a conventional Christian immortality, or Tolstoy's rationalised version in which man merges into the rest of humanity, the collective divine consciousness, past, present and future, putting off his physical body.

Here, as in *The Death of Ivan Ilyich*, Tolstoy's treatment of experience is far removed from the simplistic, somewhat bludgeoning mode of much of the later non-fiction, or of the worst parts of *The Kreutzer Sonata*. In the latter, Donald Davie has rightly argued, Tolstoy 'cheated the most valuable trait in himself, his plastic apprehension of irrationality and complexity'.[7] In the description of Brekhunov's slow, joyful death he exploits that trait to the full, making his 'conversion' something we can accept on the level of immediate, lived experience, complex, irrational, particularised, and therefore movingly convincing.

The Death of Ivan Ilyich is very close in some respects to *Master and Man*: it too posits the case of a man who has lived his life wrongly, according to trivial values, and who therefore cannot face death without fear. There, too, the late discovery of love for those around him helps him to accept death, which in the end presents itself, after the most terrible physical and spiritual suffering, as a passage to something joyful. It differs most obviously from *Master and Man* in the remorselessness with which Tolstoy presents the emptiness, the terrible pointlessness, of Ivan Ilyich's life, and the long drawn out process of his death. Until his death, Brekhunov's was a life without real values, but one lived with some kind of gusto. Ivan Ilyich's life has none of this: it is an ordinary life, which, we are made uncomfortably aware, is in its essential loneliness, its reliance on values and ambitions that in the larger view are seen to be trivial in the extreme, close to that of a modern Everyman. This is the force of the famous statement with which Tolstoy opens the second chapter: 'The story of Ivan Ilyich's life was most simple and most ordinary and most terrible', a statement which subsequent chapters persuade us to be only too close to the truth.

The desolate landscape, the snow and wormwood of *Master and Man* are used to body forth the emptiness of Brekhunov's values and life, but in *The Death of Ivan Ilyich* we are shown that emptiness more directly as we follow the course of the hero's career. What makes the ambitions, the minor successes and failures, the distractions, the sources of frustration or satisfaction, all seem so trivial in Ivan Ilyich's case is that Tolstoy begins his story from the point of his death, and only then returns to explain the life that had preceded it. The story in fact begins and ends with that death (the last word is 'died'), and the questions that this perspective inevitably raises are kept before our minds throughout. We are made to ask about Ivan Ilyich, as we rarely do about our own lives, the question which so tormented Tolstoy —what is the point, what is it all for, if it is only to end in death, this death we have already seen in the coffin-lid standing against the wall in the first pages of Ivan Ilyich's life story? That coffin-lid makes a terrible mockery of all that pleases or frustrates Ivan Ilyich; his satisfactions in life, his tastefully furnished house, his efficiency at his job, his regular games of bridge, cannot survive the kind of probing that the coffin-lid forces us to give them, not because they are entirely worthless, but because they are never seen by him in their proper perspective—the perspective of the coffin-lid, of inevitable death. For Ivan Ilyich, as for his whole circle, death is something that only happens to other people, never to oneself, as Tolstoy intimates with such absolute rightness in the pathetic yet poignant and natural reflections of Ivan Ilyich:

> 'The example of a syllogism he had learnt from Kiezewetter's Logic: "Caius is a man, men are mortal, therefore Caius is mortal", had always seemed correct only in relation to Caius, but in no sense to himself. That was Caius—man, man in the abstract, and that was perfectly correct; but he was not Caius, not man in the abstract, but a creature quite, quite separate from all others. He had been Vanya, with Mamma, with Papa, with Mitya and Volodya, with the toys, with a coachman, with a nurse, then with Katenka, and with all the joys, griefs, delights of childhood, youth and youthfulness. What was the smell of that striped leather ball Vanya had liked so much to Caius? Did Caius kiss his mother's hand like that, and did the silk of the folds of her dress rustle like that for Caius? Had he rioted like that over the pastry at school? Had Caius been in love like that? Could Caius preside at a session like that?
>
> "Caius really was mortal, and it was correct for him to die, but for me, Vanya, Ivan Ilyich, with all my feelings, thoughts—for me it's a different matter. It can't be that I ought to die. That would be quite horrible."
>
> Such was his feeling.' (Chapter 6)

The old Tolstoyan feeling for the life of the body, the love that enables him to apprehend the intimate and innocent details of the child's consciousness as it survives in the man, comes through here, even in the unnatural, unlovable Ivan Ilyich. But it comes through only to be shown as something false, a delusion we must give up if we are to understand things rightly. Ivan Ilyich's friends, who have no such understanding, respond to his death, significantly enough, with the perfectly natural if selfish feeling of complacent pleasure that 'it is he who is dead, not I'.

Those colleagues who call to fulfil the demands of propriety before the funeral have no real sense that what has happened to one of them must happen to all. It is simply an occasion for possible promotion, an interruption to their evening games of bridge, an unnecessarily depressing event that even has a kind of tastelessness about it on Ivan Ilyich's part. Only for a brief moment does the relevance of this death to his own life strike Ivan Ilyich's closest colleague, Peter Ivanovich, as he sits giving hypocritical comfort to the hypocritical grief of Ivan Ilyich's widow. Otherwise it is an air of unreality that pervades the opening chapter: the grief itself is unreal, as is the empty pomposity of the funeral arrangements, while the attempts at dignified grief and solicitude between Peter Ivanovich and Ivan Ilyich's widow are bizarrely undermined by the squeaking pouffe on which the former sits, and by the carved table on which the latter catches her black shawl. For all those concerned, death is something unreal, as it had been at first to Ivan Ilyich.

The fact that he has placed the latter's life so firmly in the perspective of death from the very outset has a considerable bearing on the way in which Tolstoy is able to tell the story of that life. For it means that there is no need to emphasise the terrible emptiness of it, the mundanity of the values by which it is lived. The pleasant, moderately gifted young man who drifts rather casually into a marriage to which he is not wholly committed, and who achieves a degree of success in his career in the law, is presented to us with relatively little comment. The keynote of *vanitas vanitatis* has already been established, and Tolstoy can gain his effect much more tellingly simply by showing than by explicit commentary. Such explicitness, the explicitness of the didactic prose of this period, would almost certainly have been disastrous, not only because of Tolstoy's tendency to become reductive as soon as he leaves the living world of his fiction, but also because it would have tended to make of Ivan Ilyich merely a target, a straw man to be hammered by the Tolstoyan moralist until he was finally converted and forgiven. That we have no sense of this happening, no sense of the work as clumsily didactic, is largely due to the fact that Tolstoy is content to leave his judgements as indirect, ironic ones, just as his whole story is constructed around the ironic discrepancy between Ivan Ilyich's own view of his life, and the reality.

It is important, too, that there should be no extremes in Ivan Ilyich's life, that he should be not simply credible, but ordinary —ordinary in his career, his marriage, his house, his pleasures, and that it should be this ordinary man, complacently settled in his way of life, that we see suddenly confronted by the one thing that is certain and yet not ordinary—death. From the time when the small knock received in decorating his house (making it as *comme il faut* and thus as ordinary as possible) develops into what would now presumably be diagnosed as cancer, Ivan Ilyich is no longer ordinary. Brought face to face with the reality of death, he is, like Brekhunov, suddenly alone, with nothing to fall back on but his own untapped spiritual resources, living 'all alone on the brink of death, with not a single person who understood or pitied him'.

For most of the second half of the story, Ivan Ilyich tries to come to terms with this terrible abyss into which he has suddenly been forced to look, staring into it and yet unable to accept that it exists. The old, accustomed habits, the 'satisfactory' way of life that had once screened the thought of death from him so effectively, no longer have that power. Whatever he is doing, whatever he tries to concentrate on, *It*, the ultimate and undeniable, breaks in to remind him of its existence. The horror that he feels in the face of that terrible *It* is reminiscent of that described in *The Memoirs of a Madman*, and there is no question but that an autobiographical immediacy comes through in Tolstoy's immensely moving descriptions of these moments of fear. For Ivan Ilyich as for Tolstoy the most terrible thing about death is its absolute reality, the fact that, knowing it to be there, waiting, one can yet do nothing whatever about it. One of the underlying reasons for Tolstoy's preoccupation with death, his wish to conquer it, as he tries to do in *A Confession* and these stories, may well have been that, like sexual passion, or the effects of music, but infinitely more so, it was something beyond his control, a fundamental threat not only to his need for a meaning, a purpose in life, but also to that irrational, Luciferian egoism that lay deep within him. Whatever his motivation, he more than any other writer, tries to take possession of death in his work by describing the process of dying from the inside. He was, his son Ilya tells us, 'always extraordinarily curious and attentive about the sensations of the dying, and, whenever he could, picked up the smallest details about their experiences'.[8] The deaths of Andrey and of Nikolay Levin, and Anna's suicide, are the preludes to the three detailed descriptions of the sensations of a dying man taken right up to and even beyond the very point of death that we have in *Master and Man*, *The Death of Ivan Ilyich* and *Hadji Murat*. Of the three, it is Ivan Ilyich's death which is described in the most detail, through the developing illness, and finally through a death agony that lasts for three days.

Before he can die, Ivan Ilyich has to spend weeks looking into the terrible abyss, something he cannot do with any spiritual calm as long as he clings to the belief that his life up to this point has been lived as it should have been. Death presents itself as incomprehensible, pointless, absurd, his sufferings an arbitrary and hideously unfair imposition on a man who has lived his life correctly, even well. Although the idea occurs to him that his adult life has in reality been 'trivial and often nasty', and that the only real happiness he has experienced lies in his childhood, although he feels that there is something wrong somewhere in his life, yet he cannot bring himself to believe that that life has been wasted, that it is all as senseless and horrible as impending death now makes it seem.

As long as this struggle goes on—the struggle which in his dream takes the form of being thrust resisting into a black sack with a light at the end—his physical and spiritual sufferings continue. Tolstoy relates the terrible physical pain to the spiritual, not in the crude sense that if Ivan Ilyich had lived a better life he would not have had his illness, but in the sense that an acceptance of death would have made his pain easier to bear, as in the end it does. As long as he cannot accept death simply and easily, as the servant Gerasim can, he cannot fall into that black sack of death. Only when, in the last few hours of his life, he comes to accept that his past life was 'all not the right thing' does he grow spiritually quiet. This is the crucial moment, the moment, we might say, of conversion, when he falls through into the black sack. As he does so, still screaming in his physical agony, his waving arm falls on the head of his son: looking at him, and at his unloved wife, he suddenly feels sorrow not for himself, but for them, and death appears for the first time as something desirable. Like Brekhunov, he dies with a sense of love for others within him, and like Brekhunov, this makes death joyful, so much so that, the fear having departed, death itself hardly seems to exist. Ivan Ilyich has, in the words of *What I Believe*, transferred his transient and trivial personal life into 'the life of the whole of humanity', a transference which is the Tolstoyan equivalent for immortality, 'the common life' of all mankind.

For most readers the defeat of death in these closing pages is not likely to be an altogether convincing one. Impressive though these pages are, the Tolstoyan resolution becomes less convincing the more we look at it. The metaphor of the black sack with the light at the bottom—admittedly a metaphor of dream and therefore not subject to logic—the statement that 'in place of death there was light', the juxtaposition of external observation of Ivan Ilyich's death agonies with his internal moment of revelation, all seem to be doing more than they really are. They chime, it is true, with Tolstoy's philosophy of death as expressed elsewhere, but here, the more we read them, the more they seem immensely skilful rhetorical devices for circumventing death, rather than a real explanation, a real acceptance. *It* is still there undefeated and unexplained at the end, despite all Tolstoy's efforts.

What is undeniably impressive about *The Death of Ivan Ilyich* is the incisive, ruthless presentation of that inexplicable *It*, and of man's helplessness in the face of it. Whatever our feelings about the ending, there can be no question of evasiveness on Tolstoy's part in what has gone before. Few works of art impinge so directly or so disturbingly on the lives of everyone who comes into contact with them as does this one, cutting down so mercilessly the screens of habit, ambition and social conformity behind which most of us live for most of the time. No intelligent reader can turn away from it without being driven to some reassessment of the values by which he lives his life, and that, for Tolstoy, would perhaps have been enough.

8

Resurrection

Tolstoy's last long novel was written in a certain amount of haste in order to raise money for the Dukhobors, a religious sect with principles not unlike his own who were being persecuted in Russia and who had, partly as a result of pressures exerted by Tolstoy and his followers, been allowed to leave the country and settle on large tracts of land which the Canadian government had made available to them. He was working on *Hadji Murat*, *Father Sergius* and *Resurrection* at the time when the money for the Dukhobors became necessary in 1898, and it seems likely that of the three he chose to finish *Resurrection* because he was least fond of it, and most willing to see it go to the press in a hastily finished, unsatisfactory state. He felt at the time that it was 'all untrue, invented, weak', and most critics have agreed with his assessment of it, seeing it as an old man's novel, a novel of hardened, dead opinions, with no real inwardness with its characters, and with a Gospel resolution foisted on it rather crudely at the end. Much of this criticism is justified, but it has become rather too easy and too conventional to dismiss *Resurrection* along these lines, seeing its only virtues as those of a kind of minor *War and Peace*, as Mirsky does.[1] For at the same time as one is aware of the flaws in it, one is aware too of a more positively creative pressure than such criticism suggests. That pressure is largely derived from the strength of an enormous, angry compassion for the oppressed, the anger and compassion of a man who suffers acutely as he sees around him a terrible betrayal of his vision of what man could and should be. It is the anger of the idealist, the seeker after perfection and truth whom we saw in *Childhood, Boyhood and Youth* and *A Landlord's Morning*, the young follower of Rousseau who dreamt so ardently of a world of love and goodness, truth and happiness, which he would somehow discover for himself.

In this sense John Bayley, who treats the novel much more sympathetically than most, is right to draw attention to its unworldliness.[2] It turns back for its motivation to that earlier, more innocent world, even taking the name of its central figure,

Dmitri Nekhlyudov, from the early novels. Indeed, it may be said to turn back even further, right back to the five-year-old boy who had been told by his brother Nikolay of a green stick, which he had buried in the grounds of Yasnaya Polyana, and on which he had written the secret of universal happiness. The green stick always provided Tolstoy with an emblem of his own search for such a formula, such a truth, and he was buried, at his request, in the place where the stick had been hidden.

But if we talk of the innocence of *Resurrection* it must be guardedly, for it is an innocence of a different kind from that of the young Tolstoy or the young Nekhyludov, one permeated less by hope than by anger. Between these two innocent worlds lies that of the non-innocent Tolstoy, the great realist whose realism is not a matter of literary technique only, but of worldliness, the worldliness that accepts imperfections in both institutions and individuals as inevitable, and builds its wisdom on the basis of such an acceptance, pushing the naïve Pierre out of his unworldly innocence into the real world of the Kuragins and the Rostovs, or Levin into the world of Kitty and Stiva—and Anna. Never abandoning their moral aspirations, they are brought to a fruitful compromise with the non-ideal, the kind of compromise the older Tolstoy was no longer willing to allow.

In the shorter novels that were discussed in the last chapter, the world is still very much a real one, but the old Tolstoy has come to reject it instead of accepting it with its blemishes. Like those works, *Resurrection* is very much a story of conversion, but it differs from them in that it posits much more clearly than they a perfectible world, a world which can and must be cured of that terrible corruption, that betrayal of itself, which strikes Tolstoy with an almost physical suffering. This is one of the reasons he goes back to the hero of *A Landlord's Morning*, that earlier attempt at a didactic novel that was never completed—unless now—and even gives Nekhlyudov another chance to fulfil his duties towards the peasants by handing over his land to them.

The Nekhlyudov of *Resurrection*, then, is not innocent as his predecessor was: the death of that early innocence is perhaps symbolised by the death, reported in the novel, of Nikolay Irtenyev, the central figure of *Childhood, Boyhood and Youth*. This older Nekhlyudov has known, and in the novel is brought to know still more clearly, the corruption of the world in which he lives. But he and Tolstoy are fiercely and determinedly innocent in their refusal to accept that world as it is, in their desire to change both it and themselves radically, and in the clear, black/white vision of things that underlies that desire. One of the irreconcilable tensions that weakens *Resurrection* is that between the extreme worldly wisdom that is involved in the observation of how things are, in the courts, in the prisons, in the government system as a whole, and the unworldliness that sees all this as subject not simply to improvement, but to a wholesale change which will remove the corrupt system completely and usher in the age of the green stick.

The detailed, fiercely ironic observation of that corrupt system is one of the great strengths of *Resurrection*. Though Tolstoy builds his novel very much around the person of Nekhlyudov, the details of the external world in which he moves—a world of courts and prisons, lawyers and jailers—exist separately from him, are much more real in their own terms, than tends to be the case in the earlier novels. This separateness makes for a certain weakness in the presentation of Nekhlyudov's character, in so far as it means we are less deeply involved in his experience than in that of Tolstoy's other aristocratic seekers. Though he is his spokesman, Nekhlyudov's experience is no longer Tolstoy's own in quite the way that that of Pierre, Andrey or Levin was. In *The Death of Ivan Ilyich* or *Master and Man* Tolstoy had already moved out of his own familiar, patrician world, the world to which he belonged by both birth and instinct, into a world he could not possess through his heroes. The city world of the professional man Ivan Ilyich, which is quite different from the stylishly corrupt city world of Prince Oblonsky, to which he was still unwillingly attracted, was quite alien to Tolstoy, the product of forces he hated deeply. It was a world he had to view from the outside, as we feel Nekhlyudov himself views it; for all his involvement in his cause, he does not seem to be engaged in that world as Levin and Pierre are engaged in theirs. Thus we have the aristocrat's contempt for the merchant classes who, his cabby tells Nekhlyudov, are even worse landlords than were the old gentry (his old master's land has been bought by a French wig-maker turned farmer), and for the liberal lawyers and others who, despite their apparent unity of purpose, are separated from Nekhlyudov by a much greater gulf than that which separates him from the older society groupings, the Petersburg *grandes dames* and the well-born military men (the cruel military men who become prison officials are not on the whole of good birth, we notice).

The result is that there is relatively little in the way of 'making it strange' in *Resurrection*, because it was all strange to Tolstoy, not merely in the sense that he had no direct experience, as Dostoyevsky did, of being in prison, but that he had no real personal experience of the classes who were directly connected with the prisons, in whatever capacity—Maslova, Simonson and the various revolutionaries are as far removed from him as are the ordinary criminals or the 'monumentally stupid' assistant Public Prosecutor. When he is in Petersburg or dealing with his peasants, Nekhlyudov seems more at home than he does in the prisoners' company, and so does Tolstoy. He built up his picture of the whole, terrible system in which 'vicious men undertook to reform other vicious men' by careful observation, by painstaking research, rather than from the knowledge of his own class, indeed his own life, on which he had based *War and Peace* and *Anna Karenina*. This is, perhaps, why there is more simple compassion to be felt in *Resurrection* than in the two earlier novels—one feels greater pity for the suffering one has not experienced and cannot experience for oneself, than for that which is already to some extent known. Certainly it is this feeling of compassionate anger with which Tolstoy, to use his own term from *What is Art?*, most succeeds in 'infecting' the reader, rather than with an interest in Nekhlyudov's somewhat solipsistic search for a cleansing of his own soul.

There are two basic techniques employed in the novel for thus 'infecting' the reader: simple factual description of Maslova's career, of the conditions in prison, of the workings of the legal system and so forth, and a more familiar Tolstoyan irony at the expense of those who operate the system, an irony sometimes clumsy (as in the description of the service in the prison), often felicitous, but always at bottom deeply and movingly angry. In the long description of the trial in Part I both strategies are employed, giving a curiously moving picture of both the seriousness of Maslova's predicament, and the almost comically corrupt system which is the instrument of her persecution. Thus, for example, as soon as the bewildered and frightened Maslova has finished giving her evidence in a way that wins our sympathy for the terrible position in which she finds herself, there is an apparently weighty deliberation between two of the three judges:

> 'A silence fell.
> "You have nothing more to say?"
> "I have said everything" she uttered with a sigh, and sat down.
> Following this, the president wrote something on a paper and, having heard a communication made to him in a whisper by the member on his left, he announced an adjournment of ten minutes, rose hurriedly and left the court-room. The conference between the president and the member on his left, a tall bearded man with large, kind eyes, was over the fact that this member's stomach was slightly upset and he wanted to massage himself and take some drops.' (I.11)

This kind of ironic dislocation, the cutting away of the false dignity of those who sit in judgement, is typical of this first part. It is this same president who to the jury, the court-room audience, and to anybody who has not the privileged eye of the omniscient author through which to see, seems a kind, dignified, impressive man, but whom we know is hoping to finish the case early because he has an appointment with a pretty Swiss governess. It is he, too, whom we have seen exercising with a pair of dumb-bells in his chambers before the case begins, an episode instantly destructive of any dignity he may seem to assume later. His kindly companion with the upset stomach has already been destroyed with the same muted but merciless irony by making him count the number of steps it takes him to reach his seat from the door of his room; if it is divisible by three, he decides, a new treatment he has begun will cure his catarrh. He manages to get in an extra short step to make the formula work. The third member of the triumvirate is similarly disposed of, his habitual gloom having been deepened that morning by his wife's threat that she would provide no dinner for him that evening unless he gave her more money.

The power of this irony lies in the fact that it is altogether plausible—so much so, in fact, that it comes to seem not Tolstoy's own, but an irony inherent in the whole business of trials, judges, accusers and accused. The three judges are not hopelessly, unbelievably corrupt: they are simply human, with human weaknesses that Tolstoy introduces at precisely the moment when they are presenting themselves to the public eye as above such weaknesses, and judging them in others. This is important, in that from it follows the implicit condemnation not just of the three men who mishandle Maslova's trial, but of all judges. Maslova's, we are to believe, is a fairly typical trial, showing us failings inevitable in the system; and Nekhlyudov is to insist later, as he argues with his brother-in-law Rogozhinsky, that 'over half the people sentenced by the courts are innocent', presumably because their judges were equally fallible, rather than positively vicious.

While the general point that Tolstoy makes about judges is a fair one, one is left uneasy about the fairness of this implication that Maslova's trial is normal, that the mistake, a gross and obvious mistake, is a typical one. John Bayley makes an interesting reference back to Stiva Oblonsky, whom one is reminded of to some extent (the governess being a common denominator) by the presiding judge in Maslova's case. Oblonsky, Tolstoy tells us, was a particularly good judge because of 'his complete indifference to the matter he was engaged on, in consequence of which he was never carried away by enthusiasm and never made mistakes'. What would have happened, Professor Bayley asks, 'if Stiva had been confronted with Maslova's case? Tolstoy does not broach the possibility, but he dare not introduce anyone like Stiva among the various officials before whom the case comes.'[3] It is a fair point: Tolstoy is so bent on showing the whole system as corrupt that he does not want to accept the possibility of the worldly man also being fair, just, and capable enough to make the fallible system work. Instead of inviting us to see Maslova's case as an exceptional miscarriage of justice (and it must surely have been so even in late Tsarist Russia), he presents it as a typical injustice, the inevitable and common product of the terrible system. In this world of clear black and white, he has no inclination to explore the varying shades of grey.

Despite this, the trial and prison scenes do convey forcefully, and in the end convincingly, the impression that the system is indeed something terrible, that the hopeless path on which the president's culpable mistake has set Maslova can have, as far as the system is concerned, no fair or equitable end to it. The crowded, squalid cell to which she returns from her trial, with the women who fight over vodka, and the small children who

are forced to accompany their mothers because they have nowhere else to go, is only the first of many such pictures by Tolstoy that have an undeniable, hopeless kind of reality about
them.

From now on this is to be Maslova's world, and to a large extent Nekhlyudov's also. It is impossible to convey Tolstoy's
presentation of that world adequately through quotation: the
descriptions of Maslova's cell, of the corridors through which
she and later Nekhlyudov walk, the men in the yard, the inter-
views in the waiting room, the transit convoy which moves off
in such scorching heat that several of those on it die of sun-
stroke, all have a cumulative effect which cannot be represented
by selection. Tolstoy's method in nearly all these cases is to withdraw himself rather uncharacteristically from the scene he is
describing, offering his sombre account in the lowest of keys, as
if to emphasise that the horror of what he is describing speaks for
itself and needs no rhetorical embellishment. It is a most effective method, his detachment, his refusal to imprint his own
personality on the scenes in some way or other as he normally
does, making them seem all the more alien to all humanity, and
at the same time all the more real. They culminate in such
passages as this, in one of Nekhlyudov's last visits to the prisoners during their transit to Siberia:

'The foul air of the political prisoners' quarters seemed fresh
compared with the stinking, sultry air here. The smoking lamp
seemed as if it was seen through a mist, and it was difficult to
breathe. In order to get through the corridor without stepping or
tripping on one of the prisoners, one had to look out for an empty
space beforehand, and having put one foot down, to look out for
a space for the following step. Three men who evidently had not
found room even in the corridor had lain themselves down in the
hallway under the stinking, leaking latrine tub. One of them was
a weak-minded old man whom Nekhlyudov had often seen on
the march. Another was a boy of about ten: he lay between the
two convicts with his hand under his cheek, and slept with his
head on the leg of one of them.

When he got out of the gate Nekhlyudov stopped and, expand-
ing his chest to the full capacity of his lungs, breathed long and
deeply of the frosty air.' (III.18)

Such images as this scarcely need the support of any rational argument against the system which can cause them: the boy with his head in the seeping ordure, or the man known to have killed and eaten another prisoner, whom Nekhlyudov has walked past only a little before, are themselves the most powerful of all arguments. But Tolstoy is too much of a rationalist to leave it at that, and this particular visit leads Nekhlyudov to his fullest meditation on the subject of the legal system, wondering whether it is he that is mad, or those who are responsible for bringing about such conditions. His perplexity is clearly not Tolstoy's, for he proceeds to put into Nekhlyudov's mouth a wholesale condemnation of the system, in which 'It was as if all these institutions had been devised for the express purpose of producing the utmost concentration of depravity and vice, such as could not be achieved under any other conditions, in order that this concentration of vice and depravity could then be spread as widely as possible throughout the population.' (III.19) The prison authorities, and society in general, seem to him to be succeeding in finding an answer to the problem of how to corrupt simple, decent men as quickly and completely as possible, so that they too can reach that peak of inhumanity that is represented by the prisoners who entice their companions to escape with them so that they can kill and eat them (Solzhenitsyn refers to a similar type of cannibalism in modern Russia in *The Gulag Archipelago*).[4]

The argument that prisons do not reform but degrade and dehumanise is of course one of the commonest and most powerful arguments against them. Tolstoy, however, goes much further than this in arguing that the prisons are not simply inefficient in this sense—doing the opposite of what they purport to do—but that they corrupt all those whose responsibility it is to operate the system, and, ultimately, the whole of the society that sanctions them. For him, the very principle of punishment, and indeed of any legal system based on coercion, is evil, making criminals out of judges, lawyers and jailers, as well as out of the people, many innocent in a moral if not a technical sense, whom they send to prison. For this reason there is no question of a liberal reform of the prison system, of 'model prisons with electric bells': such a perfected system of violence is, if anything, still more offensive than the primitive Russian one, and there is no evidence that it would be any more efficient. So Tolstoy leads Nekhlyudov up to the point in the final chapter where, reading the Gospels in the hope of finding some answer to the problem, he turns (implausibly 'at random') to Christ's answer of forgiveness in the parable of the unforgiving servant, and thence to the Sermon on the Mount and an outline of Tolstoyan Christianity, the logical conclusion of which is the abolition of the whole system of legal punishment. Society is to be held together, as in practice he believes it already is, not by laws but by human pity and love.

Most readers have probably shared Chekhov's dissatisfaction with the solutions arrived at in this final chapter, his sense that there is something arbitrary in the way they are offered. Certainly it is true that as a practical answer they seem implausible; but what is more important from a critical point of view is that they don't grow with any real inevitability out of what has gone before. If they did, we might, while still having reservations about the theory, see them as at least defensible solutions which Nekhlyudov was likely to have arrived at. Instead, they are only too obviously Tolstoy's preconceived solutions, and not Nekhlyudov's, and, defensible or not, they cannot easily be read in any other way than as a wholesale imposition from outside, a crudely didactic attempt to put a thumb in the balance and provide a clinching ending to the novel.

If the theoretical conclusions of the last chapter are unconvincing, the conclusions based on the practical observation that has gone before are not. In the novel's own terms, Tolstoy does succeed in making his point that the system itself is brutal and inhuman, and that the criminality involved in its administration is as great as, if not greater than, the criminality of those who are punished by it. Extreme though it may seem, the contention that the ultimate degradation, the cannibalism in the Siberian marshes, is the responsibility of the men who make the arbitrary decisions in the ministries of Petersburg is proved on the pulse.

The connection is made convincing most of all by the series of angrily satirical portraits of government officials at every level, from the stupid and conceited assistant Public Prosecutor at Maslova's trial, to the Procurator of the Holy Synod, Toporov, with all of whom the moral responsibility of what happens in Siberia rests. The framework of *Resurrection* consists of a whole series of such portraits linked together by Nekhlyudov's attempts to have the decision in Maslova's case altered, but it is his visit to Petersburg on this quest that gives Tolstoy the opportunity for the most concentrated group of them, and enables him to present a fairly comprehensive picture of the higher echelons of the government system. Tolstoy was never a Petersburg man, and now virtually the whole of the Petersburg society world emerges as something corrupt and corrupting. Even Nekhlyudov's good natured aunt who, 'bursting with health and energy', has much of the attractive vitality found so often in Tolstoy's earlier work, has her standing undercut by her marriage to a time-serving minister, her evangelical piety, and her inability, notwithstanding the latter, to understand her nephew's concern for the injustices done to Maslova and others. Only one person in Petersburg is really given the old Tolstoyan sympathy of the body, and with it his approval, and this is the minor figure of the aide-de-camp Bogatyrev, whose mixture of straightforward honesty, strength, health and energy makes him seem curiously out of place both in Petersburg and in the pages of *Resurrection*, so completely does he remind us of some minor character from *War and Peace*, *Anna Karenina* or any of the earlier tales of army life.

Bogatyrev (whose name is derived from *bogatyr*, a gallant, legendary hero) is a nostalgic portrait, his *samodovolnost'* bearing witness to the respect and sympathy the old Tolstoy still retained for the best kind of military man; but his main function is to act as a foil to such men as Toporov, a vicious and scarcely disguised version of Pobedonostsev, the reactionary head of the Holy Synod with whom Tolstoy had often clashed before, and who was later to be instrumental in bringing about his excommunication. In contrast to the pleasant feeling inspired by the 'unconsciously fresh and healthy' Bogatyrev, Toporov inspires only disgust in Nekhlyudov, despite the fact that he cooperates with his wishes. 'Obtuse and without moral sense', Toporov is made physically and morally repulsive: he, more than anyone, personifies the cruel, cynical abuse of power which Tolstoy sees as the rule rather than the exception in Petersburg.

The most telling of all these brief *vignettes* of Petersburg officialdom, however, is that of Nekhlyudov's erstwhile friend Selyenin. Nekhlyudov remembers from their student days his qualities of 'integrity, honesty and probity': he finds him now a part of that inhuman machine which grinds down Maslova and those like her. In a few bleak pages Tolstoy gives a concise account of the gradual corruption of Selyenin from idealistic youth to time-serving official. Its effect is out of all proportion to the space it occupies in the novel, for the credibility of the account is such as to give convincing weight to Tolstoy's whole argument: the system we see corrupting Selyenin can, we feel, corrupt anyone who is caught up in it. It is not merely the inherently evil, like Toporov, who allow it to continue functioning.

This recognition entails one of wider significance, for it points to the way in which in the last analysis it is not just the legal system but the whole society it underpins that is corrupt. Tolstoy is not merely attacking prisons and the courts in *Resurrection*: he is attacking all societies that base themselves on coercion, and in this respect it was a thoroughly appropriate book to be dedicated to the persecuted Dukhobors. The ruling social class in which we see Nekhlyudov moving in Moscow and Petersburg is a thoroughly decadent one, inexcusably unaware of, or uncaring for, the suffering on which its empty, tediously luxurious life-style is based.

But if governing classes cannot hold their power by force, by the same token the revolutionaries who seek to change society by force are at best understandably misguided, at worst just as vicious as those whom they seek to replace. Tolstoy always recognised that violent revolution in Russia was likely merely to involve the replacement of one authoritarian regime with another, and his portrayal in *Resurrection* of the revolutionary leader Novodvorov is full of an all-too-accurate foreboding. With his spiritual arrogance, his contempt for other people, and his simple desire for power, Novodvorov is every bit as corrupt a figure as Toporov. He too seeks to suppress: 'He loved no one, and regarded all talented people as rivals; if he could he would willingly have treated them as old male monkeys treat the young ones. He would have torn away all their powers and abilities, simply to avoid being eclipsed by them. He only looked with favour on those who bowed before him.' (III.15)

The 'politicals' whom Tolstoy does admire are those like Marya Pavlovna, Simonson, and Kryltsov whose desire is not to achieve power, but to destroy the existing order of things. In fact these characters tend to be less credible than Novodvorov and his like, if only because their anger and willingness to embrace violent methods runs strongly counter to the pacific character with which Tolstoy endows them, and because their unwillingness to think of power, and the practicalities of the new

175

order they seek to establish makes them extraordinarily unpractical as revolutionaries. They are really, we always feel, Tolstoyan anarchists in disguise, translated into a movement to which by nature they do not belong.

Marya Pavlovna is also used by Tolstoy as a weapon in the campaign against physical, sexual love which, along with the more obvious theme of social corruption, is a major preoccupation of the novel. Indeed, it is wrong in the last analysis to separate the two, since part of his concern is to show sexual corruption as linked to social. Marya Pavlovna, the chaste virgin who hates the very idea of sex, and who also hates the viciousness of the society she belongs to, stands at one end of a spectrum which has at its other end such people as Mariette, the Petersburg lady who tries to make Nekhlyudov fall in love with her, the old and young princesses Korchagina, and the lawyer Rogozhinsky, that 'hairy, self-satisfied man' who by inspiring a merely sensual love in Nekhlyudov's sister has stifled all the good that was in her.

Unfortunately for Tolstoy's purposes, it is the supposedly virtuous Marya Pavlovna who is the most disturbing of all these characters—perhaps, after Pozdnyshev, the most disturbing character anywhere in Tolstoy. In some respects, indeed, she is worse than Pozdnyshev, for whereas he has at least a violent individuality, she is sentimentally conceived, the crudely idealised representative of that complete chastity which Tolstoy and Pozdnyshev advocate in *The Kreutzer Sonata*. The damaging effects of Tolstoy's dualism, seen throughout the novel, in which the spiritual and good is set over against the animal and bad, are rarely seen more clearly than in those passages in which, without any suggestion of criticism or qualification, he tells us that Marya Pavlovna 'experienced a real disgust and horror at the idea of falling in love', or that without having experienced it she loathed sexual love and 'looked on it as something incomprehensible and at the same time repugnant and offensive to human dignity'. Her 'charity' is as synthetic as this would suggest, so spiritually motivated as to have an unnatural coldness about it to which Tolstoy gives an unconscious or unwilling recognition when he compares her relentless search for opportunities to serve others to that of a sportsman searching out game, or when, earlier in the novel, he stresses for no apparent reason the sheep-like quality of her eyes. The sensual, irresponsible but charming Mariette is infinitely more alive, more truly human, than this frightening and fundamentally unloving figure.

Marya Pavlovna, though, features merely as an illustration of an ideal. It is the two central figures of the novel, Nekhlyudov and Maslova, who actually have to live out the consequences of the Tolstoyan dualism, suffering in their different ways for allowing the animal instinct to take precedence over the spirit-ual, and discovering as the novel proceeds a new spiritual self-possession based on the recognition of their past mistakes.

For Maslova this is not, apparently, a difficult process: it is largely as a victim of male sexual desire, rather than as someone herself desiring, that she is presented throughout, whether as the innocent girl seduced by Nekhlyudov, or as the prostitute who hates the men who visit the brothel. She thus emerges as a decidedly passive figure who inspires compassion, but little more. Once the early pages describing her girlhood love for Nekhlyudov are past, Tolstoy never allows her that physical understanding and sympathy through which he gives vitality—an excess of vitality—to Anna, Kitty or Natasha. He cannot risk giving her a real body, a real physical presence, since to do so would at once raise the possibility of sexual as well as spiritual attraction on Nekhlyudov's part, and such complexities have no part in the scheme of the latter's resurrection. His relationship with Maslova after the sentence is one in which she really plays very little part except as the object of his pity and remorse. Her role is simply that of prompting a spiritual regeneration in Nekhlyudov by being the living evidence of his past sins. There is no convincing interaction between the two, and the complex inner life of the feelings is always with Maslova external to us as it is not, say, with Anna. The result is that we have at best only a mild interest in whether in the end she will marry Nekhlyudov or Simonson or neither. We can accept that she has learnt what Tolstoy wants her to learn, and that she too has had her resur-rection—more clearly, in fact, than Nekhlyudov has—but her fate is not a matter of real urgency for us, or, one feels, for Tolstoy.

Despite his precepts, Maslova only comes truly alive for Tol-stoy in those early chapters when the love between her and Nekhlyudov is something more than the vague spiritual relationship which dominates the prison scenes—when, that is, it has a strong physical element. However innocent it may be, the youthful love which is symbolised by the kiss behind the lilac bush or after the Easter service is a sexual love, and it is Tolstoy's apprehension of the physical joy of that relationship that gives it its charm and vitality, a charm and vitality reminiscent of the earlier work, and quite unlike anything else in the novel. He makes the early love idyllic, of course, to emphasise the more strongly what is lost by both of them, but in doing so he clearly endorses it: and in the end it is impossible to separate the love which first draws them together from the sexual desire which brings about the seduction. What is morally wrong about the seduction is not the 'animal' instinct that prompts it, but Nekhlyudov's selfishness, his lack of concern about the consequences for Maslova. Tolstoy makes it clear enough here that he sees Nekhlyudov as a good man corrupted by the society to which he belongs, and to whose values he has succumbed. He cannot plausibly blame society for Nekhlyudov's sexual desires, only for his way of indulging them. But the later progress of the novel, with its establishment of the dichotomy between the animal and the spiritual in man, seeks to show that the desire itself is evil. The prostitute whom Nekhlyudov sees in Petersburg makes him realise this with a new clarity:

' "The animal nature of man is disgusting," he thought, "but as long as it is clearly seen you can look down on it from the heights of your spiritual life and despise it, and whether you fall or resist, you remain what you were before; but when this animality hides under a pseudo-aesthetic, poetic veil and demands adulation, then, in worshipping animality you become wholly engulfed in it, and can not distinguish good from evil any longer. Then it is terrible."
Nekhlyudov saw this now as clearly as he saw the palaces, the sentries, the fortress, the river, the boats, and the Stock Exchange.' (II.28)

This is certainly Nekhlyudov speaking directly for the novelist, and not a view which Tolstoy seeks to qualify, to place by its relation to the events of the novel. And yet it is so placed, as if against his will, by the early description of the love between Nekhlyudov and Maslova, where we have a relationship which simply doesn't fit such a dualism. It is neither purely 'animal' nor purely 'spiritual' but (if we are to retain these terms) a complex mixture of the two which makes it altogether more vital than the later spiritual relationship, and which in its recognition of the complexity of motive and feeling in human affairs undercuts the simplifying didacticism of the later pages.

This contradiction is essentially the same as that larger conflict to which G. W. Spence points in his study of *Resurrection*, between Tolstoy's tendency throughout the novel to associate goodness with the simple natural life, with uncorrupted nature in general, and his final elevation of the spiritual alone.[5] The opening pages, together with such episodes as Nekhlyudov's return to his aunts' empty house or the shooting trip on which he meets Vera Bogadukhovskaya, strongly suggest that a simple 'natural' life away from the perverting influence of society is the answer. But the Rousseauan solution to which Tolstoy instinctively turns falls down in the end because it cannot accommodate the attack on sexual desire. The animal in man is undeniably a part of that natural world, as Tolstoy tacitly admits in the early love scenes, and this being so, Nekhlyudov has gradually to withdraw, like Marya Pavlovna, to a purely spiritual world of self-denial which would in the last analysis have to deny not just sexual and social corruption, but the beauty and innocence of the natural world from which he draws strength. This is why *Resurrection* cannot end with marriage and the achievement of harmony with that world as does *War and Peace*: it can only end through the contrived resolution of the Gospel text.

Being at the very centre of the novel, Nekhlyudov inevitably suffers as a character from carrying much of the burden of this unresolved conflict. Indeed, he suffers in general from having to act as a spokesman for or exemplar of a whole range of rigidly preconceived ideas of his creator, and at the same time trying to function as an independent character. The result is that he never quite emerges as a clearly defined personality in his own right, for all that we see into the development of his feelings throughout. The crucial difference between him and the other Tolstoyan seekers, to whom in theory he seems so close, is that such characters as Andrey, Pierre and Levin are never felt to be following a preconceived pattern, as, on the whole we feel Nekhlyudov is. Their search for the truth involves a genuinely explorative attitude on Tolstoy's own part, an openness to what the novel itself may discover, which makes them and their quests continually alive, in vital correspondence with life itself. Nekhlyudov's regeneration, on the other hand, seems conceived of as something illustrative rather than explorative: Tolstoy already knows just where his hero is going, and he is thus not engaged in the actual quest in the same way as he is with those other figures.

In setting Nekhlyudov on a spiritual journey of which he already knows the destination, Tolstoy denies his novel the possibility of that marvellously fresh apprehension of the complexity and irrationality of human experience which is one of his greatest strengths as a novelist. Could, for example, the almost programmatic simplicity and chastity of Nekhlyudov's feelings for Maslova after the trial have been taken so much for granted by Tolstoy in an earlier period? Would the attractions of Mariette or of Princess Korchagina have been so easily and quickly pigeon-holed under the heading of corrupt animal desire? As with the trial, things are black or white, but rarely the varying shades of grey that they once, more realistically, were.

If Tolstoy doesn't allow Nekhlyudov the uncertainty and ambivalence of attitude that he allows his earlier characters, he does himself seem to have a slightly ambivalent attitude towards him. Perhaps just because his resurrection is not done convincingly from the inside, we never have a confident sense of a really clear, controlled distance between him and his creator. There are times when, as in his judgement of Toporov and the rest, in his response to Mariette and the prostitute, or in his reflections on the cruelty and inefficiency of the legal system, Nekhlyudov certainly speaks for Tolstoy, and the distance between them is small—sometimes too small. But there are other occasions when the gap appears to widen, and Nekhlyudov's whole attitude is seen for a moment in a different light—when, for example, Maslova feels he is making use of her spiritually as he had once made use of her physically: ' "You want to save yourself through me," she continued, hurrying to pour out everything that was in her soul, "You enjoyed yourself through me in this life, and now you want to save yourself through me in the other world! You disgust me . . ." ' (I.48)

Although Tolstoy twice puts these sentiments into Maslova's mouth (cf.II.13), it is by no means clear that he endorses them himself—he doesn't pursue them, and even seems to suggest that they are a weakness on Maslova's part. And yet most readers will feel that they have a good deal of justice in them: there is something very solipsistic, narcissistic even, in Nekhlyudov's preoccupation with his own salvation of which Tolstoy does not seem to be always aware. The repetition of *moy* ('my') in the following passage, for example, is significant: ' "My business is to do what my conscious demands of me," he said to himself. "And my conscience demands the sacrifice of my freedom in expiation of my sin, and my determination to marry her ... remains unchanged." ' (II.29) This is not a matter of the familiar Tolstoyan rhetoric of repetition; the note of what is, in the overall context, an excessive self-concern is unmistakable. But is Tolstoy aware of its presence, or is it simply a reflection of his own self-absorbed egoism? The question is never really answered by the novel, and since the question of Nekhlyudov's motivation is so central, it casts a shadow of unresolved doubt over the whole of *Resurrection*.

The answer, I think, is that Tolstoy *is* uneasy about the excessive self-concern that his programme for Nekhlyudov involves, but that he does not want to recognise it explicitly, since to do so would undercut the central message of the novel, and in the end of Tolstoy's whole philosophy, which stresses the need to listen to the inner voice of conscience, that is of God, and not to be diverted either by society or by his own animal nature. The ultimate aim may be brotherly love, but goodness is only to be found inside oneself, and it is there the quest has to be concentrated. The nameless old man who appears in Part III, and who believes in 'no one but himself', is really the embodiment of a heroic and supposedly saintly solipsism. Believing completely in 'the spirit within him', he has renounced name, country, and home—he is just himself, and is the nearest Tolstoy comes in *Resurrection* to explicit justification of the kind of solipsism that Nekhlyudov exhibits. To judge such a solipsism by placing it in a wider context, though, would be to introduce a note of complexity for which he has no place in the novel. Only near the very end, when Nekhlyudov visits the governor's house for dinner, does the self-awareness which was always there in Tolstoy, even at his most extreme, break through the over-simple moral outlines of the novel to emerge with surprising ironic force. As Nekhlyudov relaxes and actually enjoys the company—his own class, as opposed to all those with whom he has been so virtuously dealing—and listens to a piano arrangement of Beethoven's fifth symphony, he falls into:

> 'a spiritual state of complete satisfaction with himself, such as he had not known for a long time, as if he had only now found out what a good man he was.
> The piano was splendid, and the performance of the symphony was good. Or so it seemed to Nekhlyudov, who liked and knew that symphony. As he listened to the beautiful *andante*, he felt a tickling in his nose from a deep affection for himself and all his virtues.' (III.24)

This is certainly Tolstoy at his most devastating, deflating all Nekhlyudov's solemn aspirations with that last simple sentence. And yet what are we to make of it? Coming where it does, only four short chapters from the end, just before Nekhlyudov's discovery of the 'truth' in the Gospels, it is too late and too little to function on its own as an ironic placing of his whole quest. Tolstoy is seriously committed to that quest, we know, and he has not previously introduced any serious qualification of Nekhlyudov's motives. But nor can it be seen as just a momentary lapse on Nekhlyudov's part: what happens, I believe, is that the honesty and self-awareness of the great artist supervenes for a moment on the demands of the prophet and teacher, as if his guard, like Nekhlyudov's, has been lowered by this brief return to more familiar surroundings. Tolstoy's attitude towards Nekhlyudov suddenly becomes more complex: his complacency here (something different from the old *samodovolnost'*) and his wish a little later that he too could have a happy family life, like that of the governor's daughter, make him more fallible and more real than he has been hitherto. Things are not, we see for an instant, as simple as he and Tolstoy would wish them to be. But it is only for an instant: the real world in which the governor's daughter can lead a good, happy life even in the shadows of the transportation prison, recedes as Nekhlyudov accompanies the Englishman around the prison, and the fierce, compassionate unworldliness of the great reformer in Tolstoy takes over once more.

One other important point is emphasised by the dinner at the governor's house, and that is the enormous loneliness of Nekhlyudov's position, a loneliness reflecting that of Tolstoy himself at this period. This has its connections, of course, with the essential solipsism of his philosophy, but here we see it in a more simple, social context. Mention has already been made of the way in which the aristocrat Nekhlyudov feels, like Tolstoy, a greater gulf between himself and his middle-class liberal lawyer than between himself and his former dissolute military friends. The whole of the Siberian journey, in which Nekhlyudov is seen in such close contact with the political prisoners, shows how far removed he is from them too: though he may feel for them, he cannot feel *with* them, or ever be one of them, any more than he can become one with the criminal prisoners. And yet his championship of the prisoners' cause removes him from any simple intercourse with his own class, as his own career had removed Tolstoy. The excessive enthusiasm with which Tolstoy makes Nekhlyudov respond to the hospitality of the governor's wife, 'a Petersburg *grande dame* of the old school', only underlines his essential isolation. He has left them, and yet can join no other group, and it is appropriate that we should last see him, having taken leave of the prisoners, alone in a poor hotel in a Siberian town examining the Gospels. Like the old man without a name, he might be an image of the old Tolstoy, his isolation such that the proposed sequel in which Nekhlyudov was to have lived a happy 'peasant' life along Tolstoyan lines could never have been written, for that too would have required his entry into a community to which he could not belong, any more than Tolstoy himself could have done.

If we look back at *Resurrection* from the perspective of the work of such twentieth-century Russian novelists as Pasternak or Solzhenitsyn, we can see that Nekhlyudov's isolation is more than just a reflection of Tolstoy's own predicament. It is a reflection too of the predicament of any sensitive and intelligent man in a society which is regulated by violence, the violence of the late Tsarist regime, of the revolution and civil war, or of Stalinism. In this respect, Nekhlyudov is the predecessor of Zhivago, and of such figures as Kostoglotov in *Cancer Ward*: it is to their new and horrifying world that he belongs, much more than to the old world, Tolstoy's world, of Andrey, Pierre and Levin. All of these characters are semi-autobiographical figures, and all may be described as seekers after the truth, but for

Nekhlyudov and his successors the search has become more urgent, the impossibility of their ever belonging to their society as Andrey, Pierre and even Levin belong to theirs, more and more obvious. Looked at from this angle, from what comes after rather than what went before, *Resurrection* seems an altogether more interesting and remarkable novel than if we approach it as a kind of third-rate *War and Peace*; remarkable, because it bears witness to the way in which Tolstoy in his seventies remains sensitive to the alienating pressures of this new world to an extent we have no right to expect, and remarkable because, for all its moral rigidity (itself partly a product, like Solzhenitsyn's didacticism, of the desperateness of the situation), it stands up so well to the comparison.

9
Hadji Murat

It is generally agreed that Tolstoy's last major work, the short novel *Hadji Murat*, stands surprisingly and impressively clear from the rest of his later work. The precise character of its achievement, and its very considerable stature, have not, however, always been so clearly recognised. Tolstoy himself seems to have had ambivalent feelings about this novel whose hero decisively violates the main tenets of Tolstoyan Christianity, but who yet appears in an altogether more sympathetic light than do the central figures of any other of his important later works. He spent, we know, a great deal of effort on it, revising it through ten drafts over the period of eight years, from 1896 to 1904, during which it was written, and then leaving it to be published after his death—partly because it would have caused further tensions within his family, partly because it would not have passed the censor, and partly, perhaps, because it would have bewildered and offended the faithful Tolstoyans, who, as Pasternak and Gorky both observed, were so totally unlike Tolstoy.[1] He explained it to them and himself as an example of what he had called 'universal art' in *What is Art?*, not on the same plane as religious art, but dealing in 'feelings accessible to all'. Despite this explanation, he remained uneasy; writing to his friend and cousin, the old maid of honour Alexandra Tolstoy, for those details about the habits of Nicholas I which are such an important element in the novel, we find him excusing himself to her, and one feels to himself, thus: 'Do not blame me, dear friend, for busying myself with such trivialities when I have one foot in the grave. These trivialities occupy my leisure time and give my mind a rest from the serious thoughts that fill it.'[2]

But the mixture of uneasiness and serious artistic commitment with which he looked on *Hadji Murat* is perhaps best brought out by the story told by Simmons of how Tolstoy reacted to a reading of parts of an unfinished version at Yasnaya Polyana: 'Tolstoy kept popping in and out of the room to listen. Once he broke in to declare the work uninteresting, and finally, with some irritation, he asked the reader to stop bothering with such rubbish. "If that is so," one of the listeners demanded, "why did you write it?" "But it is not finished yet," he replied. "You come into my kitchen and no wonder it stinks with the smell of my cooking." '3

The cooking was indeed careful in a way that would seem to belie Tolstoy's own suggestion, and that of Maude, that it was written as a 'recreation', a relief from more serious matters, though this may well have been the only way he could make it square with his teaching.4 Its seriousness is certainly of a different kind from the other work of this time; but far from being trivial, it displays a balance and a humane generosity of judgement that recall the best of *Anna Karenina* or *War and Peace*, and which, along with its formal perfection, make it possible to see it as the ripest fruit of this last period, the fitting last word of the great artist rather than the great preacher.

To say this is not to fall in with the common tendency to praise *Hadji Murat* as a marvel of aesthetic form, a novel in which Tolstoy abandoned his habitual moral preoccupations in favour of purely aesthetic ones. Tolstoy's was certainly a various nature, but it was never really in him, especially in these later years, not to be a moralist: to expend labour on a work that, though formally perfect, had no serious moral vision reaching beyond itself would have seemed to him at this time nonsensical and culpable. In fact, as has often been pointed out, his increasing preoccupation with the didactic, 'religious' role of literature leads him to a more and more fastidious concern with form, the confident, expansive disregard for convention which we see in the two great novels giving way to the wonderfully economic clarity of the parabolic tales or of *The Death of Ivan Ilyich*. What happens in *Hadji Murat* is not that the didactic or tendentious is abandoned in favour of purely formal considerations, but that the moral view is larger than that of the other late works, and that its finer balance is reflected in, is, indeed, inseparable from, the formal poise of the novel in such a way as to make us far less conscious of the intervention of the didactic Tolstoy. It is the artist as moralist, and not the Tolstoyan philosopher, whom we hear speaking. John Bayley goes too far, it seems to me, in saying that '*Hadji Murat* is less objective than anything he ever wrote', but his emphasis is a useful corrective to the glee with which less perceptive readers have seized on it as showing Tolstoy apparently abandoning all his beliefs for a francophile delight in 'form'.[5]

The escape from the rigid morality of *Resurrection* or *The Death of Ivan Ilyich* is achieved with less inconsistency than such critics tend to assume; but there can, I think, be no doubt that it is an escape, a welcome re-assertion of the intuitive morality of the great artist over the systematic morality of the teacher and prophet. The inconsistency is lessened by Tolstoy's choice of subject matter: by placing his story in the Caucasus, and making his hero an ascetic Islamic warrior, he gains what must have been a welcome freedom from the need to explore the spiritual emptiness and hypocrisy of modern Christian Russia. Whatever else he may be, Hadji Murat is neither hypocritical nor at odds with himself as he violates all five of Christ's commandments as interpreted by Tolstoy. His own culture and religion offer him a different set of values, by which he can live and die at peace with his conscience, and it is partly for this reason—because he is so spiritually self-possessed—that Tolstoy is able to give him that love, that sympathy of the body as well as of the soul, that is largely absent from his other work after *Anna Karenina*.

It is largely because of the return of this kind of love that *Hadji Murat* has been linked with *War and Peace*, and in many respects the connection is an obvious and proper one. It can, however, be deceptive: for it is important that *Hadji Murat* is not merely much shorter than *War and Peace*, but that it involves relatively little of the complex psychological exploration that characterises the latter. Though we are told that what we see is a 'terrible crisis' in Hadji Murat's life, we are only occasionally allowed into his mind. Mostly, we simply see the physical manifestations of that crisis, and this is felt to be enough: the issues are so clear for him that there is no place for introspective doubt, no divergence between thought and action. We see him in a series of vivid pictures.

Tolstoy had set out in writing *Hadji Murat* to exploit what he called a 'peepshow' technique (he uses the English word), and the metaphor emphasises the strikingly pictorial quality of the presentation not just of Hadji Murat himself, but of the whole story. Things are no longer seen in that drearily cold light which Nekhlyudov sees over Petersburg, and which hangs over the whole of *Resurrection*, but the richer, mellower light of *Hadji Murat* is just as clear: more clear, in that it is a novel based on a host of images—the thistle in the ploughed field, the childlike smile of Hadji Murat, the large, white hands of Nikolay, the black eyes of Sado's son, and many more—which imprint themselves more vividly on the mind's eye than do the terrible, documentary scenes of *Resurrection*. Nowhere does one feel that Pasternak's tribute to the unique freshness of Tolstoy's vision applies better than to this work of his supposed dotage:

> 'Throughout his life he could always look at an event and see the whole of it, in the isolated, self-contained finality of its moment, as a vivid and exhaustive sketch—see it as the rest of us can only see on rare occasions, in childhood, or at a crest of happiness which renews the world, or in the joy of some great spiritual victory.'[6]

Pasternak's father had done the illustrations for *Resurrection*: illustrations for *Hadji Murat*, though they exist, seem superfluous.

Tolstoy, however, when he used the 'peepshow' figure, was not thinking so much of the strong visual quality he would give to the novel, as of the idea of telling the story by offering a succession of separate scenes without explicit intervention on his part, and without elaborate narrative copulae. In doing this he goes almost as far in 'showing' rather than 'telling' as Henry James could have wished; only in the treatment of Nicholas I do we find much explicit moral comment, and such is the enormity of Nicholas's conceit and inhumanity as Tolstoy presents them that his condemnation seems to come as a matter of course, rather than as any kind of authorial intrusion: it is, as it were, itself part of the narrative, part of the peepshow.

The importance of this peepshow technique can hardly be overemphasised: for it is through it that Tolstoy achieves that striking equanimity that so characterises *Hadji Murat*. In speaking of its use, he himself associates it with the idea of a more balanced, more tolerant judgement than the other work of this period displays. This is the point of the statement that it would be good 'to write a work of art in which one would clearly express the fluidity of man; the fact that he is at once a villain, an angel, a wise man, an idiot, a strong man, and the most helpless of creatures'.[7] By showing Hadji Murat in a variety of roles, in a variety of contexts, Tolstoy establishes the impossibility of making the kind of simple black/white judgement of character that he makes so easily in *Resurrection* and elsewhere. The 'peepshow' becomes the vehicle for a generosity and poise that is reminiscent of the earlier work, but which is more calmly detached. Along with the dignified simplicity of the Tartar life, the martial background, and the Caucasian setting in general, this calmness makes *Hadji Murat* far closer to the Homeric epic than anything else in Tolstoy.[8]

Such a technique has its obvious dangers, however, and it is probably because of the relative formlessness that a sequence of pictures, even with a narrative connection, might have had that Tolstoy is so attentive to other aspects of formal structure in the story. He sets the whole firmly within the explicit symbolic frame provided by the thistle which he sees in the 'dead, black field', and which in its toughness, its refusal to be crushed by the cartwheel, reminds him of Hadji Murat's struggle to survive. Within this clear frame the peepshow narrative unfolds with an unobtrusive symmetry which ensures that it is never in danger of falling apart: thus, for example, from the opening chapters we move from the Caucasian village, to the common Russian soldiers, to the officers, the higher ranks and so on till we reach the Emperor, an ascending social order that implies for Tolstoy a gradual moral descent but which, until we reach Nicholas and his minister Chernyshev, he does not choose to emphasise as such. Thus the younger Vorontsov, to whom Hadji Murat surrenders, lives with his wife a life of considerable luxury, but little of the censoriousness we might expect comes through in Tolstoy's description of their household. Vorontsov's father, the Viceroy, appears rather more cynical, more corrupted by power, but again the judgement is not a harsh one: instead it is balanced and, like so much of *Hadji Murat*, apparently neutral in tone: 'he had a European education rare among higher Russian officials at that time; he was ambitious, gentle and kind in his manner with inferiors, and a subtle courtier in his relations with his superiors. He did not understand life without power and without submission.' (Chapter 9) The last sentence falls all the more tellingly because of the neutral tone, but the overall effect is of a tolerance quite out of keeping with the rest of Tolstoy's later work—it is instructive to compare the whole portrait of the elder Vorontsov, for instance, with the high officials of *Resurrection*, to whom all tolerance is denied.

Another aspect of the symmetrical structure is the close parallel Tolstoy draws between the two men of ultimate political power on each side, the Emperor Nicholas I and the Imam

Shamil. Both physically and in character the two men are strikingly alike: he emphasises their great size, the paleness and dullness of their expression, the austerity (in some respects) of their lives, and the excessive confidence that both have in their own judgement. The time-serving Minister of War, Chernyshev, knows that when Nicholas has a decision to make 'it was only necessary for him to concentrate for a few moments, and then an inspiration visited him, and the best solution presented itself, as if an inner voice had told him what it was necessary to do'. (Chapter 15) Shamil likewise sits in silence, his council knowing that he is 'listening now to the voice of the Prophet talking to him, showing him what it was necessary to do'. (Chapter 19) In both cases the decisions we see them arriving at by this means are savage ones, a terrible inversion of that intuitive moral knowledge which comes to Tolstoy's best characters. In the end, one feels it is scarcely enough to describe the two by the commonplace formula of corruption by absolute power. They are rather the deathly incarnations of the absolute evil of absolute power over others, their great size implying no vitality, but appearing as the physical expression of a diseased and swollen ego.

Of the two, it is Nicholas who is marginally the worse, as we might expect, his power being more autocratic and extending over more people. In Tolstoy's hands he appears as a man almost insane in his conceit and total lack of self-awareness. The reactionary and despotic defender of the Orthodox religion, he yet has no qualms about the 'senile sensuality' which he indulges with a young Swedish girl or with his 'established mistress', Nelidova. His sexual profligacy is routine and lifeless —'the girl was taken to the place where Nicholas normally had rendezvous with women'—but though it leaves him with an unpleasant aftertaste, it is one he can easily stifle by reverting to a thought 'which always tranquillised him, the thought of his own greatness'. He truly believes it when he says that he is the only honest man left in Russia, and sees neither dishonesty nor hypocrisy in sentencing a student to run the gauntlet of a thousand men twelve times, knowing that this means a certain and terrible death, while thanking God that capital punishment has been abolished in Russia. Such inconsistencies no longer exist for him, Tolstoy explains with cool, persuasive venom, because:

'Constant blatant flattery from those surrounding him, contrary to the obvious facts, had brought him to a state where he no longer saw his own inconsistencies, or measured his deeds and words by reality, by logic, or even by simple common sense, but was quite convinced that all his commands, however senseless, unjust, and mutually contradictory they might be, became reasonable and just and mutually accordant simply because he gave them.' (Chapter 15)

The portrait of Stalin, and his similar interview with a time-serving minister, in Solzhenitsyn's *First Circle*, is very close indeed to this whole portrait of Nicholas, and was, one would imagine, based on it, but it is a measure of Tolstoy's greater poise that, despite the wholly damning nature of his account, he does not indulge in such heavy irony as does Solzhenitsyn—thereby making that account all the more damning.

On such occasions as this, it would be ridiculous to argue that Tolstoy is not concerned to make moral judgements in *Hadji Murat*; indeed, the judgement of Nicholas is perhaps more final than anything else in his work. But it gains that finality just because it has an air of objectivity about it of which we are not always convinced in, say, *Resurrection*, partly because of the weight of historical detail behind it (the 'trivialities' he had culled from Alexandra Tolstoy and others who had known Nicholas's court), and partly because the eminent balance of which we are aware in the rest of the novel makes us less likely to question Tolstoy's balance here.

Despite the closeness of the parallels between them, Nicholas's counterpart Shamil appears in most respects in a marginally better light: he is slightly more self-aware than Nicholas, and his prayers, 'as necessary to him as his daily food', seem slightly less empty. Though he, too, has his profligate sexual side, it is indulged within the legal context of polygamy, and though the sentences he administers are cruel, they are according to the canon of the law.

The little that Shamil gains over Nicholas in this way is largely due to the virtues of the culture to which he belongs, rather than to any intrinsic superiority of character. Power is in the hands of the corrupt on either side, but throughout the novel Tolstoy shows a clear preference for the austere dignity of the Tartar society, its secure religious basis, and its clarity of moral vision, over the Russian. From the very beginning of the narrative, when Hadji Murat rides into the Chechen village on his way to make his deal with the Russians, we are aware of Tolstoy's respect for the otherness of this society, in which religious belief is a living part of everyday life, and in which the ceremonious, dignified greeting is not just an empty form of words. Sado's father and Hadji Murat pray when they meet, as naturally as two Russians might shake hands, and their conversation is terse and full of respect for each other: words, we realise, are not things to be used wastefully; they are charged with meaning, in contrast to the emptiness or hypocrisy of the words used in Russian society—at Vorontsov's dinner party, or by Nicholas, who stifles his feelings by repeating words without thinking of their meaning. ' "A rope should be long, but a speech short," ' says Hadji Murat to a Chechen who threatens to be over-effusive. Dignified and quite unembarrassed silence when there is nothing important to be said is one of the marks of his complete self-possession, and it is a virtue shared by many of his compatriots.

The contrast between the supposedly primitive world of the Tartars and the supposedly civilised world of the Russians runs right through *Hadji Murat*, and it is, one feels, Tolstoy's loneliness and alienation from the Russia of the 1890s which lead him to find a nostalgic vitality and naturalness in this world, which is not only not that of Ivan Ilyich, but is remote even from the old Russia of his youth. Only the Russian peasants survive the implied comparison with any credit. In the soldier Avdeyev's death, and the way it is received by his family, we see some of the same strengths that characterise the Tartars. Like Hadji Murat, Avdeyev shows no fear of death, accepting it quietly, as do his family when the news reaches them. His mother weeps only as long as she can spare the time, and his wife, though she grieves, is practical enough to be glad she can now marry the man she has been living with. The essential business of life goes on. Like the Tartar life, that of the peasants is permeated by their religious beliefs, and like the Tartars they are not as profligate of speech as are their masters. But that they do have masters is an important point of difference between the two, for the peasants we see in *Hadji Murat* are—another example of Tolstoy's greater objectivity—a downtrodden class, their austerity more a matter of necessity than of religion. Avdeyev's death is, like his life, passive and wasted, a final blow in a life that has been full of blows. Tolstoy's doctrines would dictate a greater regard for Avdeyev's passiveness than for Hadji Murat's aggressiveness, but in the novel his sympathies lie most with the man who fights for his independence, his life and his family.

What is curious about the way in which Tolstoy celebrates the Tartar culture at the expense of the Russian is that one scarcely notices it happening—not, at least, in the form of authorial intrusion or lack of objectivity. By taking so pre-eminent a product of his race as Hadji Murat, and placing him in the midst of an alien society, he is in fact doing the same kind of thing as Voltaire does with his Huron Indian, but the effect is altogether less didactic. Because he has become content to 'show' rather than 'tell' we accept the implied judgement as an objective one. When Hadji Murat walks out of the opera after the first act, having expressed 'no pleasure, but obvious indifference', or when he looks with dignified distaste on the low-cut dresses of the women at Vorontsov's ball, we know well enough that his distaste is also Tolstoy's. But for Hadji Murat, given his background and character, such responses are eminently natural ones, and within the context of the novel we can accept them as such.

Apart from his description of Nicholas, perhaps the closest Tolstoy comes to expressing an open hostility to the Russians is in an episode that is almost exclusively narrative: that of the destruction by Russian troops of Sado's village. The killing of Sado's son, the same 'handsome, bright eyed boy who had gazed with such ecstasy at Hadji Murat' in the opening chapter, is one of the most moving things in the novel, brief though it is, and along with the other senseless destruction—the beehives burnt, the fountain and the mosque polluted—it helps justify a passage in which a positive loathing on Tolstoy's part of war in general, and of war as waged by his own countrymen in particular, breaks through the objective facade of the narrative, the more so, perhaps, because he is, according to Maude,[9] recalling an event in which he had himself taken part:

'No one spoke of hatred of the Russians. The feeling all the Chechens experienced, from the youngest to the oldest, was stronger than hatred, it was not hatred, but a disregard of those Russian dogs as human beings, and such disgust, repulsion and perplexity at the senseless cruelty of these creatures, that the desire to exterminate them, like the desire to exterminate rats, poisonous spiders and wolves, was as much a natural instinct as the instinct of self-preservation.' (Chapter 17)

In such passages as this, one feels, Tolstoy is managing successfully to have his cake and eat it, his anger at war, and the desire for violent revenge which that anger breeds, but which his own doctrine clearly denies him, seeming an honourable enough response when it is put into the hearts of the beleaguered Chechens.

Apart from the difference of the moral code by which they live, what most serves to justify the warlike attitude of the Tartars in general is the personal nature of their fight: they are defending their homes, their families, their religion, while the Russians are simply bent on the expansion of their empire. It is, in the same way, the personal, almost private nature of his struggle to survive that is one of the most important elements in the character of Hadji Murat as Tolstoy shows it. Many critics describe him as a traitor with whom we rather paradoxically sympathise, and like Henri Troyat treat his story as that of 'a man who tries to escape from his family, traditions and faith in order to satisfy his will to power'.[10] This seems a peculiarly insensitive description: Hadji Murat shows no signs of a 'will to power' in the sense that Shamil, Vorontsov or Chernyshev does; he is not motivated by ambition, but by his desire to survive as an independent agent, and to seek revenge, a private and highly understandable desire which Tolstoy does not seek to undermine. Explaining his earlier desertion of the Russians when he had gone over to Shamil, he says 'The main thing for me was to revenge myself on Akhmet Khan, and that I could not do through the Russians'. (Chapter 13) Now, the important thing for him is to save his family and himself from Shamil, and that, he believes, he *can* do through the Russians. Governments like those of Nicholas or Shamil are for him nothing but tools which he may or may not make use of in his personal struggles, and seeing the governments, we can only sympathise with his attitude, an attitude that has something in common with that of the older Russian nobility who, like Tolstoy and his family, declined to serve the central autocracy which challenged their ancient independence.

Far from deserting his traditions and faith, Hadji Murat seems throughout a more creditable repository of what is good

and honourable in them than does Shamil. Those traditions are
not threatened by his transfer of allegiance to the Russians, because that allegiance is never for a moment rooted in any
transfer of respect for Russian ways or Russian authority. His
faith and that of his compatriots does not depend for its survival
on the survival of Shamil's government, but on its survival
within each of them, and the emphasis on the unshakeableness
and austerity of Hadji Murat's religious life convinces us that in
him at least it will survive. His prayers, we can safely surmise,
are never empty or inconvenient like those of the two autocratic
defenders of their religions, Nicholas and Shamil.

Hadji Murat's individualism, then, is of a kind Tolstoy is
likely to have sympathised with deeply. His own brand of
Christian anarchism, though finally formulated and rationalised
along Gospel lines, springs as much from the aristocrat's pride
and total inability to tolerate any governmental interference in
his life, as it does from more Christian principles. This is why
he gives us no sense of Hadji Murat's being a traitor, though
technically he is, and has been more than once. When as a
young man in the Caucasus he had heard of the historical Hadji
Murat's surrender, Tolstoy had judged him more harshly, telling his brother Sergey that it was a disappointing 'act of cowardice' by a brave man. Half a century later, his attitude towards
all forms of government different, the verdict has changed.

But if Hadji Murat is akin to Tolstoy in his fierce, proud
individualism, and his loneliness in an alien society, he is very
different in one important respect. For, like the Cossacks of an
earlier date, Lukashka or Eroshka, he is never troubled by the
doubt and introspection that had always accompanied his
creator, the questions of 'who he was and why he existed' that,
as Olenin had recognised, marked him off from his Cossack
rivals. That 'habit of constant moral analysis', destroying 'spontaneity of feeling and clarity of judgement', which Tolstoy had
recognised in himself in *Youth*, had never been suppressed by
the rather false clarity of judgement achieved in the years
following *Anna Karenina*, and his loving envy of the man who
never needs to question his motives, whose clarity of judgement
is itself spontaneous, is felt even more strongly in *Hadji Murat*
than it was in *The Cossacks*. Hadji Murat's actions, whether they
be the courteous, gentle ones that go with the 'childlike kindliness' of his smile, or the ruthless, warlike ones we see in the

closing pages, are the unquestioned product of his whole being. He may, of course, be hypocritically 'diplomatic' when dealing with potential enemies—witness his professions of faith to the elder Vorontsov, and the latter's quite proper refusal to believe them. But he is never hypocritical with himself: his motives have no ambiguity about them, and his actions are based on a clear religious code the validity of which for him, though we rarely see into it, we do not question. We may feel that we are shown very little of his soul, as we are shown those of Pierre, Andrew or Levin, but that is because there is no divergence in him between the inner life of the spirit and the outward life of action. He is what he does, and does what he is; and he has the advantage over other Tolstoyan characters of whom we might say the same thing—Eroshka, say, or even Natasha—in that his spontaneity has the spiritual strength of the austere Islamic warrior code behind it.

The richness of that code is partly brought out by Hadji Murat's dignity and bearing: he deserves, we feel, the epithets of 'courteous, wise and just' which Marya Dmitryevna bestows on him. It is brought out, too, by what we see of it in his *murids* and in Sado's family. And it is given an interesting further dimension by Hadji Murat's own recollections of his childhood; just before his flight, he falls into a reverie in which

> 'He remembered the fountain under the hill, where he used to go with his mother, holding on to her loose trousers, to fetch water. He remembered a lean dog that had licked his face, and especially the smell and taste of smoke and of sour milk when he followed his mother into the shed where she was milking the cow and heating the milk. He remembered how his mother had shaved his head for the first time, and the astonishment with which he had seen his round, bluish head in the shining brass vessel that hung on the wall.' (Chapter 23)

Tolstoy, too, was writing down his reminiscences of his childhood at this time; but what struck him as he did so was, as always, the terrible pathos of the loss of his childish innocence and hope. There is pathos, too, in Hadji Murat's memories, but it does not depend, as it did for Tolstoy, on the disparity between the world of the child and that of the man. Hadji Murat has remained, for all his bravery and intelligence, much closer to the clear, simple moral world of his childhood. The culture in which he lives has not, as it has for Tolstoy, perverted

or destroyed that world through its materialism and its trivial-
ising artificiality. The code may be fierce, but it is less corrupting than that of Russian 'Christian' society, and the smile of
'childlike kindliness' can still sort easily with bravery and
wisdom, and with the kind of spiritual self-possession that is
signified by the eyes which gaze 'calmly, attentively, and
penetratingly into the eyes of others'.

In the end, of course, Hadji Murat's plan to use the Russians
to save himself and his family cannot work: the Russians, wisely
from their point of view, do not have enough trust in his
loyalty to them to help him rescue his family from Shamil.
Trapped like the falcon whose fable he recalls—it is, like the
beautiful but prickly thistle, an apt symbol for him—he is
forced to escape and try to rescue them himself. As his men
prepare their weapons, the noise of whetstones is accompanied
by the song of nightingales: there are to be nightingales, too, in
the place where he and his men are finally trapped and killed,
their song starting up again the moment the firing has stopped.
Sad and yet celebratory, they provide a highly fitting requiem,
suggestive both of the harmony of Hadji Murat's life with that
of the natural world, and of the continuity of that world beyond
all individual endings.

Before Hadji Murat dies, however, Tolstoy is to remind us of
the prickliness of the thistle, in his murder of the escort which
accompanies him. The leader of the escort, Nazarov, is one of
the most attractively vital figures amongst the Russians, endowed with the same kind of fullness of physical life that
Tolstoy gives Hadji Murat himself, and the latter's shooting of
him in relatively cold blood comes as a sudden, violent reminder of the more doubtful qualities of Tolstoy's hero:

'The sky was so clear, the air so fresh, and the forces of life played
so joyously in Nazarov's soul as, merging into one being with his
good, strong horse, he flew along the straight road behind Hadji
Murat, that the possibility of anything bad, sad, or dreadful never
entered his head. He rejoiced that with every step he was gaining
on Hadji Murat.

Hadji Murat judged by the hoofbeats of the Cossack's big horse
nearing him that he would soon be overtaken, and taking his
pistol with his right hand, with his left he began lightly to rein in
his Kabarda horse, which was excited by hearing the tramp of the
horse behind it.

"You mustn't, I tell you," shouted Nazarov, almost level with Hadji Murat and stretching out his hand to grasp his horse by the bridle. But he had not managed to grasp the bridle when a shot was heard. "What on earth are you doing?" yelled Nazarov, clutching at his chest. "Get them boys!" he cried, and he reeled and fell on to his saddle bow.' (Chapter 25)

It is a most disconcerting use of the 'peepshow' technique, suddenly placing Hadji Murat in a different perspective from that in which we have seen him previously. Tolstoy does not judge in any explicit way, and Hadji Murat is not being inconsistent: but this side of the warrior code is not one we are likely to be able to admire from a distance, as we can so much else in it. It is impressive evidence of Tolstoy's poise and objectivity that he does not flinch from showing the ruthlessness as well as the dignity which Hadji Murat's life-style involves.

The killing of Nazarov and his men is much more disturbing than the heroic violence of Hadji Murat's final stand against his pursuers. The spirit in which he is to die has already been suggested to us by the song which Khanefi sings before they set out on their attempt to escape. In it a legendary hero, Gamzat, and his men kill their horses and entrench themselves behind them with the intention of killing as many of their Russian pursuers as possible before they die. Hadji Murat's own death is given something of the same epic quality as Gamzat's by Tolstoy's inversion of the chronology of events in the last two chapters, so that we see his battered head being displayed before we hear the account of his death:

'It was a head, shaven, with a prominent, projecting brow and black, short beard and trimmed moustaches, with one eye open and the other half-closed, with the shaven skull cleft but not cut right through, with black, congealed blood in the nose. The neck was wrapped in a bloody towel. Despite all the head wounds, the blue lips were still set in a childlike, kindly expression.' (Chapter 24)

The effect of this is not so much to evoke sympathy as to place Hadji Murat's death firmly in the past, an event to be described as Khanefi sings of Gamzat's death, and it is in this way that Tolstoy does describe it. There is no question here of the great apostle of non-violence interfering with the great novelist's account. As the nightingales sing, and he is reminded of the song about Gamzat, Hadji Murat recognises approaching death, and 'suddenly his soul became serious'. Serious, but not afraid: at no time does he seem to fear death. When Butler had asked him earlier if he was not afraid of a further attempt on his life by his enemy Arslan Khan, he had replied that 'if he kills me it will prove that such is Allah's will', and such a self-possession remains with him right up to his death.

The religious code by which he has lived has prepared him to meet death calmly, so that when he receives his fatal wound, and memories and images of his past life present themselves to his mind, his 'serious' soul has already begun to dissociate itself from his strong body with a serenity strangely out of keeping with the violence around him, violence in which his body continues to play its part. The vivid images from the past flash through his mind 'without evoking any feeling within him: neither pity nor anger nor any kind of desire. All that seemed so insignificant in comparison with what was beginning, and had already begun, within him. Still, his strong body continued to do what it had begun.' (Chapter 25)

In the final dramatic paragraphs, it is the body and its actions which Tolstoy stresses: Hadji Murat's code has taught him how to die, but it has also taught him how the great warrior must give up his life:

'He gathered his last strength, raised himself from behind the bank, and fired his pistol at a man who was running towards him, and hit him. The man fell. Then he climbed right out of the ditch and limping heavily went with his dagger directly at the enemy. A few shots were fired, and he reeled and fell. Several militiamen threw themselves towards the body with triumphant shrieks. But what seemed to them a dead body, suddenly moved. First the bloody, uncovered, shaven head rose, then the trunk, and then, grasping a tree, he raised all of himself up. He seemed so terrible, that those who were running up stopped short. But suddenly he shuddered, staggered away from the tree, and from his full height, like a thistle that had been mown down, he fell on his face, and moved no more.

He did not move, but still he felt. When the first to reach him, Gadji Aga, struck him on the head with a large dagger, it seemed to him that someone was beating him on the head with a hammer, and he could not understand who was doing it or why. That was his last consciousness of any connection with his body. He felt nothing more, and his enemies hacked and kicked at what had no longer anything in common with him.' (Chapter 25)

Even at this climax of his story, Tolstoy refrains from being didactic: only the dissociation of the conscious being from the body is affirmed. What kind of immortality that being has is not here his concern; the Tolstoyan doctrine of immortality may hover in the background, but it has no positive part to play. We are left instead with the song of the nightingales: life, the life of the natural world, goes on beyond the violence of Hadji Murat's death.

'Life asserts itself to the very end' Tolstoy had written in his diary in 1896; he was referring to the stubborn thistle that had reminded him of Hadji Murat, but for the reader of *Hadji Murat* the reference might have been to himself. In the way in which his art turns at the very last to celebrate again the strength and freshness of life as it had done at its very greatest, we have splendid testimony to the strength of that assertion. Tolstoy's last years were dominated by the attempt to propagate a rationalising, reductive moral philosophy which had none of that freshness, and very little else in common with the great art of his earlier years. But, as *Hadji Murat* shows so well, the artist who could not reduce life remained alive in him to the very end. One of his greatest strengths, arguably his greatest, is the extraordinary self-awareness which we see in him from the very outset. It is that self-awareness that prevented him from ever being finally convinced, as many of his disciples were, by the moral philosophy he had constructed for himself under such terrible pressure in *A Confession* and the works that followed it. Gorky saw how much wider than that philosophy his real vision was. So did Rilke, who visited him at Yasnaya Polyana in 1899 and 1900, and who was to write later that his meeting with Tolstoy had

'strengthened in me precisely the opposite of the impression he may have wanted to leave with his visitors; infinitely far from bearing out his conscious renunciation, I had seen, even into his most unconscious behaviour, the artist secretly retaining the upper hand, and particularly in view of his life filled with refusals, the conception grew within me of the positiveness of artistic inspiration and achievement; of its power and legitimacy; of the hard glory of being called to something like that.'[11]

Notes

1 Tolstoy and his world

1 Quoted by Edmund Wilson, 'The Politics of Flaubert', in *The Triple Thinkers* (Harmondsworth, Middlesex, 1962), pp. 85–6.
2 *Works*, LXVI, 67.
3 D. S. Mirsky, *A History of Russian Literature*, ed. F. J. Whitfield (London, 1949), pp. 251–2.
4 *Works*, III, 398.
5 Quoted by Sir Isaiah Berlin, 'Tolstoy and Enlightenment', in *Tolstoy: A Collection of Critical Essays*, ed. Ralph E. Matlaw (Englewood Cliffs, New Jersey, 1967), p. 32.
6 *Supplément au Voyage de Bougainville*, ed. Gilbert Chinard (Paris, Baltimore, Oxford, and London, 1935), p. 190.
7 Paul Boyer, *Chez Tolstoi: Entretiens à Iasnaia Poliana* (Paris, 1950), p. 40.
8 *Works*, II, 345.
9 *Works*, XLVI, 167.
10 *Ibid.*, p. 176.
11 *Émile, or Education*, trans. Barbara Foxley (London, 1911), pp. 228–78. Further references to this edition are given in the text.
12 Quoted by Berlin, *op. cit.*, p. 37.
13 *Ibid.*, p. 51.
14 Trans. Vladimir Nabokov (London, 1964), I, 272.
15 'In honour of Pushkin', *The Triple Thinkers*, p. 55.
16 Trans. Max Hayward and Manya Harari (London, 1961), p. 430.
17 *The Russian Religious Mind: Kievan Christianity, the Tenth to the Thirteenth Centuries* (Cambridge, Mass., 1946), pp. 12–13.
18 'Goethe and Tolstoy', in *Essays of Three Decades*, trans. H. T. Lowe-Porter (London, 1947), p. 117.
19 *Travel Notes in Switzerland*, quoted in Ernest J. Simmons, *Leo Tolstoy* (London, 1949), p. 176.
20 *Op. cit.*, p. 20.

2 *Childhood, Boyhood* and *Youth*

1 *Works*, XLVI, 150–1.

2 R. F. Christian, *Tolstoy: A Critical Introduction* (Cambridge, 1969), p. 32.
3 'Count Leo Tolstoi', in *Essays in Criticism: Second Series*, Everyman edition (London, 1964), p. 355.
4 *Works*, XLVI, 110, April 14th, 1852 (in English); XLVII, 71, May 12th, 1856.
5 Christian, *Tolstoy*, p. 35.
6 *The Hedgehog and the Fox* (London, 1953), p. 41.
7 *Works*, XLVI, 151.

3 The problem of happiness: *The Cossacks* and *Family Happiness*

1 *Works*, IV, 363.
2 Called *Happy Ever After* in Rosemary Edmonds's Penguin translation.
3 *Tolstoy and the Novel* (London, 1966), p. 263.
4 *Works*, XLVII, 152.
5 Maxim Gorky, *Reminiscences of Tolstoy, Chekhov and Andreev*, trans. Katherine Mansfield, S. S. Koteliansky and Leonard Woolf (London, 1934), p. 54.
6 Called *Strider: the Story of a Horse* in Aylmer Maude's translation, *Tolstoy Centenary Edition* (Oxford, 1929–37), V, 391.
7 *Op. cit.*, p. 43.
8 *Recollections* in *Works*, XXXIV, 387.
9 Quoted by Henri Troyat, *Tolstoy*, trans. Nancy Amphoux (Harmondsworth, Middlesex, 1970), p. 909.

4 *War and Peace*

1 *Works*, XIII, 238. The passage is translated at greater length in R. F. Christian's excellent *'War and Peace': A Study* (Oxford 1962), pp. 102–3.
2 *Works*, XIII, 55.
3 Berlin, *The Hedgehog and the Fox*; for another, undeservedly less well known discussion of Tolstoy's theories of history, see Nicola Chiaromonte, *The Paradox of History* (London, 1972).
4 *Works*, LXI, 180.
5 Translator's Preface to *Cavalleria Rusticana* by Giovanni Verga, in *Phoenix* (London, 1936), I, 246.
6 *Dr Zhivago*, ed. cit., p. 468.

5 *Anna Karenina*

1 Quoted by Simmons, *Leo Tolstoy*, pp. 319–20.
2 *Op. cit.*, p. 216.
3 Joyce Cary, *Art and Reality* (Cambridge, 1958), p. 162.
4 *The Appropriate Form* (London, 1964), pp. 179–80.
5 Letter to S. A. Rachinsky, January 27th, 1878. *Works*, LXII, 377.
6 April 23rd, 1876. *Works*, LXII, 269.
7 *Eleven Essays in the European Novel* (New York, 1964), p. 23.
8 F. R. Leavis, '*Anna Karenina*: Thought and Significance in a Great Creative Work', in '*Anna Karenina*' *and Other Essays* (London, 1967), p. 10.
9 *Phoenix*, I, 246, 528.
10 *Op. cit.*, p. 17.
11 'The Novel', *Phoenix*, II, 417.
12 Dostoyevsky, *The Diary of a Writer*, trans. Boris Brasol (London, 1949), II, 610. Blackmur, *op. cit.*, p. 5.
13 See Gorky, *op. cit.*, pp. 61–2.
14 *Op. cit.*, p. 203.
15 *Op. cit.*, p. 262.
16 *Diary of a Writer*, II, 792.
17 *Op. cit.*, p. 22.
18 *The Letters of W. B. Yeats*, ed. Allan Wade (London, 1954), p. 922, January 4th, 1939.
19 'Morality and the Novel', *Phoenix*, I, 528.

6 The religious crisis: *A Confession*

1 Christian, *Tolstoy*, p. 213; Mirsky, *op. cit.*, p. 299.
2 *Ibid.*, p. 299.
3 *Works*, XLVII, 37, March 4th, 1855.
4 *Op. cit.*, p. 23.
5 Quoted by Simmons, *Leo Tolstoy*, p. 114.
6 *Op. cit.*, p. 118.

7 The fruits of conversion

1 *Letters*, ed. Stuart Gilbert (London, 1957), p. 364, April 27th, 1935.

2 Christian, *Tolstoy*, p. 234; Professor Christian is mistaken in saying here that it is his wife whom Irtenyev kills.

3 *Op. cit.*, p. 66.

4 *Ibid.*, p. 46.

5 For further discussion of the relationship between the sonata and Tolstoy's story, see Dorothy Green, '*The Kreutzer Sonata*: Tolstoy and Beethoven', *Melbourne Slavonic Studies*, I (1967).

6 'Any competent sensationalist is Tolstoy's equal in this region of the mind.' *Op cit.*, p. 285

7 'Tolstoy, Lermontov and Others', in Donald Davie (ed.), *Russian Literature and Modern English Fiction* (Chicago, 1965), p. 167.

8 Count Ilya Tolstoy, *Reminiscences of Tolstoy*, trans. George Calderon (London, 1914), p. 22.

8 *Resurrection*

1 *Op. cit.*, p. 307.

2 *Op. cit.*, p. 249.

3 *Ibid.*, p. 250.

4 Trans. Thomas P. Whitney (London, 1976), II, 384.

5 *Tolstoy the Ascetic* (Edinburgh and London, 1967), pp. 128–44.

9 *Hadji Murat*

1 See Pasternak, *An Essay in Autobiography*, trans. Manya Harari, (London, 1949), p. 71, and Gorky, *op. cit.*, pp. 68–9.

2 Letter of January 20th, 1903; quoted by Troyat, *op. cit.*, p. 800.

3 *Op. cit.*, p. 688.

4 Aylmer Maude, *The life of Tolstoy* (Oxford, 1929–30), II, 420.

5 Bayley, *op. cit.*, p. 276; for the opposite view, see Troyat, *op. cit.*, pp. 800–1.

6 *Essay in Autobiography*, p. 74.

7 *Works*, LIII, 187.

8 It is curious that George Steiner does not refer to it in his discussion of Tolstoy's 'epic' qualities in *Tolstoy or Dostoyevsky* (revised ed., Harmondsworth, Middlesex, 1967).

9 *Life of Tolstoy*, I, 74.

10 *Op. cit.*, p. 801.

11 Letter of October 21st, 1924. *Letters of Rainer Maria Rilke*, trans. J. Barnard Greene and M. D. Herter Norton (New York, 1945–8), II, p. 357

Select Bibliography

Works

The 90 volume *Polynoye Sobraniye Sochineniy* (Jubilee Edition) ed. V. G. Chertkov *et al.* (Moscow, 1928–58) is the definitive Russian edition, giving the many MS variants and devoting half its space to the diaries, journals and letters.

The *Tolstoy Centenary Edition*, trans. Louise and Aylmer Maude, 21 vols. (Oxford, 1929–37) is the best and fullest English translation. The more recent translations of the major novels and shorter novels by Rosemary Edmonds in the Penguin Classics series are reliable, though somewhat freer than the Maudes'. Earlier translations than these tend to be unreliable in a variety of ways.

The diaries, journals and letters have been much less well served by translators than the rest of Tolstoy's work. Selections available in English are:

The Diaries of Leo Tolstoy, 1847–52, trans. C. J. Hogarth and A. Sirnis (London, 1917).

The Private Diary of Leo Tolstoy, 1853–57, trans. Louise and Aylmer Maude (London; Millwood, New York, 1927).

Last Diaries, trans. Lydia Weston Kesich (New York, 1960).

The Letters of Tolstoy and his Cousin Countess Alexandra Tolstoy, 1857–1903, trans. L. Islavin (London, 1929).

Tolstoy's Love Letters, trans. S. S. Koteliansky and Virginia Woolf (London, 1923). (Letters to Valeria Arseneva, 1856–57.)

Biography and Reminiscences

Boyer, Paul, *Chez Tolstoi: Entretiens à Iasnaia Poliana* (Paris, 1950).

Crankshaw, Edward, *Tolstoy: The Making of a Novelist* (London; New York, 1974).

Goldenveizer, A. B., *Talks with Tolstoy*, trans. S. S. Koteliansky and Virginia Woolf (London, 1923).

Gorky, Maxim, *Reminiscences of Tolstoy, Chekhov and Andreev*, trans. Katherine Mansfield, S. S. Koteliansky and Leonard Woolf (London, 1934; Atlantic Highlands, New Jersey, 1968).

Kuzminskaya, Tatyana, *Tolstoy as I Knew Him: My Life at Home and at Yasnaya Polyana*, trans. Nora Sigerist *et al.* (Philadelphia, 1918; London, 1948).

Maude, Aylmer, *The Life of Tolstoy*, revised ed., 2 vols. (Oxford, 1929–30; New York, 1975).

Simmons, Ernest J., *Leo Tolstoy* (Boston, 1945–6; London, 1949, 1973).

Tolstoy, Alexandra, *Tolstoy: A Life of My Father*, trans. E. R. Hapgood (New York, 1953).

Tolstoy, Ilya, *Reminiscences of Tolstoy*, trans. George Calderon (London; Philadelphia, 1914).

Tolstoy, Sergey, *Tolstoy Remembered*, trans. Moura Budberg (London, 1961).

Tolstoy, Sophia, *Countess Tolstoy's Later Diary, 1891-7*, trans. A. Werth (London; Plainview, New York, 1929).

—, *The Diary of Tolstoy's Wife, 1860–91*, trans. A. Werth (London, 1928; New York, 1974).

—, *The Final Struggle: being Countess Tolstoy's Diary for 1910*, trans. Aylmer Maude (London, 1936; New York, 1972).

Troyat, Henri, *Tolstoy*, trans. Nancy Amphoux (Paris, 1965; New York, 1969; Harmondsworth, Middlesex, 1970).

Criticism

This list is especially selective as regards Russian criticism, of which there has been a very large output in the last fifty years, much of it inevitably written in the shadow of Lenin's interpretations (see below). Where a work has been translated, I have given details of the English version. Fragments of otherwise untranslated Russian criticism are to be found in Henry Gifford's excellent collection (see below), while there is a useful survey by Gleb Struve, 'Tolstoy in Soviet Criticism,' in *The Russian Review*, April, 1960.

Ardens, N. N., *Tvorcheskii put' L. N. Tolstogo* (Moscow, 1962).

Arnold, Matthew, 'Count Leo Tolstoi', in *Essays in Criticism: Second Series* (London, 1888; Folcroft, Pennsylvania, 1910).

Bayley, John, *Tolstoy and the Novel* (London, 1966; New York, 1968).

Berlin, Sir Isaiah, *The Hedgehog and the Fox* (London; New York, 1953).

—, 'Tolstoy and Enlightenment', in Matlaw (see below).

Bilinkis, Y. A., *O tvorchestve L. N. Tolstogo* (Moscow, 1959).

Blackmur, R. P., 'The Dialectic of Incarnation: Tolstoy's *Anna Karenina*', in *Eleven Essays in the European Novel* (London; New York, 1964).

Chiaromonte, Nicola, *The Paradox of History: Stendhal, Tolstoy, Pasternak and Others* (London; Atlantic Highlands, New Jersey, 1972).

Christian, R. F., *Tolstoy: a Critical Introduction* (Cambridge, 1969; New York, 1970).
—, *Tolstoy's 'War and Peace': a Study* (Oxford; New York, 1962).
Davie, Donald (ed.), *Russian Literature and Modern English Fiction* (Chicago; London, 1965). (Essays by Lawrence, Merezhkovsky, *et al.*)
Eykhenbaum, Boris, *Lev Tolstoi, kniga pervaya, 50–e gody* (Leningrad, 1928).
—, *Lev Tolstoi, kniga vtoraya, 60–e gody* (Moscow, 1931).
—, *Lev Tolstoi, semidesyatye gody* (Leningrad, 1960).
—, *The Young Tolstoi*, translation ed. Gary Stern (Ann Arbor, Michigan, 1972; first published, Petrograd, 1922).
Gifford, Henry (ed.), *Leo Tolstoy: a Critical Anthology* (Harmondsworth, Middlesex; Gloucester, Massachusetts, 1971).
Greenwood, E. B., *Tolstoy: the Comprehensive Vision* (London; New York, 1975).
Gudzy, N. K., *Kak rabotal L. Tolstoi* (Moscow, 1936).
—, *Lev Tolstoi* (Moscow, 1960).
Khrapchenko, M. B., *Lev Tolstoi kak Khudozhnik* (Moscow, 1963).
Kupreyanova, E. N., *Estetika L. N. Tolstogo* (Moscow-Leningrad, 1966).
Leavis, F. R., '*Anna Karenina*: Thought and Significance in a Great Creative Work', in '*Anna Karenina*' *and Other Essays* (London, 1967; New York, 1969).
Lenin, V. I., *Stat'i o Tolstom* (Moscow, 1960).
Lukács, Georg, *The Historical Novel*, trans. Hannah and Stanley Mitchell (London, 1962; Atlantic Highlands, New Jersey, 1965).
Mann, Thomas, 'Goethe and Tolstoy' and '*Anna Karenina*', in *Essays of Three Decades*, trans. H. T. Lowe-Porter (London; New York, 1947).
Matlaw, Ralph E. (ed.), *Tolstoy: a Collection of Critical Essays* (Englewood Cliffs, New Jersey, 1967).
Merezhkovsky, Dmitri, *Tolstoy as Man and Artist* (London; Westport, Connecticut, 1902).
Mirsky, D. S., *A History of Russian Literature*, ed. Francis J. Whitfield (London; New York, 1949).
Myshkovskaya, L. M., *Masterstvo L. N. Tolstogo* (Moscow, 1958)
Redpath, Theodore, *Tolstoy* (London; Atlantic Highlands, New Jersey, 1960).
Roberts, Spencer E. (ed. and trans.), *Essays in Russian Literature: the Conservative View: Leontiev, Rozanov, Shestov* (Athens, Ohio, 1968).
Rolland, Romain, *Tolstoy*, trans. B. Miall (London; Port Washington, New York, 1911).
Shklovsky, Viktor, 'Art as Technique', in *Russian Formalist Criticism:*

Four Essays, trans. Lee T. Lemon and Marion J. Reis (Lincoln, Nebraska, 1965).

—, *Material i stil' v romane L'va Tolstogo 'Voina i mir'* (Moscow, 1928).

—, *Lev Tolstoi* (Moscow, 1963).

Speirs, Logan, *Tolstoy and Chekhov* (Cambridge, 1971; New York, 1972).

Spence, G. W., *Tolstoy the Ascetic* (Edinburgh; London, 1967; Atlantic Highlands, New Jersey, 1968).

Steiner, George, *Tolstoy or Dostoyevsky* (New York, 1959, 1971; Harmondsworth, Middlesex, 1967).

Sterne, J. P. M., *'Effi Brest; Madame Bovary; Anna Karenina'*, *Modern Language Review*, 52 (1957).

Trilling, Lionel, *'Anna Karenina'*, in *The Opposing Self* (New York, 1955).

Zaidenshnur, E. E., *'Voina i mir' L. N. Tolstogo. Sozdanie velikoi knigi* (Moscow, 1966).

Zhdanov, V. A., *Tvorcheskaya istoriya 'Anny Kareninoi'* (Moscow, 1957).

Index

(Italicized page numbers indicate where the main discussion is to be found.)

209